The
looniness
of the long distance
runner

THE AUTHOR

Russell Taylor is responsible for the words of the Alex cartoon strip in
The Daily Telegraph and also composes TV music. In addition to annual
collections of Alex cartoons he has also written humorous books on Russia and
the City of London. A recent recipient of the MBE in HM The Queen's New
Year's Honours awards, he lives in Muswell Hill, North London, but doesn't
advise other aspirant runners to do the same – that uphill slog on the way
back from training runs is a killer.

First published in 2001
This edition published 2003

Carlton Books Limited
20 Mortimer Street
London W1T 3JW

A CIP catalogue record for this book is available
from the British Library

ISBN 1 84442 941 5

Printed in Great Britain

The
looniness
of the long distance
runner

AN UNFIT LONDONER'S
ATTEMPT TO RUN
THE NEW YORK CITY MARATHON
FROM SCRATCH

Russell Taylor

CARLTON

To my family: Hal, Iona, Frances and Karen Taylor
(sorry, dogs don't count) ...

... and Angela Taylor (no relation),
an honorary member.

Contents

Author's Acknowledgements

The author would like to acknowledge and thank the following people:

Adèle Lang for shaming me into writing this book.

Anne Dewe, Jonathan Goodman, Martin Corteel, Charles Peattie, Catrina MacKinnon, Juliet Sychrava and others mentioned elsewhere for reading the manuscript with varying degrees of professional obligation.

Tara Spring, Becky Barrow, Mary Horlock, Chris and Raya O'Neill for cameo appearances.

Susie Plant and Bernie Clifford for additional marathon inspiration.

Cathy Holmes and Susan Roche for physiological and astrological therapy respectively.

Sophie Woodforde and all at the National Missing Persons Helpline for all their help here and everywhere.

And Callimachus.

Introduction

This all came about because I got drunk.

That's not necessarily such a bad thing. I mean, quite a few of you reading this paragraph will only have come about because someone (one, or both, of your parents) got drunk. Drunkenness can have very beneficial consequences. The problem was I made the mistake of getting drunk in the company of someone who works for a charity, namely my flatmate Angela.

Now, the first, and possibly only, rule of charitable fundraising is always get people when they're smashed. Why do you think charity auctions are invariably sponsored by gin or vodka companies? And why is it that the one-hour auction is always preceded by a three-hour cocktail reception? Because alcohol brings out all the qualities most conducive to generous charitable giving: pride, boastfulness, macho competitiveness and egotism. The City boys in suits, who are top of the guest list at all such events, want to show they are richer and got bigger bonuses than their competitors at the next table. And then they wake up the next morning with a hangover, a signed Chelsea football shirt, a cheque missing from the cheque book and a potential divorce suit. Angela was aware of all this when she asked me at 2.00 a.m. in a Soho club to sponsor her to run the New York Marathon; and I was aware of very little, probably my own name, possibly my address. After all, 500 seems a perfectly reasonable number of pounds to sponsor someone, provided your blood-alcohol count is at approximately the same level.

I lay in bed the next morning with this hideous memory fizzing at the back of my brain like the Alka-Seltzer in my glass. The huge folly of what I had done dawned on me and I started to plan damage limitation strategies. The first of these was to encourage Angela to stay out late by accompanying her to various decadent nightclubs. The idea was that this would prevent her from doing any training and she would have to abandon her marathon aspirations. I quickly realised the basic problem with this approach. Certainly Angela's training schedule began to suffer. But I calculated I would end up spending more money than I had pledged her in sponsorship on buying gratuitous drinks just to stop her going home and getting a good night's sleep. Furthermore, when after a few weeks I commented on her unorthodox Bacardi-and-Diet-Coke-based training methods, Angela informed me that she was determined to complete the marathon course even if she ended up walking it. I protested that this should entitle me to a discount, but she firmly scotched this loophole, insisting that no mile-per-hour sponsorship rate had been negotiated. So I resorted to a new tactic which involved pushing her out of the door every morning at 5.00 a.m. (no, of course I don't get up at that time. That was by now the hour at which I was rolling back in from the aforementioned clubs having been unable to shake off the nocturnal lifestyle I had acquired). My hope was that she would catch a bad cold or suffer a sports injury from running into a tree in the dark and have to cry off.

However, within a short time, I found I had sponsored two other people to run the New York Marathon. Firstly, I was buttonholed by Angela's running mate, Bernie, who demanded that I sign his sponsorship form. When I tried to refuse he pointed out that as he and Angela had agreed to run the course holding hands this obliged me to sponsor him, too, as otherwise he would feel less motivated than her and slow her down. I conceded, mainly because I admired the cunning of his logic, but as he had accosted me at lunchtime I only pledged a stone-cold-sober amount of cash.

Then a week later I was at a party, gravitating inexorably towards my customary final resting place, the kitchen. Here I noticed a woman who seemed far too attractive to be a fellow friendless kitchen-loiterer. I offered her a drink and she asked for water. This seemed to invite comment. It turned out that she was following a stringent health regime because she was in training for the New York City Marathon. Small world. After some further conversation I estimated Susie's age as 23 and star sign as Scorpio. As it happens I was correct on both counts, but this brought very little satisfaction, merely confirming that she was completely incompatible with this 38-year-old Cancerian (don't believe what you read in astrology books). Having reluctantly concluded that inviting her out to dinner would be doomed, I decided instead to sponsor her to run the Marathon and to pledge to her nominated charity the same sum of money I would otherwise have blown on a candle-lit evening of listening to her telling me what a bastard her prop-forward boyfriend is. Fifty pounds seemed a reasonable figure (okay, I'm a cheapskate dater) and this way the money would go to fighting multiple sclerosis rather than into the pocket of some poncey celebrity chef. And although I still drop the fifty quid, at least I get to keep my dignity.

I now had a huge financial exposure to the NYC Marathon. So I decided I might as well throw good money after bad, get on a 747 and present myself along the route with stopwatch and megaphone in hand to ensure that my three sponsees actually completed the distance. I hoped I might also be able to take embarrassing photos of them in the final stages of undignified collapse with which to blackmail them later and mitigate my loss.

The other factor that inspired me to make the trip was my Secret Shame: I had never been to America. Having Never Been To America at the age of 38 is a bit like Not Having Lost Your Virginity or Not Having Passed Your Driving Test. You feel you have missed out on a crucial rites of passage experience without which you cannot presume to call yourself an adult. You harbour paranoid fears that you will find yourself at a dinner party one evening where the conversation gets on to fellatio or three-point turns. Suddenly someone will turn to you and ask your opinion. You will say something asinine in reply and everyone will realise... As it turned out almost everyone I confessed my guilty secret to said that they, too, had Never Been To America, or else they had just made their first visit the previous month. I was outraged to find I had been hanging around with such a bunch of L-plated virgins.

America seemed a strange prospect. I've seen the place millions of times in movies and on TV, heard its cities and freeways glorified in pop songs and feel I know it really well. Yet at the same time I had a sneaking suspicion that it might not actually exist, but could just be some huge version of the *Truman Show*, devised to entertain the rest of the world, and that the American tourists one bumps into over here in Europe are just strolling actors in the pay of the Walt Disney Corporation or whoever runs the place.

I was none the wiser when I finally got there as New York looked exactly as it is supposed to: the taxis were yellow, the buildings tall and the A Train even went to Harlem, just like Duke Ellington said in the song. On Sunday morning I equipped myself with a subway map and a bunch of energy-boosting bananas and set off to support my protégés in the New York City Marathon. Susie ran like the wind and I completely failed to spot her as she was always some miles ahead of her modestly predicted position. Angela and Bernie wafted like a gentle summer breeze and consequently managed to finish some way behind an 80-year-old man, two one-legged athletes and a competitor who was running in a full-sized rhinoceros suit. Still, annoyingly, all three of my sponsees completed the course and I had to pay up.

I'm not sure at which stage I decided that the experience of watching a marathon (a pleasant stroll in Central Park in the late autumn sunshine, dispensing bananas and encouragement to the competitors) was in some way equivalent to the experience of actually running a marathon (a nightmare ordeal with aching limbs and bladder, complete with idiots on the sidewalk shouting "way to go" at you). But I found myself inexplicably quite fancying a shot at doing it. At the time, I put this weird whim down to anxiety about my rapidly approaching 40th birthday – clearly just some sort of early-onset midlife crisis.

On the plane home I was suddenly struck by a positive and practical reason for doing a marathon: I could write a book about it. The negative corollary immediately followed: this book, my first solo writing opus, would be bound to feature a front cover photo of me wearing shorts and looking knackered, worse still, being carried away on a stretcher with an ambulanceman holding a drip-feed aloft – not exactly how I wish to be seen and remembered. To be honest, I'd always fancied one of those posed author shots on the dust jacket, nicely lit like in a corporate brochure: sitting at my desk, chin resting on hand, with a mug of sharpened pencils in the foreground (incidentally, contrary to what you might think, the modern writer does still use pencils: they're handy for prodding the "reset" switch at the back of your laptop when it crashes).

Then, while trying to work out which of the six in-flight movies I'd least prefer not to watch, I had a second idea: I could give all the royalties from the book to charity. This was a decision taken for practical as well as philanthropic reasons. Normally when embarking on a charitable fund-raising venture you will go round all your friends with a sponsorship form and ask them to pledge some money. I vividly recall the reluctance and suspicion with which you are greeted. We like to get something for our money here in this Nation of Shopkeepers and will resort to the most desperate evasive action when asked for a freebie. "I haven't got any money on me." "You don't need any, just sign the form." "I don't have a pen." "Here's one." "I've sprained my wrist." "I can't remember my name." "I'm illiterate." The excuses flow freely. The cash rather less so.

But all this is nothing in comparison to when you attempt to collect your pledges. People will cross the street to avoid meeting you. They will change jobs, their names, move house, emigrate – anything to get out of coughing up that £25. Collecting sponsorship money reduces you to the leprous condition of the people you are collecting for. You become that plaintive African child in a charity ad that your friends turn the page to avoid seeing. But in my case, I thought, as a dreadful Sylvester Stallone movie started, this awkward situation will not arise. My friends will merely have to pledge to buy my book. After that, it's up to their consciences. I won't be policing their bookshelves. The more I thought about it, the better the idea seemed. The charitable status of the book also puts me in a guaranteed win-win position. If the book sells well, I can claim it is due to the sheer brilliance of my writing. If it flops, it is because we're a nation of Scrooges. Not you of course, dear reader. You've bought it; or if you haven't and are just flicking through it in a bookshop I have hopefully now shamed you into buying it. Of course, your decision to do so may have been motivated by the desire to gain an insight into the Gandhi-esque karma of an author who would give away all his royalties to a good cause. Well, as it's now too late for you to ask for your money back, I can reveal the truth.

A few years ago at a party in North London I met a journalist who had been the author of a best-selling, humorous coffee-table book back in the seventies. He revealed to me that, contrary to popular belief, he had not actually benefited hugely well financially from the book. As an unknown author at the time, he had been given no advance and secured only a derisively low royalty deal. But, he went on, after the vast sales of his initial book, his publisher rashly chucked at him an advance the size of Microsoft's annual pizza bill for the follow-up volume. Naturally it bombed, but its author was laughing all the way to a three-storey town house in Islington.

This is how I intend to play it. So if this time next year you see a book on the shelves by me about taking part in the London to Brighton Vintage Car Rally or something, don't feel guilty about not buying it. It won't be for charity and I'll have already banked my money.

CHAPTER 1

Midlife Crisis

As I mentioned earlier, this is clearly part of a midlife crisis, but a productive sort of crisis. More like a midlife wake-up call. There are so many things you never get around to doing in your life and with many of them, frankly, by the time you are pushing 40 it is too late. For example, reluctantly I shall have to cross the following items off my To Do list:

a) *become a pop star;*
b) *play football or cricket for England;*
c) *become a millionaire.*

But why run a marathon, you ask? Isn't this a bit of an overreaction? Running is very bad for you, everyone knows that. It does irreparable damage to your knees and lumbar vertebrae. A perfectly tolerable level of fitness can be achieved by just walking briskly for 20 minutes three times a week. True, but to be honest even this is more than I have undertaken for the best part of 25 years. In fact, apart from an annual game of tennis with my mother and sister, I have participated in no form of physical exertion since school (and even there I expended large amounts of mental energy finding ways to avoid it).

Thinking it through, I realised that there are several advantages to doing a marathon. Firstly, it is one of the few aerobic sports in which you can still turn in a credible performance at an advanced age. Clarence DeMar actually won the Boston Marathon at the age of 41. Admittedly he'd put in quite a bit of training over the previous 20 years, but marathoning excellence is clearly something, like wisdom, that comes with age; or maybe it's just that today's channel-surfing youngsters do not have the attention span to run all that distance.

Secondly, the marathon is the only event where you can compete in the same race as the world record-holder. Okay, it's likely that he will cross the start line 20 minutes ahead of you and finish some two and a half hours in front of you with 20,000 runners in between and you will never lay eyes on him except on the TV coverage on the evening news, but officially you were in the same race. After all, if you were to take up sprinting, your chances of finding yourself on the blocks alongside Maurice Greene and Donovan Bailey in your first attempt at the distance are absolutely zero.

Thirdly, the marathon possesses a unique glamour, because not only is it the longest running race in the Olympics, it is the only one that has a name. All other track events go under a bald description of the distance to be covered: 100 metres, 1500 metres etc., with maybe a terse clarification, like "Hurdles" or "Steeplechase" appended. The marathon, however, has a brand – and a very successful one which has cross-marketed itself over the last century to various other activities. We talk about a marathon shopping expedition, for example, or a dance marathon. Of course, it is likely that the reason for the race having a special name is that no one in their right minds would agree to run it if it were called the 26.2 miles.

Last, but not least, the marathon is the event where you get maximum appreciation for your efforts. Spectators all along the route clap and cheer the runners as they pass. And the worse you are, the greater the amount of applause you get. The dodderer who comes home in six hours will get three times as much appreciation as the élite athlete who does it in just over two. This is really quite Marxist when one thinks about it: to each according to his needs. I estimate I should get at least four hours of continuous applause. Four hours! No West End actor racks up anything like that in curtain calls. The most sycophantic standing ovation at a party political conference never went on that long. Not even Josef Stalin at the 18th Congress of the Communist Party of the Soviet Union was that feted by the delegates, even though they could validly be sent to the Gulag for stinting on their audible appreciation of the Great Leader.

So, marathon it is then. But which of the many hundreds held worldwide? I have decided to follow Angela's example and run the New

York City Marathon. Why not London, you ask. It's nearer and more convenient. True. But the London Marathon is run in April. This would mean that I would have to do all my long training runs in the dark, cold and wet of the British winter, and frankly, I know myself well enough to know that I wouldn't bother. The New York City Marathon, by contrast, is held in early November, thus the bulk of my preparation will involve jogging through pleasant parks in the summer London sunshine. Also training in wintertime involves wearing a tracksuit and a cap or woolly hat to keep out the cold. This gives rise to the risk that passers-by might think I am just endeavouring to look trendy by wearing sports casuals. A 38-year-old trying to belatedly get fit is a sad enough spectacle, but one attempting to appear hip is beneath contempt.

My second reason for preferring New York is that I do not know the city, having been there just once. I find it hard to visualise the distances involved. Okay, 26.2 miles is 26.2 miles wherever you run it, but some-how Staten Island to Central Park doesn't sound that daunting – it doesn't conjure up any sort of a mental picture. On the other hand, Greenwich to the Mall, via Docklands, sounds totally terrifying. I have lived in London for 15 years and can visualise every mile of that journey in agonising detail. I can see how long it would take me to drive it (long enough), how long it would take to cover it by public transport (forever) and the idea of running it just does not bear thinking about.

My first resolution is to tell nobody about this foolhardy notion of mine before I have established whether this objective is remotely com-patible with my unconditioned body. The initial fitness assessment I can do discreetly in my local gym. I will not have to face the British outdoors in winter and the possibility of being spotted by my neighbours in the initial stages of the endeavour which are bound to be fairly undignified.

Before embarking on even this mild course of unfamiliar exertion I decide to break myself in gently with some light research into the origins of the marathon race. Once, this would have involved a brisk morning stroll down to the public library, but these days, thanks to the Internet, I can do it all from my home computer and thus put off for a while longer breaking my quarter century of lethargy.

CHAPTER 2

The History of the Marathon

Many battles have things named after them. Stamford Bridge has a football stadium, Balaclava has a hat, Marengo has a casserole, Sedan has a type of car. But only the Battle of Marathon has had its name immortalised in an international sport (and also, until 1990, a chocolate bar). There is no Olympic discipline called the Hastings where competitors have to try to shoot arrows into each other's eyes. There is no Somme event at the Games where competitors crawl very slowly through mud and then kick a football around. Yet hundreds of thousands of people every year run 26 miles 385 yards in the so-called marathon. Why do we do this? If the truth be told, it has virtually nothing to do with the Battle of Marathon which was fought in Greece 2,500 years ago.

By the beginning of the fifth century BC the Persian Empire under King Darius I had overrun most of the known world from the river Indus to the Oxus (oh...look them up in the atlas). In a relatively unhindered expansion it had suffered only one setback, some nine years before Marathon, when an army of Athenians and Eretrians had burnt the city of Sardis which was under Persian rule. Darius was so miffed by this act of defiance that he appointed a servant whose job was to utter these words to his master every day: "Sire, remember the Athenians."

His memory thus jogged, Darius dispatched envoys to all Greek towns to demand their submission to Persian rule. These heralds would arrive in the marketplace and announce that King Darius, "the Lord of all Men from the Rising Sun to the Setting Sun", demanded fealty from the inhabitants. Had the townspeople thought this claim through they would have realised that the horizon is only about 11 miles away, so Darius was boasting of an empire that would have been about 22 miles across and was thus about the size of the Isle of Wight. But on the whole, the townsfolk didn't think it through and instead handed over a symbolic offering of earth and water as a sign of their acceptance of the Persian yoke. Of all the Greek towns, only Athens and Sparta refused to contribute to Darius's sandpit. On hearing this, the Persian King flew into a great rage (well, we don't know this for sure, but kings tended to in those days) and commanded that an invasion force of 600 galleys set sail to punish the Greeks for their insolence.

In September 490 BC, having stopped off on the way to raze Eretria, Darius's army, under the command of General Datis, landed on the plain of Marathon. The Athenian army was encamped on the hills above. From where they stood, the outlook was not promising. The Greek force consisted of about 10,000 men of Athens, plus a thousand Plataeans. The army of the Persians and Medes included soldiers from all their conquered realms, 46 nationalities in all, including tribesmen from Hyrcania and Afghanistan, horsemen from Khorassan, archers from Ethiopia and swordsmen from the banks of the Euphrates and the Nile, the Indus and the Oxus (seriously, look them up). Its total strength is estimated to have been between 25,000 and 100,000 men.

The Greeks' problems were compounded with the return of Pheidippides, a professional runner who had earlier been sent to run to Sparta to ask for military assistance. He started off by relating some half-arsed story about having met the god Pan on the way back. The main part of his news, however, was more sober. The Spartans would love to attend, he reported, but had a bit of a mix-up in their diaries. It was only the sixth day of the moon and their religious customs forbade them to fight before the moon was full. This must have made them a pushover for any enemy with a calendar, but for the moment the Athenians were on their own. It was to be a pivotal moment in history. Just a handful of free men stood before a huge evil empire which threatened to engulf the rest of known civilisation. This would be a conflict whose significance was to stretch long into the future. After all, it had just invented the plot of pretty much every science fiction movie that would ever be made.

The 10 generals commanding the Athenian force debated their

predicament and were split. Five of them, tunics brown, were against engaging a vastly superior army in suicidal combat. The remainder favoured giving battle immediately. The casting vote thus went to Callimachus, who was a civilian and the current incumbent of the annually rotated post of "War Ruler" of Athens, a sort of Minister of Defence. Miltiades, one of the hawkish generals, implored him with the following words: "It now rests with you, Callimachus, either to enslave Athens, or, by assuring its freedom, to win yourself an immortality of fame such as not even Harmodius [who he? Ed] or Aristogeiton [ditto] have acquired." Had Callimachus had our advantage of twenty-first century hindsight he would have realised that he was in fact destined to become *exactly* as famous as those other two people that nobody has ever heard of and he would probably have elected to sit it out until the year was up and it was someone else's turn to be War Ruler. As it was, he was won over by Miltiades' blandishments and, after a few quick sacrifices to ensure the blessing of the gods, the Greek army prepared for battle.

As if things weren't already bad enough, the Athenians had another serious military disadvantage. Unlike the Persians, they had no cavalry (if they'd had any horses they'd obviously have lent one to Pheidippides and the marathon race would never have come into existence). Thus their only advantage in the forthcoming engagement was surprise and the dubious fact that the land on which they were to give battle was sacred to Heracles.

Their troops were hastily drawn up into a line and then, contrary to military practice, charged the Persians at a run. To cut the match report to a minimum, the Greeks broke through on the left and right wings and encircled the Persian centre. Despite their numerical superiority the Persians were routed and fled back to their boats in disarray. It was at this point, with victory assured and the thought of immortality in his head, that the luckless Callimachus took the first step towards it by getting himself killed. The Persians set sail round the coast to Athens, hoping to catch the city undefended. But Miltiades guessed their intentions, marched his troops through the night and got there first.

And that was about it. The casualty figures were 6,400 Persians dead and 192 Greeks. The Persian cavalry took no part in the battle. No one knows why. The Spartan army turned up in time to inspect the burial mounds, stayed for tea and then went home again. Darius died five years later to be succeeded by his son Xerxes, who became legendary for being the only person ever to have two Xs in his name. Athens and Sparta rejoiced and then a few years later declared war on each other.

This, the most detailed account we have of the battle, comes from the Greek historian Herodotus writing about 65 years afterwards, and for our purposes is noteworthy for its failure to mention anything about anyone running 26 miles 385 yards. Heracleides Ponticus, 85 years later, muddied the water by claiming that the messenger sent to Sparta was called Thersippus of Erchia. Pliny the Elder failed to note the event at all in his essay on Great Running Feats of History (but how can you take seriously a man who called himself after a tree?). The historian Plutarch made no mention of any messenger called Pheidippides being sent to Sparta, but did report that after the battle a runner was dispatched to Athens to relay the good news. This individual (Plutarch says he was called Eucles) ran all the way to Athens in full armour and on getting there was able to pronounce only the words "Rejoice! We conquer" before dropping dead of exhaustion. Sadly, he expired before mentioning to the Athenian populace the bad news, i.e. that a lot of seriously aggrieved Persians were sailing round the coast with the intention of laying waste the town. Luckily, thanks to Miltiades' prompt return, the messenger's premature demise did not prove costly. Plutarch's story, though more dramatic, was written some 500 years after the events took place and so could well be complete tosh.

Lucian, writing in the second century AD, decided that the runner's name was Phillipides (not Pheidippides, but this could be a copyist's error) and follows Plutarch in saying that he ran to Athens. Then the situation is further confused in the nineteenth century when Robert Browning tackled the subject in a rather ditsy poem entitled "Pheidippides". Browning amalgamates various versions of the legend and has his hero Pheidippides running to Sparta, bumping into Pan on the way back, fighting in the battle itself, then running back to Athens and finally pegging out. The poet also throws in a few touches of his own. He has a strange obsession with fennel and goats. So the length of the original marathon run depends on whose account you choose to believe. The distance from Marathon to Athens is about 24 miles. The round trip from

Athens to Sparta is approximately 145 miles. The combined journey would be about 169 miles (not including any additional distance run while chasing fleeing Persians).

This problem didn't really worry anyone until 1894.

At that time the Frenchman Pierre de Coubertin was actually worried about something else, namely his country's embarrassing recent record of military defeats against their traditional foes the British and the Germans. Things had started to go wrong at Waterloo and culminated with the French being whopped at the battle of Sedan in 1870 by the Prussians. Coubertin had visited Eton and Rugby and was impressed by the British public schools' emphasis on physical training and sport. These disciplines were snootily looked down on in the more academically oriented French *lycées* – which, Coubertin thought, might explain his nation's general uselessness on the battlefield. His interest in young men in skimpy shorts happened to coincide with the discovery by archaeologists of the original Olympic stadium. The site was excavated between 1875 and 1881, annoyingly for Coubertin by a German, but it gave him the idea he had been searching for. The ancient Olympic Games had been held every four years between 776 BC and AD 261. Coubertin proposed to resurrect this tradition, adding some modern disciplines, with the inaugural games to be staged in Athens.

The marathon as an event had no precedent in the ancient games, where the longest race was 4,800 metres. The idea came from Michel Bréal, a French historian and linguist, who proposed to immortalise Pheidippides' feat (eat your heart out, Callimachus) in a long-distance running event. He also offered to present a gold cup to the winner. This was a clever sop to the lukewarm Greek government, who immediately agreed to host the games and got very excited about this event in particular and its commemoration of Greek heroism to the world. Had marketing people existed at the time they would probably have proposed that the race be named the Athens, but luckily they didn't and so the marathon was born.

Despite the non-existence of those marketing people, the Greek government was nevertheless aware of the huge PR value of a home victory in this inaugural event and they set about organising trials and heats among local athletes. They really needn't have bothered. Just four foreigners entered the marathon and of those, only one, a Hungarian, had ever previously run the distance, which had been set at a nice round sensible 40,000 metres (luckily for modern marathoners, Coubertin had decided to go with the Plutarch/Lucian account of the battle, otherwise we'd all be running ultra marathons to this day).

There were 17 participants in this first marathon (well, second technically) which took place on Friday 10 April 1896. The other non-Greeks were an American, a Frenchman and an Australian accountant named Edwin Flack. These three, who hadn't read their marathon training books (as none existed at the time), made the basic error of setting off too quickly and eventually paid the price. The American dropped out before halfway. The Frenchman led for a long time but eventually collapsed. Flack took over the lead but succumbed to exhaustion about four kilometres from the stadium. So in a fairytale ending the Greeks took first, second and third places – until, that is, the Hungarian Kellner, finishing in fourth place, spoiled it by pointing out that the Greek who had beaten him had done so by riding part of the way in a carriage. Thus it was that Spiridon Belokas had the honour of becoming the first person to be disqualified in a marathon.

The winner was Spiridon Louis, a farmer and water deliveryman from Amaroussion. His training method consisted of running alongside his mule on his twice daily 14km delivery trips from his home village to Athens. As well as the gold cup he was promised free haircuts and meals for life and various other goodies by jubilant Athenians, but humbly he asked only to be given a horse and cart, a request which King George duly granted. Louis never ran another marathon, maybe in honour of Pheidippides' single race or perhaps because his training method had been rendered obsolete now he could ride on his new cart. He would have vanished into dignified and modest obscurity like a true hero had he not blown it by showing up again 40 years later, in full Greek national dress, presenting a laurel wreath to Adolf Hitler at the opening ceremony of the Berlin Olympics.

Incompetence by officials, over-enthusiasm by spectators and some blatant cheating by participants are just some of the features which were to characterise the early years of the marathon. The second Olympic marathon in 1900, held in a 101˚ heat, was a disorganised shambles in the backstreets of Paris. Accusations flew that the winner, a local baker's delivery man named Michel Théato, had used his familiarity with the city to take several short cuts along the way. The fact that there were three French athletes in the top four finishers gave some credence to this theory. The seventh-placed runner, Dick Grant of the United States, even went so far as to sue the International Olympic Committee, claiming that he had been run down by a bicycle while attempting to overtake Théato. Most of the competitors had no idea that they were running in an Olympic marathon. The Games had been largely ignored by the press and the various sporting events that were being held in Paris were assumed to be part of the International Exposition which was taking place in the city at the time. Michel Théato only found out that he was an Olympic champion when he received his medal in the post 12 years later.

St Louis four years later was even more chaotic. One runner had gambled away his travel fare in a crap game in New Orleans and had to hitchhike to the start line. He arrived in his civilian clothes and had to have his trousers cut down into shorts by another athlete, delaying the start by several minutes. When the race got under way, the 32 participants found themselves slogging along dusty roads in a 90° heat. The accompanying officials' vehicles churned up the dust into a dense acrid cloud which asphyxiated several runners. One competitor, a Zulu tribesman named Lentauw, who was in St Louis as part of a Boer War exhibition, was at one point chased off the road and through a cornfield by two large dogs. Despite this unscheduled detour he still managed to finish ninth.

Fred Lorz, a New York bricklayer, collapsed with exhaustion after nine miles and was picked up by a passing truck. When the truck in its turn broke down 11 miles further on, Lorz felt sufficiently revived to jog back to the stadium to pick up his kit. His arrival was greeted ecstatically by the spectators who took him for the lead runner. Lorz omitted to dispel this misconception and it was only after he had had his photograph taken with President Roosevelt's daughter and just before he was about to mount the winner's podium that the mistake came to light. He was handed a life ban by the American Athletics Union, which was repealed just in time for him to win the Boston Marathon the following year.

In the meantime, the real winner had entered the stadium – an

English-born American named Thomas Hicks. In the absence of doping regulations, his accompanying team had *en route* administered liberal doses of strychnine (then used as a stimulant) washed down with brandy, which had rendered him pretty much gaga. He staggered over the line and vowed never to race again.

In 1906 there were the first and only "Intercalated Games", which gives most of us our first and only opportunity to use the word "intercalated". The games were held in Athens and the marathon was won by a Canadian called Billy Sherring who managed to pay his fare to Greece by betting the $75 raised for his trip by his local athletics club on a horse called Cicely. The horse won at 6–1 and so did Billy, in 2 hours 51 minutes. The Greeks were less enthusiastic about his victory than that of Spiridon Louis 10 years earlier, but still presented him with a statue of Athena and a lamb.

The 1908 Olympics in London featured the first marathon to be held over the modern distance of 26 miles and 385 yards. This figure was, however, arrived at fairly arbitrarily. The race was originally planned to be run over a standard distance of 25 miles and a course was duly devised that began at Windsor and finished in the newly built Olympic stadium in White City. But then Queen Alexandra let it be known that she would like the race to start on the lawn at Windsor Castle so that Princess Mary and her children could watch from their nursery window. In order to gratify this royal whim an extra mile had to be added to the beginning of the course. Then an additional 385 yards was appended to the end of the race so that it would finish under the royal box and Her Majesty wouldn't have to go to the effort of raising her lorgnette to watch it. Some Olympic official probably got himself an earldom for this display of fawning, but we marathon runners got ourselves an extra 1.2 miles to run. This has led to a tradition which survives to this day where marathoners shout "God Save the Queen" (or some less respectful observation about Queen Alexandra) as they pass Mile 25.

The 1908 marathon, better organised than in previous years, seemed by Mile 18 to have become a two-horse race. Charles Hefferton of South Africa led a 23-year-old Italian confectioner named Dorando Pietri by almost four minutes. Just when he looked certain of victory, Hefferton's advantage was destroyed by the intervention of spectators.

First he accepted a glass of champagne from a bystander which within a mile had caused him to suffer from stomach spasms. Then on the home straight into the stadium he was so pummelled by slaps on the back from enthusiastic supporters that he became completely enervated and was passed by the little Italian. Dorando (whose name had mistakenly been entered in the official records as Pietri Dorando and who would henceforth forever be known by his first name) stumbled into the stadium, himself in the advanced stages of collapse.

First of all he turned the wrong way and had to be redirected by track officials. Then he fell. He was helped to his feet by officials, but fell again and again. By this stage the crowd were rooting for him, not that they really knew who he was or had any particular love of Italians, but mainly because he was not American. The 1908 Olympics had seem bitter rows erupt between the British and American teams, with the strong suggestion that the exclusively British judges were prejudiced against the ex-colonials. As Dorando collapsed for the fifth time, just a few yards from the finish line, a second runner appeared in the stadium. To the horror of the crowd he turned out to be John Hayes, a 22-year-old New Yorker. At this point a track official took matters into his own hands (literally) and carried the hapless Dorando over the finishing line. Naturally the Americans protested and even the British judges could not think of a reason not to disqualify Dorando, who by this stage was literally at death's door.

Dorando soon recovered sufficiently to grumble that he would have been quite capable of crossing the line on his own, but still he accepted a special consolation prize of a gold cup from Queen Alexandra. Ironically, it did not seem to occur to him that the only reason that he had failed to complete the race legally was because over a mile had been added to the distance at the whim of the very woman who was presenting him with the prize. Still, Dorando went on to become much more celebrated than the man who actually won the race and even had a song written about him by Irving Berlin.

The 1912 marathon in Stockholm was marked by tragedy and treachery. In the Portuguese runner Francisco Lazaro the event boasted the first modern marathoner who truly entered into the spirit of Pheidippides. Lazaro sadly died of exhaustion and dehydration shortly after the race and was unable to emulate the feat of his biblical namesake. The "not cricket" award went to the eventual winner Kenneth McArthur, an Irish-born South African. McArthur had run most of the race alongside his compatriot Christian Gitsham. Two miles from the stadium Gitsham stopped for a drink of water and his comrade sportingly agreed to wait for him. When the refreshed Gitsham looked up he found that McArthur had vanished in the general direction of the finishing line, managing to open up a one-minute gap which Gitsham was unable to close. It is not recorded whether the two ever spoke again.

The interruption imposed by World War One and the new world order that followed seemed to bring a maturity and dignity to the marathon that leaves me very short of amusing stories to relate. There followed a series of dull races in dull cities (Antwerp, Amsterdam). By the Paris Olympiad of 1924 the distance of 26 miles 385 yards, arrived at by royal decree in 1908, had been fixed as the official marathon distance, further evidence that though we Brits are not very good at playing sports (football, cricket, tennis, rugby etc.) we are jolly good at making up the rules that govern how foreigners will beat us at them.

The next race of any note was in Hitler's Olympics of 1936. The Japanese were an emerging running nation, but their dreams of marathon glory had been constantly thwarted. Their runners had finished in fifth and sixth place in the Los Angeles games of 1932 and in fourth and sixth place in Amsterdam four years earlier. Medals seemed to elude them. Of course, the secret of eventual sporting success is to lay down strong roots and Japan's annexation of Korea some 25 years earlier now paid dividends as a couple of promising Korean runners, Kitei Son and Shoryu Nan, were press-ganged into running in Japanese colours. They duly finished first and third for the glory of Emperor Hirohito. Inspired by this example, Japan went on to invade most of the rest of the Asian continent in search of continued marathoning glory.

The 12-year interruption to the Olympics brought about by World War Two ushered in the modern sporting era, but still marathon competitors showed an impressively slapdash approach when it came to preparation. Neither the gold nor the bronze medallist in the London Olympics of 1948 had ever bothered to run 26.2 miles before.

This casual approach was trumped in Helsinki four years later by the

Czech Emil Zátopek. Zátopek had already won the 5,000 metres and 10,000 metres and his wife Dana had won the javelin. Three gold medals might have been enough for the average Czech family in the austere post-war years, but Zátopek quite fancied a shot at the marathon. The fact that he had never run the distance before was easily remedied – he decided to tag along with the current world record-holder, Jim Peters of Great Britain. This made sense. In each of the previous three Games the Brit had finished second in the marathon, so Peters was the ideal pacemaker for a man intent on the gold medal. Zátopek sought out Peters at the starting line and introduced himself to his unwitting running partner. Peters, who had lopped a staggering five minutes off the world record just six weeks previously, thought he'd teach this Central European upstart a lesson and set off at a blistering speed. He was most miffed when at 15km Zátopek appeared alongside him and politely enquired whether this pace was fast enough. Peters was already pooped, but his masculine dignity did not allow him to do anything other than agree that the pace was too slow. Zátopek asked him if he was sure. Peters just about had breath left to grate out a monosyllabic affirmative. The Czech thanked him and sped off into the distance.

From then on the novice built up an unassailable lead. Despite his strange head-rolling, tongue-lolling running style, which made him look like he was permanently about to "do a Dorando", Zátopek was quite comfortable and chatted affably with cyclists, policemen and spectators along the way. He ended up winning his first marathon by two and a half minutes and had the lack of common decency to set a new Olympic record as well. By the time the second runner reached the line, Zátopek had already signed several autographs and was waiting for him with a slice of orange, thus setting a precedent for very patronising behaviour by winners. Sadly for British consistency, this silver medallist was not Jim Peters as he had dropped out after 20 miles, exhausted and demoralised, his race plan in tatters. When later asked how he had found his first marathon, Zátopek replied: "Boring".

Zátopek again distinguished himself in the marathon at the Melbourne Olympics of 1956. He didn't win, but managed to finish sixth, just six weeks after undergoing an operation for a hernia he had sustained while pioneering a novel training technique which involved running while carrying his wife on his shoulders (and it should be recalled that his javelin-throwing spouse was no lightweight). According to his doctors, he should not even have resumed training by the marathon date. Had Zátopek lived in the West he might now have looked forward to retiring to an agreeable existence of after-dinner speaking and charity golf tournaments. Sadly he lived in communist Czechoslovakia and due to his failure to see eye-to-eye with strict Marxist-Leninist ideology he found himself demoted from army lieutenant colonel to garbage collector. The moral of his life story has to be: children, don't try this at home.

Just for the record, the winner at Melbourne was Alain Mimoun, a Frenchman of Algerian birth, and the first of four consecutive African victors over the next 16 years. At 35 he was the oldest man ever to win an Olympic marathon and, as was practically a prerequisite for gold medallists in this event now, had never run the distance before.

The winner in 1960 could practically have been accused of cheating because he had actually competed in two marathons previously. Abebe Bikila, a member of Ethiopian emperor Haile Selassie's bodyguard, surrendered something of this advantage by not wearing any shoes or socks. He led the field through the torch-lit streets of Rome along with the Moroccan Rhadi Ben Abdesselem from 18 kilometres but did not overtake his fellow African until they reached the symbolic obelisk of Axum, which had been pinched from Ethiopia by occupying Italian troops. When he won in a new world-record time, many Italians were wishing they'd held on to Abyssinia a bit longer so they could claim the victory. Not wishing to be outdone by the illustrious Zátopek in the complacency stakes Bikila, when asked how he felt, replied, "I could have gone round again without any difficulty."

Sensibly Bikila deferred going round the Olympic course again until Tokyo four years later where he not only won an unprecedented second marathon victory, but also outdid Zátopek by crawling off his sickbed to do so (he had had his appendix removed only five weeks before the race). He wore shoes and socks this time and broke the world record of Basil Heatley, who re-established the plucky British tradition of coming second. Despite the fact that the event was won by the holder, the Japanese band had not bothered to learn the Ethiopian national anthem and had to play the Japanese one instead when Bikila was on the podium. Probably no one who was not Ethiopian or Japanese noticed.

Bikila had to drop out of the Mexico City marathon in 1968 with an injury, thus allowing his compatriot Mamo Wolde to take gold. With this the third Ethiopian victory in a row, luckily the band had remembered to bring the sheet music with them. A Japanese runner, Kenji Kimihara, came second so by rights they should just have played the Ethiopian anthem twice to redress the balance.

The 1972 Olympics were held in Munich where Frank Shorter of the United States had been born. With the absence of any serious German competitors in the field he might therefore have expected a rapturous welcome from the home crowd when he won the marathon. The special thrill of that once-in-a-lifetime moment was rather spoilt when he entered the stadium to be greeted by boos and whistles of derision. The crowd's disapproval was actually directed at a hoaxster named Norbert Sudhous who had pretended to be the leading runner and was in the process of being removed by security men. But for Shorter the moment was ruined forever.

In Montreal four years later he arrived in the stadium just in time to hear the cheers for the East German, Waldemar Cierpinski, who took the gold medal a minute ahead of him in a cunning piece of Cold War *realpolitik*. Cierpinski accidentally ran an extra lap of the track and so actually crossed the line after Shorter. The real surprise was the absence from the podium of Lasse Viren who had entered the marathon with a qualification which would once have rendered him unbeatable and have pretty much guaranteed a new world record – he had never run a marathon before. But times had changed and this marathoning virgin, who had won the 5,000 and 10,000 metres, came in a humble fifth.

The Americans boycotted the next Olympics, in Moscow in 1980, so Shorter didn't get a chance to take his revenge on Cierpinski who won narrowly. Despite his two victories (a feat achieved before only by Abebe Bikila), Cierpinski was apparently described by a fellow member of the East German team, a little harshly one might feel, as a "living example of mediocrity".

The favourites in Los Angeles in 1984 were Rob de Castella of Australia and Toshihiko Seko of Japan, who had between them won their last nine marathons in a row. One of them was going to be disappointed today. As it turned out, both were. Punters with a good knowledge of Olympic marathon form might have cast their eyes down the list of unfancied runners – for example, Carlos Lopes of Portugal, who had only completed one marathon previously, and Irishman John Treacy who had never run one. The smart money was on them for first and second place and thus it transpired (an Olympic record of course being throw in). If this had been horse racing there'd have been a steward's inquiry. The happiest competitor of all was Dieudonné Lamothe of Haiti. His first name means god-given but this could not have been a reference to his marathoning gift as he crossed the line in 78th and last place in a time of 2:52:18. Years later he revealed that he had been ordered to finish the race under pain of death by his country's dictator Baby Doc Duvalier (a ploy that might be dubbed the Pheidippides Incentive).

Favourites for the Seoul Olympics marathon in 1988 were the European champion Gelindo Bordin (Italy), the world champion Douglas Wakihuri (Kenya) and the World Cup winner Ahmed Saleh (Djibouti). They finished first, second and third. Bookmakers were furious and romantics everywhere mourned the passing of the golden age of the amateur.

Hwang Young-cho, the winner in Barcelona in 1992, paid homage to Dorando Pietri by collapsing and being stretchered off but, with an admirable sense of professionalism, he remembered to cross the finishing line first. His victory for South Korea by 22 seconds over Koichi Morishita of Japan was symbolic revenge for the 1936 Olympics where the Korean winner Sohn Kee-chung had been forced to run under the Japanese flag (and the Japanese name of Kitei Son). Although it was no longer under Japanese occupation, Korea was now partitioned instead, so probably someone else would have to try all over again one day.

Josia Thugwane of South Africa was determined to make Bikila with his appendectomy and Zátopek with his hernia look like wimps. Thugwane had managed to get himself *shot* in a carjacking in his home town of Bethel five months before the Atlanta Olympics in 1996 but still recovered to take the gold medal. Possibly he was not so good at his day job as he was at marathon running – Thugwane, standing 5ft 2ins, worked as a security guard. Abdul Baser Wasigi of Afghanistan broke an

88-year-old world record to complete the slowest marathon in Olympic history, finishing in 4:24:17. It is not recorded what his country's liberal, enlightened regime thought of this performance.

Women's marathon

A Greek woman named Melpomene supposedly ran a time of four and a half hours a week before the first marathon in 1896. Unfortunately for any Olympic aspirations she may have had, women's track and field events were not admitted into the Games until 32 years later. Even then, any distance over 800 metres was considered too difficult for the ladies. In fact, the sight of women looking exhausted after the 800 metres in 1928 was deemed so unedifying that the Olympic Committee immediately rethought their progressive innovation and women were not allowed to race over any distance greater than 200m for another 32 years.

Violet Piercy of Great Britain ran a marathon in 3:40:22 in 1926 at a time when it was still considered far too unladylike to attempt such a thing. Her record stood for 37 years, mainly because no woman thought to run one again until Merry Lepper of the USA in decadent 1963. This must make it the world's second-longest standing world record, being eclipsed only by Pheidippides whose (unrecorded) marathon record stood for 2,386 years.

Once they'd got going, the women were no slouches. Mildred Sampson took the record down to 3 hours 19 minutes the next year and, by the time of the first women's Olympic marathon 20 years later, almost another hour had been lopped off the record. Joan Benoit of the USA won that inaugural race in Los Angeles and immediately set two Olympic records: the marathon record (obviously) and, at 5ft 3ins and 105 pounds, the record for the smallest Olympic champion ever.

In Seoul four years later, gold-medallist Rosa Mota managed to shave over an inch and eight pounds off Benoit's record, being only 5' 1 ¾" tall and weighing 97 pounds. Whether her weight was recorded before or after the marathon which was run in heat is not known. In 1992 Lorraine Moller of New Zealand gave hope to all armchair slobs by taking the bronze medal at the advanced age of 37.

Other marathons

At the time of the first Olympic marathon, distance running was believed by doctors to be extremely dangerous to the constitution and likely to induce a heart attack. It should be remembered that this was the same era when smoking cigarettes was promoted as a health aid. Marathons were thus considered to be for the mad and innately suicidal. The Boston Marathon, which began in 1897, attracted large crowds around the turn of the twentieth century in the same way that the lunatic asylum at Bedlam used to in the eighteenth. After 1908, when the image of Dorando Pietri, exhausted and half dead, appeared on the front pages of newspapers across America, attendance figures at Boston rose to 300,000 in the hope of seeing a fatality or two.

Exhibition races were set up between the leading runners of the day, including Dorando, Johnny Hayes and Canadian Indian Tom Longboat. Marathon runners became celebrities and were even featured on cigarette cards. Armchair fans eagerly followed the latest results from the host of city marathons that sprang up in the early 1900s. As they sat puffing on another cigarette from the pack they had bought just to complete their collection of marathoner cards, they gave silent thanks that they were not risking their health like their foolish heroes who indulged in all that dangerous cardiovascular exercise out in the fresh air.

Marathons quickly became a focus for gambling. As there were no regulations concerning prohibited substances, doping and even suspected poisoning of runners was commonplace. The favourite in the 1901 Boston Marathon, one Ronald McDonald, collapsed and had to retire from the race after a spectator handed him a sponge which later turned out to have been laced with chloroform. Amphetamines and strychnine were commonly used stimulants. The long distances involved and the fact that much of the course was run away from the supervision of race officials made races easy to fix. Even without nefarious intrusion, runners were frequently impeded by spectators or vehicles. In 1907 at Boston Robert Fowler, who was running a tactical race, hanging back from the leader Tom Longboat and waiting to make his break, suddenly found his path blocked by a freight train cutting across the road which delayed him for several minutes. He was unable to catch up and finished second.

To the disappointment of many spectators it turned out that the doctors had been wrong and marathon runners did not expire on any sort of a regular basis. That Clarence DeMar was able to win the Boston Marathon on seven occasions over three decades tended to scotch the popularly maintained theory that marathon running shortened your life (he still finished in the top 50 in 1950 at the age of 62). Apart from the odd runner being mown down by an over-enthusiastic cyclist there was very little gore. But increasing numbers of spectators decided that they quite enjoyed watching even if no one died. By the early 1930s Boston was attracting crowds of over a million.

The guinea pigs in the early days of the marathon were largely from the working classes: milkmen, bricklayers and miners. By the 1930s, when it was realised that it was not strictly a kamikaze event, some thought began to be given to preparation, technique and diet. It was no longer enough just to be able to outplod the rest of the field. Speed training came to be considered as important as endurance work. Clarence DeMar pioneered the carbohydrate-loading diet whereby he lived on non-starchy fruit and veg for a week and then introduced bread and potatoes just before the race. Gradually the social profile of the event began to change and by the 1950s marathoners tended to be college students, teachers and even those once-sceptical doctors. In 1970 the first- and second-placed runners at Boston had PhDs. The start of the New York City Marathon in the same year and Frank Shorter's Olympic victory in 1972 ushered in the American jogging boom and a worldwide renaissance in marathon running. This led to the establishment of the London Marathon in 1981, Chicago in 1984 and a succession of US presidents in shorts looking undignified at photo calls. By the end of the twentieth century marathons were as popular as they had been at the beginning.

For a long time, women were able to compete in marathons only by infiltrating them. Bobbi Gibb famously hid in the bushes in Boston in 1966 and jumped the race, which started a tradition of unofficial female participation in the event until women were officially admitted in 1972. The most famous of these modern-day suffragettes was Rosie Ruiz, who hopped over the barrier and into legend at the Boston Marathon. She chose to do this not at the start line as was traditional, but a mile from the finish – and this in 1980, eight years after the ban on women had been lifted. Probably she had merely intended to get herself a finisher's medal without having to go to all the fag of actually running 26.2 miles. Unfortunately she got her timing wrong and found herself not only winning the women's race, but actually beating the course record by two and a half minutes. Despite the suspicions of hardened runners, one of whom described Ruiz's legs as "Cellulite City", she was awarded first prize. A week later she was disqualified amid allegations that she had also cheated in the previous year's New York City Marathon by riding the subway for part of the distance.

Ruiz has always insisted that she won Boston fairly. Her credibility as a wronged woman was not enhanced when two years later she was given a probationary sentence for stealing cheques and cash from her employer. And her judgement was once again proved lacking in 1983 when she sold cocaine to an undercover police officer. To this day she remains a household name and a butt of jokes in the US. How ironic that the most famous American marathoner is one who never actually ran a marathon. Likewise in Britain most people have vaguely heard of the bloke who almost died in the London Olympics. And worldwide I suppose the best-known marathoner is the original messenger who ran to Athens.

So, there we have it: the three most famous marathoners in the world. One cheated; the second cheated and almost died; and the third just died. Why did the rest of them bother? And why on earth am I so keen to join their ranks?

CHAPTER 3

Going to the Gym – A Methodology

The preliminary stage of my marathon odyssey (if that's not a mixed metaphor) involves a little exploratory light exertion in the gym. Now, going to the gym is actually enjoyable, but sadly you only remember this fact *after* each visit. The pleasurableness of the experience is certainly not uppermost in your mind first thing in the morning when you are trying to persuade yourself to get out of bed a whole hour and a half earlier than you actually need to. Even if you manage to force yourself to do a work-out and feel correspondingly good afterwards, it still occurs to you that in order to gain any long-term benefit you will have to continue doing this three times a week for the rest of your life. And even though you may extend your mortal span through being fitter, how much of that extra time will have been spent on the pec deck watching terrible Mariah Carey videos? Therefore you need a motivation to go to the gym, a short-term goal, a financial inducement. Up until now I have operated on the following theory, which involves playing on one's own essential meanness.

Go to your local gym and ask what their rate for a single, one-off visit is. Write down this figure and immediately sign up for a whole year's membership. My local gym charged me £300 for the year as against £7 for one session.

Now before your first – and every subsequent – gym session you must repeat the following mantra: "THIS IS MY *LAST EVER* VISIT TO THE GYM."

This is not so unlikely really. For an unfit person, a visit to the gym is a degrading, depressing experience. You are in agony for days afterwards and you feel you have already become a complete laughing stock in front of your future peers in the world of workouts. So, a simple calculation will tell you:

Cost of first visit: £300.

Coming away after just half an hour of gasping and sweating on exercise machines, calibrated to their lowest possible setting, you realise how comprehensively you have been ripped off. You are never going back again (remember) so that means the single session has set you back £300. Think of all the things you could have bought for that money – a television set, a two-week package holiday, a black-market cup final ticket. Instead of which you got 30 minutes of pain-racked, public humiliation.

Cost of second visit: £300 ÷ 2 = £150.

One hundred and fifty pounds? They really saw you coming a mile off, didn't they? Okay, you weren't taken for as much money, but shouldn't you have known better this time? Overall you feel just as wretched as after your first visit.

Cost of third visit: £300 ÷ 3 = £100.

You really are a glutton for punishment of the financial as well as physical kind. The ton you've just blown could have bought you a television licence and, frankly, lying slumped in an armchair is more your métier isn't it?

Cost of fourth visit: £300 ÷ 4 = £75.

You complete mug. That £75 could have been invested in a decent seat at the ballet where you could watch some other people exerting themselves and think fondly of the pair of pre-paid Bloody Marys lined up for you in the crush bar.

Cost of fifth visit: £300 ÷ 5 = £60.

Improving, but you could still have gone out to an okay restaurant, had a drinkable bottle of wine, surprised a friend by picking up the tab and have had change for a taxi home.

And so on. If you can maintain your sense of outrage for enough visits, you will eventually get the session cost down to under £7 (or whatever the price of a one-off visit at your gym might be). This means that you have actually managed to save money and you can now stop going. Thus, from a motivation of sheer meanness you will have visited the gym approximately 50 times and hopefully have got yourself into some sort of shape.

On this occasion, however, I should need no such self-deluding pretexts. My motivation for getting down to some serious training could not be clearer. In just under a year's time I will have to force this body, whose previous competitive race was the 880 yards (school sports day 1971 – time unrecorded), to run the ultimate distance of 26.2 miles. I renew my lapsed membership at my local gym.

CHAPTER 4

Thoughts from the Treadmill

10 November

Cost: £300
Bike: 0 mins
Running machine: 0 mins
Shower: 5 mins

After all the usual vacillation, my first visit to the gym comes about because, typically, my boiler has broken down at the onset of winter and I need somewhere to take a shower. I contemplate using this opportunity to commence my training programme but my cunning brain manages to talk me out of it. Exercising today, it argues, would be counterproductive as it would only build up a backlog of sweaty T-shirts and underpants at a time when there is no immediate prospect of having any hot water to wash them in. Good point, my body meekly concurs, and we do no exercise today. All in all, that is probably among the most expensive ablutions in the history of the world. I expect I could have showered in ass's milk or champagne for less.

19 November

Cost: £150
Bike: 12 mins
Running machine: 3.5km (20 mins)
Weight: 73.5kg

My boiler has now been fixed so I have no excuse for not embarking on my first serious gym session.

I have decided to coincide my fitness regime with a structured programme of popular music re-education. Rather than subject myself to the vagaries of MTV I have brought my portable CD player to the gym. There is a handy flat surface next to the control panels on the running machine which seems purpose-built for my Discman. Unfortunately, as soon as I start running, vibrations course through the machine and cause the Discman to shuffle slyly towards the brink. I take my eye off it for a second and it has crashed to the ground like a naughty baby's dinner. This is an unforeseen setback. But quickly I have an idea: bring some Blu-tak next time to stick the CD player to the running machine. Ingenious. This, I anticipate, will be just the first of my many triumphs over adversity in the coming months. I think I may have that marathon licked.

So, just for today, I abandon the Discman and rely instead on the ubiquitously piped MTV. Although the TV is on a wall bracket behind me, I can watch it by making use of the full-length mirror directly in front of me, the ostensible function of which is to allow me to admire the athletic grace of my body as it pounds the running belt. Obviously I prefer to watch pop videos. For a few dim moments I puzzle over how many left-handed guitarists there seem to be in bands these days and wonder if an overly politically correct Musicians Union is conducting a positive recruitment drive among this socially disadvantaged group. Then I remember that I am watching the TV in the mirror and everything is reversed. The downside of this viewing arrangement soon becomes apparent. When the caption comes up at the end of the video informing viewers who the artist was, the name appears as back-to-front gibberish. I swing round to read it before it fades, forgetting that I am balancing on a track moving at 12km/hr and fall off the running machine in an undignified manner.

I hop back on to the belt in time to see the first mile tick off on the digital display. Just as I am feeling quite pleased with the effortless ease with which I have vaulted this first psychological barrier an annoying small voice inside my head says, "How do you know they're miles? They might be kilometres."

"This is Europhobe Britain", I retort jingoistically. "They have to be miles."

But now the seeds of doubt have been planted and liberally doused with Biogrow. I decide I would prefer to remain ignorant for the moment about whether they are miles or kilometres. Anyway, the best thing is not to clock-watch. I force myself to look away from the display and my eyes immediately alight on a sign fixed to the wall, featuring a cartoon of a man scratching his head. I read the caption underneath and any tiny crumb of morale-boosting self-delusion is crushed (and just imagine how small crumbs are once they're crushed). It reads "All our machines have been reset to metric measurements. We apologise for any confusion caused." Apologise for confusion? At this tentative stage in my grand design, confusion is my only ally. If I have to face up to the reality of how far I am attempting to run, I will give up immediately. Besides, I reason, there are wider-reaching benefits of not informing gym-users that the machines have been reset to metric. For example, the extremely unfit ladies who coyly subtract several stones when programming their weight into the machine. The figure they enter in pounds might actually approximate to their real weight in kilograms.

Shuffling through 20 minutes on the running machine seems an achievement and, not wishing to overdo it on my first proper visit to the gym, I head for the changing rooms. Here all the physical needs of the male gym-goer appear to be catered for. There are lockers, showers, loos, sauna, even one of those ironing boards to change nappies on for the New Men among us. Somehow, though, I can't help feeling that our psychological needs are being neglected. For example, there is a condom machine. This seems perfectly sensible. The fundamental reason why people bother to torture their bodies in this place is to make themselves more sexually attractive. Any of us Adonises leaving this place after a hefty work-out run the risk of having complete strangers making themselves sexually available to us and we would need to be prepared. But I am disappointed to find the condom dispenser issues prophylactics in the standard packets-of-three, just like the vending machines in pubs. Surely the one here in the gym should sell them in tens at least? Are we body-worshippers really being told that our sexual expectations, or indeed performances, are likely to be on a par with that of a fat bloke who's on his way to relieve a bladder bursting with 12 pints of lager? This is not the message we want to hear.

21 November

Cost: £100
Bike: 15 mins
Running machine: 4.5km. (25 mins)
Weight: 71kg

One hears a lot about the Mental Challenge of running a marathon; of the need to train one's mind as well as one's body. I just hadn't appreciated how quickly this would be required. My ingenious plan to get my Discman to remain stationary by sticking it to the running machine with Blu-tak has backfired. I was correct in my assumption that the Blu-tak would cause the Discman to forsake its lemming-like shuffle to the edge of the machine every 30 seconds. What happens now is that the vibrations from the running machine no longer make the Discman topple off; instead they transmit themselves directly into the player and cause the CD I am listening to to jump. This is even more irritating than having constantly to bat the machine back into position while running. I puzzle over this dilemma for a while, my concentration not helped by the stuttering song playing in my ears. I can think of no solution, short of Blu-takking the player to the ceiling from where it would no doubt fall on to my head. By the time I finally abandon fiddling with my Discman altogether, I am surprised to notice that eight minutes and 1.5 kilometres have elapsed. Maybe this is the way I can get through the sheer tedium of running 26.2 miles, by setting myself various forms of intellectual distraction. I wonder if I could persuade the trainer on duty to switch the TV set onto the Open University? Doing differential calculus backwards in the mirror, I'd have run a marathon before I knew it. Somehow I doubt there'd be many takers amongst the rest of the gym's clientele, though.

I manage to endure 25 minutes on the running machine with only two (admittedly quite long) walking breaks and one water stop. I decide my sterling efforts have earned me a relaxing sauna. Following the recent refurbishment of the gym the sauna room has now gone over to being mixed. Contrary to what might be supposed this is not necessarily an arrangement desired by the men. Men actually quite like sitting around nude in the company of other men, and there's nothing inherently homoerotic about it. I remember once going to a stag night when a group of about 20 blokes watched politely for half an hour as two strippers went about their routine. However, what really got the men going was a game played afterwards which involved the groom and best man stripping naked, standing on bar stools and throwing pints of beer over one another. Turning away from the reception with which this spectacle was greeted, which would not have shamed a Roman circus mob, I noticed one of the strippers sitting at the bar, still naked, sipping a drink and chatting to the barman. Not one of the revellers was paying her a scant bit of attention. Now there is no good biological explanation for this peculiar behaviour that I know of and, according to strict Darwinian principles, the genetic line of males who show more interest in other beer-throwing males than naked females would probably be expected to die out. But blokes just seem to be like that. And we've survived so far.

There is another problem with the mixed facilities which I encounter today. I am alone in the sauna when a good-looking woman enters clad only in a very small towel which leaves little to the imagination. She asks me if I would mind if she poured some more water on the coals. It's already pretty hellishly hot in there but I could hardly refuse and retain my manhood. So I agree and try to make it sound like I was about to suggest the same thing myself. The woman then lies down in such a position as to render the imagination's small contribution to what's under the towel pretty much redundant. I begin to panic. Obviously if I exited the sauna now, it would look as if I was a total prude or, worse still, a complete wimp who couldn't handle a couple of extra degrees of Celsius. What I fear, though, is that if I look at her (and, apart from a load of stripped pine there's not a lot else to look at in a sauna) I will develop an erection. After that, even if the thermostat goes haywire and the sauna melts down, sheer embarrassment would prevent me from moving and I would have to sit there until my flesh seared and my blood boiled away. I leave immediately. On balance, prudery or wimpdom is preferable to death by broiling.

24 November
Cost: £75
Bike: 15 mins
Running machine: 30 mins (5.2 km)
Weight: 71.5kg

I manage a credible distance today, over 5 kilometres. By the way, I've now accepted that they are kilometres, not miles. This is bearable because the imperial/metric conversion chart in the gym only goes up to 10 kilometres and I am refusing to allow my brain to calculate exactly how many kilometres equate to 26.2 miles, although I have an uneasy fear that it's rather a large multiple of five.

The problem with these theoretical distances is they mean nothing to me because, despite being brought up in the country, I have lived in London for the last 15 years. In the capital all distances are calculated either in the number of tube stops or taxi fares. When giving directions, you tell people it's five stops on the Piccadilly Line or a tenner in a black cab including tip. No one has any idea how far away anywhere in London is from anywhere else in miles. Taxi drivers are aware of this, which is why they are not at all fazed by the theoretical regulation that they must accept all fares within a 10-mile radius of Charing Cross and will brazenly drive off, leaving you threatening to report them. They know you're not going to get an ordnance survey map of London, a pair of dividers and a calculator and work it out. It seems to me it would be more sensible to replace the electronic display on running machines in London gyms with a Hackney cab taximeter which would tick off your running performance in pounds and pence instead of meaningless units like kilometres and calories burned. That way, after a healthy half-hour jog, you could be heartened by telling yourself that you ran from Soho to Camden Town. And you wouldn't have to leave a tip.

I find the only way to invest these distances with meaning is to imagine that I am starting from my parents' house in the village of Streatley in Berkshire where I grew up. Today, for example I ran past Bishop's Farm, past my old school, the petrol station, across the railway bridge and got as far as the Fair Mile Hospital. As this is a psychiatric asylum it is probably not a good place to be found lying slumped by the roadside exhausted and dazed. This should give me an incentive to run further next time.

My weight has increased, I notice, but is that good or bad? Does it mean I am putting on that vital muscle bulk? Or that my post-gym food binges are cancelling out all the calorie-burning value of the exercise? Hmm, I think I need to do some more research here.

2 December

Damn. Less than a month into my fitness programme and I have already missed a whole week's training. My fall from virtue has been brought about by a glut of early Christmas parties. I am already starting to appreciate the inverse relationship that exists between alcoholic intake and successful visits to the gym the next morning. I know that I should give up booze, but that would be a Scrooge-like act just a couple of weeks before Christmas. Besides, stopping drinking all at once would give as big a shock to my system as trying to run 26.2 miles straight off. The only sensible way to proceed, I decide, will be to phase out alcohol gradually as I phase in exercise.

9 December

Cost: £60
Bike: 15 mins
Running machine: 5km (28 mins)
Weight: 73.5kg
Item forgotten: towel

One of those pieces of popular knowledge which everyone knows but no one knows how they know, or indeed if it's actually true, is the human brain can only retain 11 ideas at the same time. Sadly for the runner, there are *twelve* items to take to the gym for an effective workout. This means that I inevitably seem to forget one of them. The items are:

1) *shirt (preferably branded, sleeveless, if you have decent upper body development)*
2) *shorts (skin-tight, if decent lower body development; baggy if me)*
3) *sports socks (branded and matching one another if possible).*
4) *trainers (branded and not the same ones you wear during the day)*
5) *towel (not sure if there are any brands, but sports companies no doubt working on it)*
6) *swimming costume (to preserve modesty in sauna)*
7) *shampoo*
8) *change of underwear*
9) *shaving kit*
10) *deodorant*
11) *water bottle*

12) *Damn! What is that twelfth one? Only kidding… a good book (to read on the exercise bike). And, oh yes…*

13) *gym bag (well, by definition, you can't forget this without forgetting everything else as well).*

As I mentioned before, one of the things you gradually realise when you start exercising is that it is actually pleasurable. Once you've got over how much you resent it intellectually (you could have stayed in bed, made some phone calls, played a computer game, done your laundry), you realise that you enjoy it on a natural and instinctive level. After all, running is what bodies were designed to do (even mine). My brain might enjoy going to see a film, but my body finds remaining motionless for two hours a bit dull. Sadly this feelgood factor is belied by my image in the mirror. As the minute counter on the running machine trips over into double figures I see myself start to fall apart in front of my own eyes: red-faced, hair plastered with sweat, eyes popping, mouth gasping. There before me is my very own Picture of Dorian Grey to remind me of my mortality. It's like in that weird Michael Powell film *Peeping Tom* where the sadistic murderer forces his victims to watch their own death agonies in a mirror as he kills them. (Sorry, for those of you who haven't seen the movie: I've just given away the ending.)

Only after I have finished my work-out and am back in the changing rooms do I realise that the 12th item I have forgotten today is my towel. I end up having to dry my entire body with the gym's hairdryer, which takes ages and frankly looks odd. Blow drying your pubic hair is an especially unusual affectation and attracts odd looks from other men.

Now, exercise makes you hungry, but sadly it doesn't make you hungry for all the healthy organic things they optimistically serve up in the gym's own cafe, such as salads, quiches and yoghurts. No, millions of years of evolution has instilled in you the desire to eat animal flesh after exertion. After all, in prehistoric times you wouldn't have run all that way after a bit of lettuce, would you? No, you are conditioned to expect meat; your prey; protein and fat. You crave something with a pulse, and we're not talking about the type you find in a mixed bean salad here. Conveniently located a few hundred yards from the gym is a fish and chip shop. I am powerless to resist. No doubt they have industrial fans blasting the aroma of scalding animal fat in the direction of the ravenous clientele down the road.

11 December

Cost: £50
Bike: 15 mins
Running machine: 5.25km (30 mins)
Weight: 71kg
Item forgotten: water bottle

I haven't yet plucked up the courage to tell anyone that I am planning to run a marathon, let alone write a book about it. I'm afraid of their reaction. Obviously the idea of the book is to generate laughter, but only once it is written and people are actually reading it. Laughter at the very idea of me undertaking this project would be a very different and altogether more dispiriting thing. The advantage of this project is that I can write the book as I am running, killing two birds with one stone. But which comes first: the chicken or the egg? The bird or the stone? Am I going to the gym in order to write the book or writing the book in order to go to the gym? One shouldn't puzzle over such philosophical conundrums while trying to balance on a belt slipping under your feet at 12.5km/hr.

I have forgotten my water bottle today so I have to go over to the water dispenser for liberal refreshment after my half-hour on the running machine. My eye is caught by a notice on the wall which invites the gym's clientele to "Do the Marathon challenge". At least 20 people have already signed up for what I had assumed was a pretty daunting undertaking and, amazingly, several have already completed it. I immediately feel disheartened. *That* many people from the gym have done a marathon? Then I realise that this is a progressive marathon. You just have to do a bit each day on the running machine until you rack up the necessary 42.2 kilometres. Damn! I've done it now. I've accidentally found out the fact I have been trying to hide from myself, namely how many kilometres there are in a marathon. And the magic number is 42 – the answer to life, the universe and everything according to Douglas Adams. Incidentally, as a hardened pub-quizzer, I can also tell you it is the number of days in the gestation period of a ferret.

13 December

Cost: £42.86
Bike 15 mins
Running machine: 5.5km (30 mins)
Weight: 71.5kg
Item forgotten: deodorant

It's a miracle that I make it to the gym at all today, the morning after the *Daily Telegraph*'s Christmas party. I set the machine to walking pace for a long time before I embark on any running. This is, of course, important preparation for the Big Day. The New York Marathon has a field of over 30,000 runners and it can often take 10 or 15 minutes to cross the start line, so one might as well get used to setting off at a stroll. Exercise is painful today and I have to force myself to stick out my allotted half-hour. I feel as if I am sweating neat vodka and could wring out my shirt and make a decent martini with the result.

Which is the laziest organ in the body, I am led to wonder. Not the feet (okay feet aren't really an organ, but you know what I mean) or the heart or the lungs or even (on this occasion) the liver. No, the laziest organ in the body is actually the brain. It is constantly looking for excuses to give up. I keep having to make little pacts with it, giving myself intermediate targets: let's just keep going till 10 mins, 15 mins, 3km, 4km etc. Then when we reach that mark I have to think of some new ruse to persuade it to continue to the next target point.

I wonder if I am discovering the existence of the soul. There are definitely three warring entities within myself: the Body, lumbering and dull; the Brain, sly and lazy; but between them is something else, calm and purposeful: the Will, maybe. While my brain is listing reasons to stop (general Yuletide lack of fitness, dangerously high blood-alcohol level, don't want to overdo it too early in the regime, etc.), this third entity is gently telling me to go on. And it seems to get its way.

I have forgotten my deodorant. But it's not my problem. It's the problem of anyone who sits next to me on public transportation for the rest of the day.

23 December

Cost: £37.50
Bike 15 mins
Running machine: 6km (34 mins)
Weight: 71.5kg

Interestingly, I don't seem to have gained any weight over the pre-Christmas hospitality season. Could my training be paying off already? I examine my running stance in the mirror. Is it my imagination or does it look more professional? I decide to concentrate on my technique today. How should I hold my hands? Karate style for cutting cleanly through air? Or fists clenched for punching my way through crowds of dawdling runners? I find I have now got to a stage where I can run my 30 odd minutes without having to slow down to a walk at any point. Walking is bad, mainly because it is a much more pleasurable activity than running, and is in turn superseded in the attractiveness stakes by a nice sit down with a drink and a TV remote.

The counter on the running machine I'm using today measures distances in metres rather than kilometres. This gives it the uncanny appearance of ticking off years instead of distances. I watch centuries flit past in seconds: 476 – the fall of the Roman Empire; 663 – the Synod of Whitby (the date is embedded in my memory but I've no idea what it was); the Dark Ages, the Middle Ages, the Renaissance slip by in their turn. I test myself on how many dates I can identify as they flash up: 1492 – Columbus sailed the ocean blue; 1644 – the Battle of Marston Moor. So this is what school history was for – to make the first painful couple of kilometres on the running machine more enjoyable. 1770 – Beethoven is born. He writes all his great works and dies within the space of a few bars of Gabrielle on the in-house sound system; 1805 – Battle of Trafalgar; 1815 – Waterloo; 1929 – my father is born, then my mother, then me, I'm an adult and then, a few strides later (even by the most optimistic estimates), I'm dead and time rolls on uncaring. There's something profoundly morbid about running.

29 December

Cost: £33.33
Bike: 15 mins
Running machine: 6.3km (33mins)
Weight: 71.5kg

It is possible to explain almost anything with statistics. My absence of weight change I now attribute to the fact that I am shedding fat and laying down muscle at an exact gram for gram ratio.

The problem with running in a gym is that you have nothing to look at except MTV or your own reflection in the mirror in front of you. Both are depressing. I resolve to wear more interesting T-shirts in future, or at least ones that look good in reverse. Then I hit on the idea of printing special T-shirts with reversed-out text (a bit like on the front of ambulances). Just imagine, one could brush up on one's knowledge, learn poems, historical dates, chemical formulae, post-war FA Cup winners. There are all manner of things that one could commit to memory in that otherwise dead exercise time. A sonnet would fit nicely on a T-shirt. Not only would my range of shirts be useful in the gym, they would also be a conversation piece outside it (along the lines of "Excuse me, I think you're wearing your T-shirt inside out"). There's money to be made out of this lark yet.

As I start to run distances in excess of half an hour, new problems, relevant to a marathon, start to emerge. My water bottle balances nicely between two parallel bars on the running machine. Being able to take a drink is an occasional herring with which one can reward the recalcitrant performing seal of one's body. But these days I easily get through a small bottle of Evian in half an hour. I start to worry about the size of bottle I'm going to need to lug around if I ever get any further in this. I'll need one of those huge plastic tanks you get in office water dispensers strapped to my back. Then at some point I'm going to need to address the direct corollary of water consumption: needing to go to the loo. Proper marathon runners, I have read, just pee down their legs on the move. This seems an unnecessarily antisocial thing to practise at this early stage in my training regime. Besides, for the moment, none of the water gets as far as my bladder but seems to come spurting straight out of my pores, like a cartoon character who drinks a glass of water after being shot.

The first couple of kilometres trip past pretty quickly these days and I find myself starting to resent them. Just a month ago they were eagerly welcomed friends and companions on my journey; now I view them irritably like street beggars in Calcutta, that I have to force my way past to get to my ultimate destination. Though it is very bad for posture, it is hard not to fix one's gaze on the distance counter on the running machine as it wearily clicks over the Clicks. I have come to the conclusion that if I stare intently at it, it turns over quicker. Maybe I have some telekinetic ability to make the counter move faster by sheer willpower. It is dubious how useful this skill would be in an actual marathon where distances are measured in real metres of asphalt, but I could be a great discovery to science.

I am starting to discover that, once one gets over the discomfort of the first 20 minutes or so, running becomes quite effortless. In fact, it's possible to forget that you are running at all. The dull physical activity occupies your body and frees your mind to ponder the meaning of universal issues, such as: why do all pop songs at the moment seem to have a tin whistle accompaniment and a Spanish guitar solo over the middle eight?

2 January

Cost: £30
Bike: 17 mins
Running machine: 7km (38 mins)
Weight (revised): 75kg
Item forgotten: spare underpants

This is my first run of the New Year and I have two problems. Firstly, chronic alcohol poisoning after Hogmanay revels. Dripping manly sweat on to the running machine is all well and good, but throwing up over it is not on. Secondly, a bunch of other people, probably equally the worse for wear, who have rashly made New Year's resolutions to get fit and will be slogging and struggling feebly on the machines for the next week or two until they give up for another 12 months.

For a change there is no MTV today and instead the TV has been switched to the sports channel where they are showing a Great Sporting Disasters video – stock cars piling up, skiers falling over, rallycross riders being thrown off their bikes etc. I presume this is a deliberate ploy to get rid of the people on New Year's Resolutions as soon as possible after they've paid up their membership. If camcorders had been around in ancient times I suppose footage of Pheidippides clutching at his chest and writhing on the ground would probably have made it on to *It'll be All Right on the Night*.

Nowadays I find I can get through the first 10 minutes on the treadmill without degenerating into a physical wreck in front of my own eyes. This is important. The Ostensible Dignity Factor is all that matters in the gym. No one else can see how many miles you've already run or what difficulty level your machine is calibrated to. All they can see is how red-faced and knackered you look. If you are cruising along surveying the world benignly or, better still, having a relaxed conversation with your neighbour then you are cool, otherwise you are dismissed as a New Year's Resolutioner.

By the end of the session I am able to congratulate myself that I have now completed the Marathon Challenge. In other words, if you add up all the distances I have run so far, it amounts to 42 kilometres. The bad news for my athletic aspirations is that it has taken me 53 days to achieve this target. Clearly I must improve my performance before the Big Day, lest it become the Big Month and a Half.

In the changing rooms I belatedly discover the real reason for the strange consistency of my weight over the few weeks. It turns out that I have been using the weighing maching incorrectly. It is one of those old-fashioned jobbies with little weights that you have to slide along a scale. Once I position the weights correctly, I find that I weigh 75kg. More than before. But I still don't know if this is a good or a bad thing.

6 January

Cost: £27.27
Bike: 12 mins
Running machine: 7.25km (38 mins)
Weight: 75kg
Max. heart rate: 162bpm

My parents have given me a heart-rate monitor for Christmas (after I begged them for one using all the resources of "pester power" available to a 38-year-old). Over the past fortnight I have finally figured out how to work it and so now have a new statistic to ponder on in addition to times, distances, weights and cost. I attach the sensor strip across my chest and read off my resting heart rate from the wristwatch display: 62 beats per minute. Once I start running my heart rate climbs rapidly. I watch it contentedly for a while as it edges up beyond 100 and then realise with a frisson of alarm that I have no idea how high it should be going. I recall seeing a chart with various coloured bands relating to different fitness objectives (cardiovascular workout zone, fat-burning zone, etc.). I also remember that for my age group there was a red band labelled "improved performance" which ended at about 160 beats per minute. My heart rate is creeping steadily up past 150 and I begin to wonder what happens if I exceed 160. I don't recall the colour of the next zone. Could it have been black and emblazoned with skulls and crossbones? What exactly happens if you go beyond your limit? Do you immediately keel over with a massive coronary? Or spontaneously combust?

My lazy brain jumps at the chance to recommend immediate cessation of exercise in order to appraise the situation. Not that it cares about my body, but it realises that their survival is mutually dependent. I calculate what my heart rate would be at the end of a marathon. If it continued to increase as it is currently doing (at about 60bpm per 7km), I estimate that at 42km I would have a theoretical heart rate of 460bpm and would have matched Pheidippides' feat an hour or two before. Luckily it settles down at around 160bpm.

I have read that the important factor in an athlete is how quickly the heart rate returns to normal after exercise. So, back in the changing room, I sit down and, spurning even the lightest effort of opening my locker, stare at my wrist monitor. My pulse rate stubbornly refuses to fall below 90bpm. It could just be a case of a watched pot never boils I suppose, but I can think of two alternative explanations:

1) *I am still chronically unfit and this whole endeavour is doomed.*

2) *Unbeknown to myself I am struggling with my sexuality and am excited by the naked male bodies on view around me in the changing room.*

Neither explanation exactly appeals, so I conclude logically that the monitor must be faulty.

8 January

Watertight excuse for not going to the gym this week: splinter in foot.

Splinters are just one of the perils of living in North London these days with the obligatory bare floorboards. Despite the inconvenience of a sliver of wood decomposing inside my sole, I am secretly quite pleased because I have a good excuse for not going to the gym. Now this is a condition that I call Imaginary Boss Syndrome. I rehearse the excuse to my Imaginary Boss in my head. Sorry, I tell him, but I couldn't go to the gym this week because I was possibly in the early stages of gangrene. That's all right, says the Imaginary Boss, take the rest of the week off. Thanks very much, I say and punch the air as I leave his Imaginary Office. Of course, the problem with Imaginary Bosses is, well, that they are imaginary. I'm really only cheating myself.

15 January

Watertight excuse for not going to the gym this week: head cold.

I have a caught a heavy cold (I told the Imaginary Boss that it was 'flu). Angela has been to the doctor with the same thing and has been sent away with the traditional doctor's excuse that it is a viral infection and therefore antibiotics would be useless. This is no doubt a way of saving money on prescriptions, but I think rather short-sighted by the medical profession. After all people don't go to see their GP to be given medical advice, they go to be given some medicine. Taking this will make them feel better, psychologically if not actually physiologically. Think of the profits that could be generated from hypochondriacs like me if doctors regularly prescribed placebos. A viral infection, the doctor would say, ah, there's a new drug for that, Mr Taylor. And he would scribble out a prescription for some gelatine pills. It doesn't matter what it is as long as I *think* it's medicine. I'd willingly hand over £6 for the stuff, and it'd probably do me the power of psychosomatic good as well. This scheme could put the National Health Service back in the black.

Anyway, in the meantime I have a viral infection. My friend Tara warns me that training in this condition could be very dangerous. She knows about this because she is a radio producer, whose long service on phone-in programmes has made her an expert in fields such as incontinence, cellulite and other intimate afflictions beloved of daytime audiences.

24 January

Cost: £25
Bike: 12 mins
Running machine: 8km (45 mins)
Weight: 75kg
Max. heart rate: 171bpm

Amazingly it is two and a half weeks since I last visited the gym. Doesn't time fly when you're having fun (i.e. not flogging your body to death on a treadmill)? Strangely enough, in this period of inactivity I have developed athlete's foot and this morning I have a sore left knee. How can this be? Is my body mocking my pathetic lack of physical exertion over the last fortnight? I decide that getting athlete's foot is a badge of honour. Not many people in this world can claim to merit this affliction and my efforts over the last few months have clearly allowed me to join their exalted ranks. As for the knee, it is probably just pining for the feel of the running belt being pounded below it.

Today the first kilometre on the running machine is never-ending. I am convinced that the gym staff have sneakily re-set the machine to miles in my absence. My fortnight of indolence also shows in my physical response to the first 10 minutes of running as revealed by my friend who never lies – the mirror. It is like the bit at the end of *Raiders of the Lost Ark* where all the Nazis turn into ghouls and their faces boil away to reveal hideously grinning skulls. I am a wreck again and everyone around me can see it.

As I start to run, a pretty mixed-race woman steps on to the adjoining running machine. Excellent, I think, a race. I begin shooting sly sideways glances towards her. "Men are all such sad oglers." she thinks, catching one of my over-lingering looks in her direction and assuming it was aimed at her cleavage. Actually men are far sadder than she could ever imagine. My gaze was directed at the display on her running machine to check what distance she had managed to clock up and to be sure I was beating her. Sadly for me, just as I am making serious ground on her she gives up and walks off, probably to report me for sexual harassment. She is replaced by a tubby woman who sets her machine to 3km/hr. Now, this is actually less than normal walking pace so the woman appears to be moving in slow motion. Maybe I've just become over-confident after my pathetic two months of training, but seriously this is zimmer-frame pace. What's the point? She'd get a more thorough cardiovascular work-out shuffling round her house in carpet slippers smoking a fag. This thought seems to communicate itself to her and she, too, departs.

I persevere without a pacemaker and manage to record a distance of 8 kilometres which, if it were a batsman's tally in cricket, would be described by Richie Benaud as having been "ground out" rather than scored. Hobbling back to the changing rooms with my left knee now throbbing, I realise that I had completely misinterpreted its earlier message. Recognising the route to the gym and the ordeal awaiting there, it was actually saying: "Please don't do any exercise ever again... and I think I speak here for the right knee and most of the ligaments as well." As a runner, it's important to listen to your body.

Back in the changing rooms I eavesdrop on a typical blokes' gym conversation. This pair probably met in the squash tournament last year and have been exchanging nods over the exercise bikes ever since. Now they find themselves towelling down at adjacent lockers and it would seem rude not to strike up a conversation. After a few awkward opening pleasantries Bloke Number One hits on an inspired gambit (and for this I feel I have to apologise on behalf of my sex to the whole of womankind). He asks Bloke Number Two, "What are you driving at the moment?" This is exactly what Bloke Number Two wanted to hear and the two of them immediately launch into a passionate heart-to-heart on competition air filters, free-flow exhausts, low-profile tyres and other incomprehensible things. (Okay, I probably just feel excluded because I don't have a car. When asked what I drive, I always reply, truthfully, that my last car was a Porsche. It was actually the first, and in my opinion most stylish, car designed by Ferdinand Porsche – the Volkswagen Beetle.) But back to the Blokes who are still droning on in similar fashion. Why do they need to talk about their cars, I wonder? I mean, they saw each others' dicks in the shower earlier and therefore already know who's got the biggest.

16 February

Cost: £23.08
Bike: 12 mins
Running machine: 8.5km (47 mins)
Weight: 74.5kg
Max. heart rate: 168bpm
Item forgotten: sports socks

Shockingly it is over three weeks since my last training session. What went wrong, I ask myself, shaking my head in sad disbelief like an England manager after a 4–0 drubbing by Moldova. My brain dutifully produces its sick note. Okay, it's true that about three weeks ago I had a mild bout of food poisoning which took a while to clear up. And last week I went to the USA for a wedding, and somehow all the gaps in between have been neatly polyfillad in with valid excuses for non-exertion. I realise now my brain's crafty ploy. It has understood that once I am actually in the gym a certain measure of the "well, why not, as I'm here?" thinking will creep in. Its trick is to prevent me from ever getting there in the first place. As before, my body has started aching despite the lack of appreciable exertion over the previous three weeks.

The music playing in the gym as I start my session today is not a song I recognise. It features a heavy techno beat, to which the singer is counting from one to eight over and over again before exhorting us to "work it out". "Nine?" I hazard, presuming this is some pre-nursery numeracy tape. The arithmetic seems a tad easy. I mean, the people who come to the gym aren't necessarily the brightest around, but I presume they can count from nought to 60 or at least know how quickly their cars can do it. Then I realise that this is an exercise tape that someone has thoughtfully provided for us and we are being asked to work out our bodies, rather than any sums. With some trepidation I start running, only to be pleasantly surprised that it is not the ordeal that I feared. Maybe running is like riding a bike – once learnt, never forgotten. On second thoughts I decide to put cycling analogies out of my head, as riding a bike seems an infinitely more sensible way of traversing the impending 42.2 kilometres.

The in-house sound system is now pumping out a song entitled "I'm Horny". This is strangely inappropriate. Although the gym is the Temple of the Body and is today particularly well stocked with beautiful high priestesses, it is not a place where I can imagine feeling sexually aroused. For a start all available blood is being frantically pumped to my muscles and there is none left for other appendages. I know men are supposed to think about sex every 11 seconds (or something) but this does not apply on the running machine.

My neighbour today is a Nordic Ice Queen who at the time of my arrival has already notched up an impressive 25 minutes on her machine. Occasionally she stops her belt, squats down and tugs at her legs. I can't work out whether this is part of some advanced in-training stretching exercises or whether she is crippled by cramps with trying to keep up with me. We have been exchanging what I have assumed to be competitive glances for some minutes. It suddenly strikes me that maybe she just fancies me. I dwell on this notion for a minute or two before rejecting it. Two places where I am never destined to pick up women are the gym and the dance floor. Only on occasions where zero bodily co-ordination is required am I able to maintain the requisite dignity to have a chance with the opposite sex. Probably the Ice Queen was just looking in puzzlement at my Argyle socks – I forgot the white towelling ones.

Such is the pressure to compete with her that I find I have run for a whole 22 minutes without a break. I am well beyond mere oxygen debt and am now into oxygen heavy overdraft with rude letters from my bank manager. Suddenly, mercifully, my rival steps off her machine leaving me with only 5 kilometres to make up – a distance I should easily attain. It must be admitted, though, that aesthetic victory is hers and the wall mirror leaves me in no doubt of this. She still looks like a shampoo advert, whilst I resemble a boiled lobster.

Now she has gone, my will to win is sapped and I struggle to pound out the remaining kilometres. I invent intellectual distractions to keep me going: am I running fast enough? I have selected a default speed of 12km/hr. This would theoretically get me through a marathon in under four hours (though I am aware that even with today's personal best run, I have still completed only a fifth of the distance). But what about the effect of running on asphalt and concrete rather than a smoothly yielding running belt? What about the retarding effects of those constant high fives with spectators? Isn't there some Newtonian law about opposite forces? How much faster will I have to run to compensate for this?

In my determination to surpass my previous distance record, I push my three-weeks-out-of-condition body. My work-shy brain is now panicking and it dredges up something it once read about overtraining and how it is actually more harmful than training too little. Much as stopping appeals, I ignore this ruse. If my brain had its way my training would be limited to a stroll down to the newsagent's every morning. I finally slip off the running machine after three-quarters of an hour and experience that sensation of "moonwalking". This is a bit like sailors trying to get their land legs after a long voyage at sea. I feel as if I am floating across the floor as I walk over to the water dispenser at as dignified a pace as possible. I complete my programme with a "warm down" (why isn't it called a "cool up" I've always wanted to know). This includes three sets of sit-ups. The advantage of the sit-up is that it is the only form of valid exercise which allows you to lie flat on your back. As long as your hands are behind your head and your knees bent you can lie there for as long as you want, looking as if at any moment you are about to jerk up into a punishing set of crunches. In fact you are just crashed out in a state of exhaustion. I stare at the ceiling and can hear the words of the Beatles song filling my head: "She said: I know what it's like to be dead."

Back in the changing room, once again my heart rate refuses to fall below 90bpm inside the first 10 minutes. Eventually I give up. It's hardly my fault. I have been exercising for a total of about 90 minutes (47 minutes running, 12 on the bike, another 30 minutes of stretches and weights) which equals 5,400 seconds. Now on average I should have been thinking about sex every 11 seconds which makes a total of 490 seconds (assuming I thought about it for one second each time). So, at a conservative estimate, I have at least eight minutes of thinking solidly about sex to catch up on. No wonder my blood is still racing.

25 February

Cost: £21.43
Bike: 10 mins
Running machine: 4.5km (4 run, 0.5 limped) (25 mins)
Weight: 75kg
Max. heart rate: 160bpm
Item forgotten: swimming costume

I am conscious that I have begun to strike an altogether more athletic figure in the mirror. For once my chest looks broader than my waist. Of course, it could be that they just use fairground distorting mirrors at the gym to create a flattering effect for the more out-of-condition patrons. The occasional woman mounts one of the adjoining machines, but like lusty Arthurian swains stepping up to the stone, after a few token heaves at the sword, they retire shamed.

In short, everything appears to be going well. I arrive at my fourth kilometre and 20th minute feeling so refreshed that my brain doesn't attempt to use either of these milestones as excuses to take a walking break. But it has been secretly leafing through my medical records and has unearthed details of a sporting injury to my left calf which I sustained two years ago on an ill-fated tennis camp in Portugal. It has pulled a few strings with the relevant muscles (possibly hamstrings) and got them to collude. In any case I suddenly feel a sharp twinge from the offending limb and, mindful of the fortnight I spent on crutches on that previous occasion, decide to abandon my run.

With hindsight I realise that what I have probably done is overtrained. Trying to run a greater distance every visit to the gym is a typical beginner's error (this is male competitiveness taken to its ultimate extreme: being competitive with *yourself*). A proper training schedule, which I will shortly be adopting, demands that every third week you reduce the distance run in order to consolidate the gains made. Despite my capitulation on this occasion, I have a quiet word with my sneaky brain and warn it that nothing short of total physical disability or death is going to stop me from doing this marathon. And in the first eventuality I could always enter the wheelchair event. I saw several one-legged competitors run rings round able-bodied athletes (well, not literally obviously – that would be silly and rather dangerous in a linear road race).

I walk another half a kilometre on the running machine to prevent the muscles from seizing up and then retire to the changing rooms to lick my wounds (again, metaphorically: I'm not that supple yet.) Of course, the obvious recuperative thing to do now would be to take a sauna and apply heat to the afflicted muscles. But naturally, today of all days I have chosen to forget my swimming costume and thus the mixed sauna is out of bounds.

4 March

Watertight excuse for not going to the gym this week: calf injury.

Angela suggests I should do some walking to strengthen this recalcitrant muscle. She tells me how she walks to the tube station every morning and evening – a healthy 30-minute constitutional. This, of course, is what *real* exercise is about: the freedom of the open road. And it's truly free – no gym subscriptions to be paid. So I stroll to Highgate underground station. But then, half way there, I suddenly remember that earlier in the week I rashly purchased a weekly season ticket. This means that my round bus trip from my house to the underground (cost 60p either way) is already paid for. So, this exercise, far from being free, is actually costing me £1.20 a day. I complete the distance, but my saunter has become a resentful trudge.

11 March

Watertight excuse for not going to the gym this week: sore back.

This week's affliction is due not to any physical exertion but because my cat, Doo, has taken to sleeping on my bed. She tends to stake out her strategic position early in the evening, so that by the time I retire she is already lying there bang in the middle of the bedspread, snoring gently. Loath to move her, I arrange myself in a question mark shape around her under the duvet. The real question mark is why I bother to injure myself just to avoid disturbing a creature whose only interest in me lies in the fact that somewhere back in prehistory my species developed a thumb and hers didn't, thus making me better environmentally adapted to purchasing and opening tins of Whiskas.

18 March

Watertight excuse for not going to the gym this week: er…To be honest I haven't really got one. General apathy I suppose. My back is still a little tender, and I've developed athlete's foot again. I really think this condition has been misnamed, as it only seems to appear during weeks when I have done positively no exercise whatsoever. I know there are such things as psychosomatic illnesses where you become so convinced you are suffering from an illness that you actually develop the symptoms, but do ironic psychosomatic conditions exist, where your body is essentially taking the piss? I think I must be suffering from a previously unknown condition which I shall call Slacker's Foot. There. At least I have made a contribution to medical science this week. Or perhaps I should name this newly discovered illness after myself: Taylor's Syndrome. The problem with having such a common surname is that there is no doubt already a disease, probably of the pancreatic lining, called Taylor's Syndrome discovered by some ambitious forebear of mine. Even so it's not very memorable. Better to have a cool and exotic name like Dr Alzheimer. I mean no one's going to forget that illness – except people suffering from it I suppose.

I'm also feeling a bit demoralised because almost everyone I tell about my marathon ambition says that they were a good distance runner at school. In fact, quite a few of them mention modestly that they ran for their county. How can this be true of so many of my friends? Did they all grow up in Rutland or other small county? Or in some left-wing inner city borough where in a spirit of socialist non-competition anyone, regardless of ability, was allowed to be in the athletics team? My Russian friend Larissa goes one better and casually lets drop that she used to be Under-16 1500-metre champion of the Soviet Union.

Of course, it is easy for someone to say that they were once a competent distance runner. After all, this is not a claim that is ever likely to be put to the test. A boast of being ex-school 100-metre champion could be scuppered by the person in question having to run for a bus and pulling up wheezing and gasping after 20 metres. But a distance running capability is unlikely to be verified in any everyday situation. It's not as if, having missed your bus, instead of waiting for the next one you're going to run 10 miles to your destination.

I'm definitely going to the gym tomorrow, come rain or come shine.

14 April

Cost: £20
Bike: 12 mins
Stepper: 107 floors (20 mins)
Running machine: 6km (33 mins)
Weight: 75kg
Max. heart rate: 163bpm
Item forgotten: water bottle

I don't remember what the weather was like the next day. It was too long ago. The only thing I'm sure about is that I didn't go to the gym. I'm following my own exercise regime which stipulates that one mustn't do any training in any month which has five letters in its name. It's over six weeks since my last session. I can scarcely remember where the gym is and I have been getting sarcastic mailings from them. They have clearly sussed that I am no athlete and are now offering me reduced-rate facials and invitations to take part in quiz evenings. I console myself that I am one of those vital clients who makes money for gyms by paying up front and then not using any of the facilities for months on end.

Before leaving home today I have a spoonful of some new energy concentrate I bought a few weeks back, riddled with guilt about my absence of recent exercise. It seems to me that these things are a contradiction in terms: anyone strong enough to lift the huge barrel down off the shelf in the health food shop by definition wouldn't need it. The only other contribution I have made to my marathon regime in the meantime is to have my hair cut very short. It turns out that having the right haircut is psychologically important. I decide that I cut quite a cool figure on the running machine. After all, when did you last see a serious athlete with floppy hair? Sebastian Coe, you reply. Yes, but he was only practising to be a Tory MP.

So out of practice am I that I have forgotten the most essential item of all – my water bottle. Obviously there is a water dispenser at the gym but this means that I have to hop off the running machine after 20 minutes. I moonwalk over and lie under the tap for what is hopefully not too undignified an amount of time. By the time I am sufficiently rehydrated someone quite muscular has pinched my treadmill so I have to finish my session on the stepping machine. Climbing stairs is actually easier than running but far duller. Vertical distance achieved is somehow less satisfying than horizontal. Perhaps this is because stair climbing is the one gym exercise that doesn't imitate any form of sport. On the running machine you can fantasise about the roar of the crowd as you enter the Olympic stadium at Mile 26. On the exercise bike you can imagine the Maillot Jaune on your back as you sprint down the Champs Elysées to the finishing line in the Tour de France. Even on the cross trainer you can picture yourself on overland skis with a rifle strapped to your back in one of those winter Olympic events that only Norwegians enter. But stair climbing? What sort of a discipline is that? Quite useful training for firemen maybe, but that's about it. Oh well, I console myself, as I stump up the floors, it's all good practice for New York sightseeing in case the elevators are out of order at the Empire State Building.

I have decided not to overdo it. The desire to exceed my previous distance on each visit to the gym is probably what has been exacerbating my knee and calf. The problem is that my friend Mary has taken up running and phones me up daily to report the distance she has achieved. She has a job working in Liverpool which she hates and so is probably motivated by imagining herself sprinting down the M62 in the general direction of London. Despite the fact that she is 200 miles away I still feel competitive with her, and eight kilometres would be easily manageable. But all the same I decide to restrict myself to six today. I am learning to read the little twinges from my various joints and to judge whether they are serious or just malingering.

16 April

Cost: £18.75
Bike: 15 mins
Running machine: 8km (42 mins)
Weight: 75kg
Max. heart rate: n/a
Item forgotten: heart-rate monitor

Over the period of my absence, the gym has upgraded its equipment. There is a new running machine called a Technogym which has lots of advanced features, including a gradient button to simulate uphill running. This seems a piece of sadism too far: as if it weren't difficult enough just running on the level. Why don't the manufacturers go the whole hog and have a couple of electrodes that the runner can attach to his testicles and receive electric shocks if he falls below some predetermined speed? The Technogym also has a large and comforting red knob with the word STOP written on it which you are instructed to push in an emergency. No doubt it is merely wired up to a huge deafening World War Two style klaxon and flashing arrows that point at you, and a huge sign over your head which lights up with the word "WUSS".

What I like about this machine is that the clock counts *down* from the time you programme in. Psychologically this is very important. I just have to keep going until it gets to zero and there is no temptation to try and exceed this target. One frequently reads about the coming war between man and machine, when all the computers will decide that pandering to the fleshly whims of their creators is a waste of time and will wipe us all out. The final showdown is normally predicted to lie somewhere early in the twenty-first century. In my opinion the battle has already been fought – some 20 years ago – and the machines won. The first Space Invaders machines, which began to appear in pubs in the late 1970s, were the turning point. For the first time here was a game it was impossible to win. No matter how many invaders you shot down they kept coming. At no point did the evil hordes stop and a message flash up on the screen saying: "Okay Earthman, you win." No, as countless 1950s B movies warned us, aliens are evil and relentless in their desire to exterminate humanity. The little spaceships just came faster and in bigger numbers and dropped more bombs until you lost all your lives and had to scrounge another 10p off a friend to play again.

I hear that there are some games these days where a good player, after spending a virtual lifetime in front of the VDU, can get to the final level only to emerge blinking into the daylight and find that the rest of civilisation has invented faster than light travel and gone off to live on Alpha Centauri. But even in these cases the incentive is just to sell you the new version of the game. I think it is very likely that computer games were invented by extraterrestrials to sap humanity's will to win. When the alien starships do finally descend from the skies we will merely look up weakly from our PCs and say, "Oh, is it you?" before being transported off to their slave planet.

My point is that I had been using the running machine like a computer game. In trying to run a greater distance each session I was trying to beat the machine, whereas it was always an odds-on bet that I would keel over with a heart attack long before it ran out of numbers on its digital display. Now I am in serious training. I'm just trying to do eight kilometres three times a week. No more, no less is acceptable. I am like the darts players practising hitting that treble 20 time after time or the spin bowler in the nets learning to land the ball on a 10p piece just outside off stump.

21 April

Cost: £17.65
Bike: 12 mins
Running machine: 8km (45 mins)
Rivals seen off: 3
Weight: 75.5kg
Max. heart rate: n/a (forgot to look at monitor)

It is three days since the London Marathon so I expect the gym to be empty as all the successful participants will be taking a well-earned break from training and all the useless ones will be in hospital or still running. I arrive to find the place packed out. Unfortunately, it seems to be the same as going down to your local tennis courts the week after Wimbledon. Every court will be crammed with kids sporting headbands, caps or vacant expressions (according to the year) and fighting over who's going to be Bjorn Borg, Andre Agassi or Pete Sampras. I decide that this influx of hopeful but very unfit people is good for my ego so I decide to see how many other runners on the adjacent machine I can see off. In my 45-minute run I manage three. The first of them is a middle-aged man who has already clocked up close to an hour on the machine plodding along at a dogged 8km/hr. He has a peculiar habit of emitting a huge bark like a sexually aroused sea lion every three minutes. After almost falling off my running machine the first time he does this, I soon find it has the effect of Chinese water torture in that I am waiting in tense anticipation for his next ejaculation. To my relief he gives up a couple of minutes shy of his hour and retires to the stretching mats. I watch his highly charged warm-down in the mirror as with much eye-rolling and thrashing around he recreates in mime the orgasmic ecstasy that exercising clearly brings him.

Tennis is showing on the TV today, a clay court match between two players I have never heard of. It was the same with the pop music channel that was playing last time, I reflect – most of the names of the bands and artists were completely unfamiliar. It's like being in one of those science-fiction films where the hero awakes to find he has been transported to a parallel time continuum which is exactly like the Earth apart from the fact that Hitler was never born or something and so everything is subtly different. Or it may just be that I'm getting old.

CHAPTER 5
The Tower Jog

London
5 May
Distance: 10km (certified)
Time: 55 mins (guessed)

There is a syndrome which a friend who has run the London Marathon describes as "Get the Womble". It goes as follows: in Mile Two of your first marathon you are overtaken by a runner wearing ludicrous fancy dress, your dignity is compromised and you determine at all costs to beat this particular competitor. You cast aside your carefully calculated race plan and take off in hot pursuit. Ten miles later you collapse and have to retire from the race. What you never find out is that the person in the Womble suit was a member of an élite running club whose mates over a lot of beers a few weeks earlier had bet him he couldn't break three hours dressed in a silly costume of their choice. To avoid this sort of mishap it is vitally important to take part in a few competitive races before the marathon itself in order to hone your big-match temperament.

Over the last week my left knee has embarked on a kamikaze mission and launches itself at anything likely to damage it permanently. Yesterday it was the cast iron lion's head on the leg of my garden table. I pray it will behave today for the Tower Jog where I have elected to make my racing debut. Actually I already have my suspicions that this may not be the most gruelling event in the road running-calendar. Theoretically the race, which is a charity run in aid of the British Heart Foundation, consists of 10 laps of the moat around the Tower of London. However, closer inspection of the promotional leaflet reveals that competitors may start and finish whenever they like between the hours of 9 a.m. and 7 p.m. and undertake as many or as few laps as they wish (up to a recommended maximum of 10). We are also invited to "jog, walk or even crawl" the course.

I arrive in the early afternoon to discover that most participants have plumped for the middle option, which is unsurprising as a good proportion of them are aged over 60. To add further insult to my competitive aspirations many of them have not even bothered to change out of their everyday clothes and a few are even accompanied by dogs or infants. All in all, hardly a world-class field. A lap consists of running about two-thirds of the way around the Tower, round a marker post, then back again. This equates to roughly a kilometre. There are a couple of refreshment points along the course and even a tent equipped with sleeping bags half-way round – in case anyone, hare-and-tortoise-like, fancies a sleep, I imagine. In order to keep a record of individual distances achieved, after each lap you must submit a chit to be signed off by a team of ladies sitting in picnic chairs at the start line. The presence of the Old Dears merely adds to the not-taking-it-seriously ethos of the occasion.

Not really sure how to play this one, I set off at a non-committal trot. A spectator on Tower Bridge Road shouts down a pointless exhortation to "come on" addressed to no one in particular. Not that anyone seems to have any intention of increasing their pace. In fact, the only thing that separates the occasion from a stroll in the park is that all the participants (dogs excepted) are proceeding in a uniform direction. Considering that the average age of the field is probably greatly more than my own 38 years (even allowing for the dogs and kids), it is no surprise that I find myself overtaking other participants by the dozen. Even though many are wearing slacks and some are walking with the aid of a stick, I must acknowledge the pathetic pleasure I derive from leaving them in my wake: that vital competitive element of the road-running experience denied to me in the gym. My elation is temporary and by the third lap I am feeling pretty weary. I resolve to study a map after the race and establish exactly what shape the Tower of London is. From here at ground level it appears to be in the form of a highly irregular polygon, which is a pentagon on the outward part of the lap but somehow becomes a hexagon on the way back. There is always an extra stretch of wall to run along which I could swear wasn't there on the outbound leg. I try to get my suffering into perspective by reminding myself that conditions down here in the moat are far more pleasant than they would have been in medieval times when we'd have had the additional inconvenience of having burning hot pitch poured on us from the castle walls.

In this so-called race, the forward motion of which amounts to little more than a gentle migration, I am overtaken on two occasions. The first time is by a short, thickset, shaven-headed man. In defiance of my own advice I immediately decide to use him as my pacer and increase my stride to follow at his heels. Then, at the end of the lap, when we are getting our chits signed off, I overhear him mention to one of the Old Dears that this is his 16th lap. Over 10 miles… I change my plan and allow him to run on ahead of me as he is clearly a psycho and I have no desire to be near him when he keels over with a heart attack and be the one that has to give him the kiss of life.

On my fifth lap a second person lopes past me, a pretty, fit-looking teenaged girl, fresh of face and lithe of limb. I latch on to her, resolving not to let her get more than a few paces ahead of me. For the next lap I run a brilliant tactical race in her wake weaving my way adeptly through the packs of dawdling pensioners. Fit Girl seems fresh as a daisy (and looks like that could be her name). I wonder how many laps she has already completed. I hope she is just on her second, hence her unflushed elegance. She is still so young that her body has not yet given a thought to child-bearing and its morphology is still designed to outrun priapic boys in playground games of kiss-chase. Unsurprisingly, within five minutes she has left me so far behind that, as I struggle round one corner of the Tower, it is only to see her disappearing around the next. I renegotiate the deal with my male dignity and decide it will remain intact just so long as Fit Girl doesn't actually lap me.

By the beginning of my seventh lap I have totally lost visual contact with her and decide to walk for a bit, resolving that I will start to run again as soon as she passes me coming in the opposite direction. She appears sooner than expected, across on the other side of the grass, on the homeward leg of her lap, wriggling past the other lumbering runners with an effortless ease. I stumble into a run and worry about how soon it will be before I meet her coming the other way. I am genuinely scared of this anonymous creature who cannot be more than 17. To my surprise and gathering delight I round the far marker post, traverse one...two...three sides of the Tower and still she hasn't reappeared on her outbound leg. I am now well past the point where we last crossed. I round the last corner into the home straight of my seventh lap, hoping to see her limping along clutching at a heavy stitch in her side, or better still lying prostrate on the grass being attended to by the St John Ambulance Brigade. But no, she is gone; finished her allotment of laps. Please God tell me that she didn't do 10 and still look that good. I am torn between remorse at the fact that I will never see this beautiful creature again and relief that I can now trot out my remaining circuits without feeling terrorised.

I hand over my chit to have my lap signed off. By now I have a nodding acquaintenceship with several of the Old Dears. I joke that I am collecting their autographs. As I set off on my next lap I am suddenly poleaxed by the thought that every single one of the other runners for the whole of the day must have been making exactly the same joke. Charitable as they are, it is probably all the Old Dears could do not to trip me up or kick me in the groin and snarl "for God's sake say something original". The mortification that stems from this realisation bites more sharply than any stitch.

By the time I get to my final lap I have got my second wind (actually it's about my fourth) and I put on a bit of a spurt, powering past the rest of the field. This is a totally pointless exertion really as everyone else is ambling along chatting and being as infuriatingly uncompetitive as ever. The Shaven Headed Psychotic is still haring round, his lap count must by now be well into the 20s. I think they will have to fire tranquilliser darts into him to get him to stop. I finish the race, as the English gentleman does his dinner, feeling that I could have managed just a little more. I hand in my chit and accept a cup of tea and a boiled sweet (to replenish my saccharine apparently). I see Fit Girl lolling on the grass in the finishing area. She is alone, probably waiting for a slower friend. I could go over and talk to her, but what's the point? She'll just head off to the changing tent and then emerge wearing a school uniform, like the girl in *Trainspotting*.

In all the excitement I realise I have forgotten to look at my watch. Damn. My first race and I don't even have a finishing time. Well, under an hour, definitely. I take a shower in a nearby health club which has offered its facilities for free. This is a seriously macho gym. The hairdryer in the changing room weighs as much as a rocket launcher. You need to be built like Sylvester Stallone to lift it. And if anyone claims blow-drying hair is namby, you just say, "Yeah, *Viet*-Namby," and blow them away with a blast of hot air.

CHAPTER 6
Buying the Kit

If you are taking up running seriously there is no point in buying your trainers at a general sports store where the 18-year-old sales trainee will be able to advise you only on the street credibility of the footwear you are purchasing. We all run differently. For example, some of us are supernators, others are pronators. I know Super Nator sounds like a character out of a Japanese computer game, but it actually refers to the condition where the foot has raised arches. Pronator is just a polite way of saying flatfooted. Each foot type needs a special running shoe to avoid its owner picking up long-term injuries. The only way to be sure of purchasing the correct footwear is to visit a specialist running shop. It is also important to buy your running shoes in the afternoon. This is because your feet swell during the course of the day. They also swell when you are running so trying on your trainers late in the day will ensure that they do not end up pinching at Mile 15. You should also take your current running shoes with you as the trained eye of the salesperson will be able to infer data about how you run from examining them.

I turn up at Runners Need in Camden Town just before closing time on a Friday afternoon. There are only a few minutes to go till free parking so I leave my dad's car (which I have borrowed for the weekend) on a meter just over the road from the shop, knowing the chances of getting a ticket are infinitesimal. Surprisingly for this late hour the shop is devoid of customers, all of whom obviously have bought their shoes earlier in the day and are even now feeling the blisters rising. I am served by the manager, Brad, a kindly faced, softly spoken South African. He is wearing shorts and trainers and has the sinewy tanned legs of the seasoned runner. He asks me what sort of running I am intending to do. I hesitate for a split second before I say, the New York Marathon. This is the first time I have confessed my ambition to a person who is professionally qualified to cast a trained eye over my body and burst out laughing. Brad does no such thing but instead nods encouragingly and asks me to take off my old running shoes.

Brad picks up one of them and squints along the sole like a rifle-maker checking the barrel for trueness. "You're a pronator," he pronounces knowledgeably. "Both feet," he adds examining the other shoe. I'm not sure how to feel at this verdict. I don't know if being a pronator is good or bad for running or if being a double-footed pronator is better or worse than being a monopedal one. Of course, a pronator is certainly a pretty handy (or should that be footy?) thing to be immediately before the outbreak of a world war because flatfooted people don't have to join the army and get killed. "Most people pronate," Brad comforts me in reply to my unspoken anxiety. If most people pronate, then I'd rather supernate (because that's the sort of person I am) but I suppose I'm stuck with it.

Brad disappears into the stock room and comes back with a couple of shoe boxes. As he unpacks the trainers and threads the laces he tells me that he too used to run marathons until injury forced him to give up. He invites me to examine his left leg. I do and it feels almost hollow to the touch. The few remaining bones probably rattle when he runs. He could be a Morris dancer without the need for any silly bells. Brad goes on to enthusiastically detail his various other running injuries. Now, this is possibly not part of conventional sales patter from someone trying to sell you a pair of running shoes. Imagine if a car dealer described to you in graphic detail exactly how James Dean slammed his Porsche Spider into an oncoming Ford Wagon as part of a sales pitch to sell you a sports car. Maybe it's all just part of the macho thrill of the experience; or perhaps this is a sort of a Government health warning that purveyors of running shoes are obliged to issue to all their customers. I slip the trainers on and walk around the shop in that gingerly way you do with new shoes, as if they might suddenly turn nasty on you and break your ankles.

"Let's take them for a spin," Brad says, indicating the door. He leads me out on to a side street where he asks me to run up to the next junction and back again. Now I realise why Brad, too, is wearing trainers. Inviting your customers to run away with your merchandise before they have paid for it is not good business. But I reckon you'd have to be pretty fleet-footed to out-run Brad. I jog up to the end of the road and back again, feeling his practised eye on me. "You're an abductor," he tells me as I return. I am about to protest that I have brought his shoes back safe and sound, when he goes on: "It means you run with your feet splayed. Oh and you've got one leg shorter than the other", he adds breezily as we walk back to the shop. Sorry, did I come here to buy running shoes or to have my self-esteem semtexed? "Has anyone ever run away with the shoes?" I ask him, thinking that this might be a neat alternative to sponsorship deals for those élite runners who are able to out-sprint the sales staff. "No", he replies, as if the thought of such dishonesty had never occurred to him.

Back at the shop Brad goes off to fetch a different pair of shoes which he says will suit my running style better. A pair of clown's boots maybe? But he comes back with some quite trendy looking trainers which, he explains, have added cushioning in the instep to protect my collapsed arches. He tapes some little plastic inserts to the undersides of the insoles for added support. As if feeling that he has been a little harsh on my feet and that he might be losing a valuable repeat customer here if he deters my running aspirations at this early stage, he tells me that I have Morton's Toe. This is the condition where the second toe is longer than the first and, according to Brad, is a Greek sign of fertility. The things a salesman will say to a customer just to flog him a pair of shoes. Still I forgive him for all the other horrid aspersions he cast on my feet. After briefly road testing the new pair I decide to take them.

On impulse I buy myself a new running vest. So far I have been doing all my training in various old cotton T-shirts. The problem with cotton is that it is very absorbent and after an hour or so your shirt will be so saturated with sweat that you feel as if you are running in chain mail. I select a blue vest made out of a wicking material – this is a cunning man-made fabric which by magic allows sweat and air to pass through in opposite directions.

As I leave the shop I glance across the road and see a tow truck parked next to my dad's car in the process of winching its hook into position. Instinctively I sprint over, jump into the car and drive off before the Vehicle Removal Officer can say a word. Those few extra seconds my new shoes gave me were probably enough to stop him attaching the hook. They've already saved me more than they cost within two minutes of purchasing them. Thanks to them and these abducting, pronating feet of mine, attached to my unequal legs, I avoided getting Morton's Towed away.

Inspirational Viewing No 1

The Loneliness of the Long Distance Runner (1962)

Probably the seminal film about running, it is all set in that strange sixties black and white world where there are no middle-class people. Everyone is either surly and proletarian (boys in borstal, factory workers, shopkeepers) or plummy and effete (borstal governor, factory owner, boys from posh school, all people on TV).

The hero Colin Smith, played by Tom Courtney, is a petty thief and joy rider from Nottingham who is thrown into borstal for robbing a bakery with his mate Terry out of *The Likely Lads*. His fellow inmates in Ruxton Towers young offenders' institution are a bunch of cockneys and scousers who constantly refer to each other as cockneys and scousers (presumably for the benefit of the plummy and effete sixties cinema audiences). At first Colin is assigned to the workshop where boys uselessly dismantle machinery for scrap, but then he proves himself to be rather a useful runner. This surprises everyone, especially us viewers, as the only exercise we have seen him perform in the film so far is to lose his virginity in Skegness and run (unsuccessfully, obviously) away from the policeman trying to arrest him for the bakery job. Yet in his first race he pips Stacey, Ruxton Towers' champion runner, at the finishing post. Stacey throws a punch at Colin, followed by a huge strop and then does a bunk.

The plummy governor, Michael Redgrave, has his heart set on winning the cross-country challenge cup off the toffs from the local posh school. Colin quickly becomes his new blue-eyed boy and is promoted from the workshop to the cushier gardening detail. But Colin is no stooge of the system. His role model in the class struggle is his dad. At the beginning of the film we see Mr Smith Senior in his sick bed rebelling against the tyranny of the capitalist state by refusing to go to the hospital and thus dying in pain with working-class dignity rather than getting better with the aid of bourgeois drugs.

This is a kitchen sink drama and the kitchen sink is constantly chucked in when it comes to the heavy-handed symbolism. When Colin is being introspective we know this because he stares hard at his reflection in the bedroom mirror. He burns a pound note (symbol of capitalist oppression), roughs up his mother's new fancy man (symbol of patriarchal oppression) and gets moody with his girlfriend (symbol of emotional oppression). In short, he's a bit of a rebel. In fact the film was released in America as *Rebel with a Cause* which is to rob it of the best thing about it, i.e. its title. Even this is something of a misnomer, though. There's not much about loneliness here. In fact, whenever Colin is out running on his own he seems pretty happy. He turns cartwheels, lies in piles of leaves, flounces about and generally bonds with nature. These scenes are accompanied by a jazz soundtrack which presumably is supposed to evoke a feeling of freedom and spontaneousness. By contrast the oppressive borstal scenes are overlaid with the hymn "Jerusalem" which of course symbolises The Establishment. Sadly for the film's subtextual message, musical trends have evolved over the 40 years since it was made and these days the jazz sounds very "Establishment" while the sparse avant-garde string arrangements of "Jerusalem" are rather cool.

To be honest there's not a huge amount about running in this film. The director is more interested in showing us flashbacks to Colin's disaffected adolescence than concentrating on his training as he builds towards race day. All we are able to ascertain is that his diet comprises the meat and potatoes served in the dining hall (definitely too much fat there) and his training seems to consist of touching his toes and star-jumping in the general callisthenics classes held by the thuggish PT instructor Mr Roach. "That was a good sprint just now. You put it on just at the right moment," Michael Redgrave tells Colin after his first victory. "It just happened, sir," explains Colin. So much for his technique then. Working-class people are just instinctive is the film's message, and don't need poncey things like race plans. As for Colin's running stance, well this film was made before the days of the Method and Tom Courtney's wild lurching style is not to be commended to aspirant athletes.

Finally we get to the big dénouement – the five-mile cross-country race for the challenge cup. The plummy kids of Raneleigh School arrive in their white flannels with their posh parents – mums in check coats with lapdogs and dads in military uniform or trilby hats. The race gets under way and quickly becomes a two-man contest between Colin and plummy James Fox. It should be stressed that this is a film about winning symbolic victories within the context of the class struggle rather than actually breasting the tape first and thus Colin's methods should not be followed by any runner with less ideologically laden objectives. He takes the lead and we get a montage of flashbacks to various symbols of authority. "How'd you come to be here?" one of the plummy voices enquires of Colin. "I got caught. I didn't run fast enough, sir," replies Colin. However, Colin has now come to the conclusion that the way to defeat authority is actually to run slower. Well in the lead, he deliberately stops within sight of the finishing line and lets James Fox pass him. The message is that you do not attain freedom by running away from the repressive regime of the establishment, as Stacey did. No, freedom comes from defying the system from within. Thus in the last scene we see the triumphant Colin, er, back in the workshop dismantling gas masks. Are you sure you've got this right, Col?

All in all, it's probably better to read the original book by Alan Sillitoe on which the film was based, which is rather longer on musings on the nature of solitude – "loneliness is the only truth and only realness" – and much shorter in length. In fact, the most pleasing thing about the book version is that it turns out to be just the first in a collection of short stories and not a novel, as I had presumed when I bought it. Wouldn't it be nice if marathons were like that? You get to Mile Five anticipating a long slog ahead, round a corner and find miraculously it's all over.

Summary

Artistic merit ***
Marathoning relevance ***
Kitsch factor **

CHAPTER 7

Chase Corporate Challenge

Battersea Park, London
14 July
Distance: 3.5 miles
Time: 39 mins

The Chase Corporate Challenge is an annual 3.5 mile run organised worldwide by Chase Manhattan, the American Investment Bank. The British leg is run over two evenings in Battersea Park. Technically it is a corporate event open to bankers, lawyers, management consultants and other upper-tax-bracket individuals. Fortunately for me Becky Barrow, a journalist colleague, finds me a place on the *Daily Telegraph* team, which would otherwise have consisted of just her.

To prepare myself for this, my first genuinely competitive race, I invest in some energy-boosting sports drinks. Unable to restrain myself until the prescribed five minutes before the race I sample one at home and am disappointed to find that it tastes exactly like the weak, flat orange squash we used to be served at school break time. Throughout the day I am haunted by a ghastly foreboding which no doubt every runner gets (but, of course, only one person can actually achieve): what if I finish last? Statistically this is extremely unlikely, I reason. Becky has told me that there are 17,000 runners in the event. And if by some amazing piece of bad luck I *do* come last, then I will just have to shoot myself.

It seems that everyone on my District Line train is also running in this race. I can tell this because they are all already kitted out in shorts and T-shirts emblazoned with company names, corporate mission statements and their race numbers. I overhear a woman sitting next to me confide the "What if I'm last?" fear to her colleague. I am heartened when she goes on to reveal that she hasn't run for five years. Good, someone guaranteed to do worse than me. I mentally note her race number which is in the high 20,000s. With only 17,000 runners actually taking part in the event this sadistic touch by the organisers is clearly just to create a fear in the participant of exactly how humiliating last position will be.

I find I have left my new sports drink at home, but already have a need for its 33 per cent performance-boosting properties (can you become addicted to something just because you read an advertising slogan?) so I buy a bottle of Lucozade at Sloane Square tube station. Heading towards Battersea Park, everyone walks in little corporate crocodiles, many dozens of them, all keeping to the same side of the street. I cross over and walk along the empty pavement on the other side, but no one follows my lead. The nail that sticks out gets hammered down, as the Japanese say.

All this corporate-ism has depressing associations of school. My prep school was housed in a single building, yet it still it had three "Houses" (Amundsen, Bering and Cabot, as they were stirringly named) and all pupils were assigned to one or other of them, even non-boarders like me. Various sporting and academic fixtures were arranged between the houses and keen rivalry was encouraged. To this day I do not understand why I was expected to show loyalty to something which had absolutely no physical existence and was just an arbitrary list of pupils' names divided into three categories pinned on the Masters' notice board. Surely only a deranged person would compete fiercely for the honour of a dead, foreign explorer? At least the corporate clones accompanying me down Lower Sloane Street have sold their individuality for large salaries. I wonder if they have a race plan. Will they run it in a pack like Roman foot soldiers? Or maybe roped together in single file, mountaineer-style? Or all attached to a giant rod like table footballers? As I muse I open my sports Lucozade and it explodes all over me.

By the time we have crossed Chelsea Bridge and entered Battersea Park thousands more pasty-legged investment bankers and accountants have joined us, all lumbering in the same direction. It resembles the scene in *Invasion of the Bodysnatchers* when all the zombies, summoned by some secret signal, begin to assemble silently for the final destruction of the human race. Maybe a better analogy would be recruits in World War One heading off to the trenches, about to subject themselves to some fate they neither desire nor understand at the arbitrary bidding of their masters. I follow them towards the starting line. I try to call my running mate Becky, but the mobile phone network has clearly crashed as several thousand Yuppie bankers try to locate their colleagues simultaneously.

I find myself in a central arena enclosed by corporate marquees which resembles a huge army boot camp. Thousands of people in little squadrons of purple, red or green corporate colours are rushing round purposefully. Some are doing push-ups or flailing-armed callisthenics in organised groups of up to 30. A central loudspeaker booms out propaganda, which they mindlessly assimilate: "Wear your number on the *front* of your running vest... Make sure you drink plenty of fluids... Seven-minute milers please take their positions at the start now." In the centre of this vast muster cheerful T-shirted recruits sling out bottles of Volvic from a huge central dump as if doling out rounds of ammunition. It feels like everyone's going to go out and invade Poland.

Amid all this Nuremberg-style activity I feel totally lost. Not only can I not find the rendezvous point where I am due to meet Becky, but I am aware that I am unique in having no number, no corporate vest, no mission statement. I don't even know whether I am a seven-minute miler or a ten-minute miler. I do not belong. If I was James Bond I would biff a passing runner on the head, drag him round the corner and reappear a moment later dressed in his kit and look for some way to blow this whole evil place up. The loudspeaker continues to issue instructions about the importance of displaying our race numbers *at all times*. "I am not a Number, I am a Free Man," I mutter to myself in an attempt to cling on to my sanity.

With everyone but the 10-minute milers lined up ready to run, I finally locate Becky who had been delayed by a press deadline. She gives me my numbered bib and we hurriedly change into our running kit in the Press tent. Briefly we worry about leaving our valuables unattended until Becky points out that everyone else in the race is much richer than us and we are more likely to get a hand-out from them than be robbed.

We stroll towards the start line. The race has actually already begun but somehow running before you even get to the official start seems a bit desperate. On the way Becky confides in me her fear that she might come last. I feel reassured. In the distance we can hear an excitable American commentator yelling out exhortations over the public address system as competitors less tardy than ourselves get under way: "Let's hear it for Goldman Sachs… there go the guys from Morgan Stanley… c'mon give them a big cheer." His zeal contrasts strangely with the total absence of spectators. Becky and I finally cross the deserted starting line with seven minutes already showing on the large digital clock suspended above it. So anticlimactic is this moment (no starting gun, no massed cheer of spectators or triggered release of helium balloons, even the commentator has given up by this point) that we can't galvanise ourselves into actually running for another two or three hundred yards.

Finally we break into a jog and spend the first mile or so chatting as we begin to catch up with the dead-beats and no-hopers. I realise that running with a friend is always going to be a problem. You are both too embarrassed to set off at a blistering pace because (a) it might seem like you were taking it seriously (which would be very un-British) or (b), worse, your companion might turn out to be better than you. So you maintain a conversational flow to show that you can run without hyper-ventilating and at the same time throwing down an unspoken challenge to your partner to reply without audibly gasping. We proceed along in this fashion for a while, debating the theory that investment banks might be using the race as a novel method for headcount reduction, with the last 20 runners from each organisation being handed their P45s at the finishing line. A sign announces Water Ahead. We wonder whether the race involves wading across the pond, but find it is just a Refreshment Point, where more bottles of Volvic are being handed out.

From my hugely superior experience of running (one race more than her) I point out to Becky that 3.5 miles is an annoying distance for a race. Ironically, it is easier to run longer distances, in that the first 20 or so minutes of any run are the worst bit. It's apparently something to do with switching from anaerobic to aerobic breathing, but feels more like profound spiritual despair. Walking, stopping, dying all seem like preferable options to continuing. Once you get past this stage, though, the whole process becomes quite enjoyable. On a short run like today, where the race ends before you get to the nice bit, you reap none of the benefits.

After a couple of miles Becky is showing symptoms of succumbing to this condition: eyes glazed, breathing laboured, cheeks flushed, utterances sporadic. I find myself in one of those Antarctic expedition dilemmas: my colleague has severe frostbite and snow-blindness. Do I struggle on with her or hurry on ahead to fetch help? I decide to abandon her and see if I can make any sort of a time out of this race. Sadly, once you have started at the back of the field it is impossible to emerge with much dignity on the official results sheet. Even attempting to do so is likely to cause injury. My ankles risk being turned and calf muscles torn as I attempt to sidestep and weave a path through all the dawdling yuppies in front, who have slowed to a dodder through exhaustion or having spotted a business contact they want to network with.

The other problem of being at the back is that all the seriously unfit people, rapidly dehydrating, are prone to grab a bottle from each Water Point, take a gasping slurp and then hurl it sideways. Overtakers run a serious risk of being brained. As I shimmy my way purposefully through the perspiring pack, the slogans and mission statements on the backs of T-shirts I pass become more ironic as they become more sweat-soaked: "Powerhouse", "The Team that Likes to Stay Ahead", "We're Always in the Running" they proclaim unconvincingly. Burning up these workoholic slobs is far more satisfying than in the Tower Jog, as they are a whole generation younger on average. The Thrill of the Chase – now, how come none of their highly paid marketing people thought of that one?

For the last mile and a half I run an improvised *fartlek* (that is short bursts of speed, interspersed with controlled running). I sprint every time I sight a chink of daylight through the sweaty wall of flesh ahead, slowing down again once they close ranks. I am tut-tutted irritably several times as I barge past people who are attempting to set up global deals with fellow runners. I reach the final straight and see the finish line up ahead. Now, this may be my first competitive race but I have already worked out who I Hate the Most: the runners who having finished the race some minutes before you then lean over the barriers shouting patronising encouragement as you flounder up red-faced to the line.

I manage to put on a bit of a sprint for the tape. The physical uplift this brings is quickly doused by the stentorian tones of the public address system which takes over the administration of our lives again after this brief interlude of free will: "You are responsible for noting your own finish time" it warns us as we cross the line. "Do not remain in the finishing area or you may risk disqualification of your entire team." Some corporate Cogs are clearly too overwhelmed by the individualistic possibilities of being responsible for their own times and reel around dazed after crossing the line, in strict defiance of Edict 2. The clock shows 39 minutes 4 seconds as I finish. Luckily, runners' times in large-scale events like this are like sub-atomic particles in quantum mechanics: there are always external factors which prevent them from being measured accurately. Minutes taken crossing the start line, periods of enforced walking when bunched in by stragglers, stopping for drinks, queuing for the loo and so on can all be deducted from one's official timing.

Becky and I meet up in the Press tent and compare heavily doctored performances. She reckons she finished in 35 "adjusted" minutes (once she'd given herself an allowance for our late start). I have awarded myself a generous 29 minutes (because I did *try* to run a bit at the end). We both failed to register our times officially, partly out of a generally iconoclastic spirit but mainly to prevent awkward questions being asked by colleagues in possession of a results sheet. Shower facilities don't seem to be available but luckily Becky has an entire extended family in the locality and, after a quick phone-round of the Chelsea Barrows, she locates a nearby uncle with a bathroom and a fully fired-up boiler.

As we leave the park the digital clock is showing over an hour and puffed-out runners are still crossing the line clutching at where they hope crucial ligaments might be, trying to imply that injury rather than sheer uselessness has impaired their performance. We stroll across Albert Bridge in the late afternoon sunshine with our race numbers still pinned to our chests, the symbol of our new-found conformity. A couple of joggers pass and we feel infinitely superior. "I am not a Free Man..."

CHAPTER 8

Visit to the Doctor

Obviously one should seek one's physician's approval before undertaking any unaccustomed strenuous activity. Unless of course you live in the USA, where presumably no doctor would ever give approbation for a patient to undertake a marathon, as even a stubbed toe sustained during the event would occasion a multi-million dollar law suit against the hapless practitioner.

The previous time I had been to my local surgery was two summers before when I was struck on the forehead by a tennis ball after failing to get out of the way of a forehand smash by my sister, Karen. A few days later I began getting headaches and naturally concluded that I was suffering from a brain haemorrhage. As I would be unlikely to live long enough to wait for an appointment with my usual doctor, Dr Wilder, I instead took one with another practitioner in the surgery who was conveniently – and, I might add with hindsight, suspiciously – available immediately. After conducting the briefest of examinations which did not actually involve making physical contract with his patient, the doctor declared that I was suffering from nothing more than a case of labyrinthitis (whatever that is) which was going round the community and that it should pass within a few days. And he sent me on my way without even the comfort of a prescription clutched in my fist. Emerging empty-handed from the consulting room had the effect of signalling "neurotic time-waster" to the receptionist and other waiting patients. Worse still, as I left the consulting room the doctor's parting words were: "Let's hope it's nothing more serious, eh?" Hope?? Er, shouldn't you know, Doctor? I realised now why there is a permanent two-week waiting list to see Dr Wilder. So when I came to get the medical all-clear for the New York Marathon I put my name down well in advance for an appointment with her.

I arrive promptly at the surgery for my appointment at nine o'clock and spend an enjoyable 15 minutes in the waiting room reading leaflets about illnesses I don't have. Then Dr Wilder's voice calls my name. I jump up, pleasantly surprised at this shorter-than-average wait, and follow her into her consulting room. She takes her seat and opens a drawer in her desk.

"Did you hear me the first time?" is her unexpected opening line.

"I'm sorry?" I mumble, taken aback.

"How long have you been out there?"

"Er… about fifteen minutes."

"I called you ten minutes ago. Twice. I didn't get any reply so I've seen another patient in the meantime. Is your hearing all right?"

Before I can reply she has inserted a probe with a little torch on the end down my left ear. I squirm away like a daydreaming schoolboy finding his earlobe suddenly tweaked from behind by an irascible Latin master.

"When was the last time you had your ears syringed?"

"Er… I'm not sure I ever have." This consultation is not going quite to plan.

I find myself fixed up with an appointment to see the nurse to have my ears dewaxed. By now I feel a total fraud. I had come here to seek confirmation of my physical soundness for the ultimate sporting feat and find myself diagnosed with at least one serious medical condition before I have even opened my mouth. What chance for the rest of me? I console myself that at least unclogged ears will enable me to savour the plaudits of the public as I sprint for that finishing tape.

My medical examination itself is much briefer and more perfunctory. When I announce my intention to run a marathon, a glance from the doctor briefly questions my sanity but stops short of a referral to a behavioural psychiatrist. Instead she briskly takes my blood pressure, checks my pulse and within minutes has declared me fully fit for the endeavour. Strangely my reaction is one of disappointment. That is partly because I am a Cancer and thus a hypochondriac who values quality time with my physician and would have liked to have had a few more tests lavished on me, maybe having my knees banged with a little rubber hammer, getting to read letters off one of those eye charts … just so long as it's not a blood sample.

But there is another reason. Secretly, I realise, I had been hoping for the following scenario. Dr Wilder prods at my chest with a stethoscope listening to my heart in several places. A frown crosses her features. She listens again more attentively, maybe consults a medical book, then shakes her head and begins to scribble something on my medical record card. As she writes, she explains to me that I have an irregular heart rhythm which will prohibit me from ever being able to undertake any strenuous or prolonged sporting activity. Of course, there's no reason at all why, if I avoid all forms of physical exertion, I should not live to a contented old age. And then I would have it – a lifelong sick note.

Back in the real world not only am I deprived of this comforting get-out, but checking over my medical records Dr Wilder finds I am overdue for a routine blood test.

"We might as well do it now as you're here," she says, getting a syringe out.

CHAPTER 9

Running in the Outside World

Once you have plucked up the courage to start running in the real world nothing will persuade you to go back to the running machine – not even the thought that, in my case, I have ended up paying £17.65 per gym visit and have thus been consummately ripped off. For a start, in the great outdoors you are breathing clean fresh air and, even with a healthy admixture of traffic fumes, it is still a sight more palatable than the sweat and steroid-laden fug that passes for air in the gym. Secondly you have nature in all its glory to gaze upon. Even if you're running round a derelict housing estate it is less soul-deadening than staring at your own sweaty reflection for hours on end or watching MTV. Thirdly, you're actually getting somewhere by running. This brings a marvellous sense of achievement (until you realise you've got to get back – also by running). Running eternally towards your image in the mirror but never getting any closer no matter how high you crank up the running machine just adds to the hamster-on-a-wheel frustration of the gym experience.

Possibly the greatest boon of running outdoors is that you are able to think. Gyms always have the TV on, usually tuned in to some dire station like Select TV (if this is what they selected, what the hell did they reject?) with the volume turned full up. This ensures that you rot your mind at the same rate as you hone your body. Outside you are blissfully free from the brain-dead cable channels. The brute activity of running keeps your body happy and allows your brain to float free. Okay, that sounds a bit poncey, but scientific research has shown that activity in the right brain (the creative side) increases after 20 minutes of exercise. I'm reminded of a science fiction story I once read in which a team of astronauts is sent on a voyage to Alpha Centauri. Because they have none of the trivial distractions of everyday life and have nothing to do all day but think, the astronauts all become super-intelligent and solve all humanity's problems. Of course, in reality they would have ended up murdering each other over which old episode of *Little House on the Prairie* they were going to watch yet again. But it's a nice theory.

Naturally running in the outside world has some disadvantages: the whim of weather, the dangers of traffic and the possibility of mockery from passers-by to name just three. The biggest problem posed by external reality, though, is that you swap the two decimal point precision of the running machine for the vagaries of woods and parks. Training for a marathon requires specific mileage to be run each day, but how do you measure these distances? There are several options, all of them pretty useless.

Running track

The simplest solution is to run in a place where distances are conveniently marked out for you. This could be a main road – where your life expectancy will be about a week – or more practically your local running track. Now the problem with running tracks is that they are frequented by serious athletes. Most of these individuals will not only be better than you, but since they are inevitably running much shorter distances they will seem *much* better than you from the frequency with which they power past you. Definitely not an experience to be recommended, except for when you're fine-tuning your pedometer. The running track has all the disadvantages of the gym (monotonous repetitive environment) and none of the advantages (a roof).

Pedometer

A pedometer is a portable gadget that clips to your belt and estimates the distance you have run by counting the number of strides you take. In order for it to be effective not only do you need to measure you stride accurately but you must maintain this exact stride length throughout your run. Even if you manage this unlikely feat the device will still not give you an accurate reading as it works by simply notching up a stride every time it is jogged. Thus it will rack up the theoretical metres whenever it is tapped, nudged, dropped, while you are jiggling up and down on the spot waiting for pedestrian lights to change, taking a walking break or doing your stretches. Having experimented with this gadget on several runs I can only conclude that it serves the same function as those indicators they now have at bus stops that inform you how many minutes you will have to wait for the next bus. Most of the arrival times displayed bear no relation to the actual running of buses on the route. The indicator just flashes up random numbers to create a sense of reassurance among waiting passengers and stop them taking a taxi. I persevered with my pedometer for a long time, liking its old-fashioned mechanical simplicity in this digital age. But in the end I threw the useless bastard away.

Opisometer

Measuring on a map is the simplest way to establish distances, except that most of the places one tends to run (woods, parkland etc.) are created by Nature rather than Man (well, that's why we like to run there, isn't it?) and are thus very difficult to measure accurately on a map. I experimented with curling various bendy things (little bits of string, paper clips) around various green bits of North London on my A-Z map and then holding them against a ruler. This was not a success as it's difficult to get the string to go straight, and impossible to get the paper clip to bend to follow the exact contours of your route. An alternative is to buy one of those little wheely things that you roll around the map and it lets you read out the distance in kilometres or miles. Let me advise you it took me ages to find one of these in a shop. My search was hampered by the fact that I didn't know what the things are called. Only after I finally located one in a shop and pointed at it did I discover that it is called an opisometer – a fact which will now never be of any use to me unless it comes up as my £1,000,000 question in Who Wants to be a Millionaire? It turned out that the opisometer's corner handling is very bad so, unless you have very large-scale maps or are running huge distances, its measurements are not very accurate. I ended up spending less time using mine to measure things that I had done searching for it in shops.

Sports watch

In the end, the best way to quantify runs done in the outside world is by time. After a month or two of jogging on running machines with digital read-outs in the gym you should have an idea of what speed you run at comfortably. Thus all you need is a standard wristwatch to time your runs and you can estimate the distance achieved. Now on your first run you will notice that your watch has stopped. At least this is how it will seem to you. You simply cannot believe that you have been running for only three minutes. It feels like at least 10. If your watch hasn't stopped then time has slowed down. Now, according to Einstein's theory of relativity, time does indeed slow down from the point of view of a moving observer, but to be honest it is not really noticeable at 10km/hr. Convinced that your watch is defective, you will now go out and blow £50 on a sports watch. The main advantage of wearing a sports watch is that it makes you feel like a proper athlete. This sort of psychological preparation, though a bit wet, should not be spurned. The only practical benefit of a sports watch is that the advanced ones will allow you to read off your split times. In other words, when you are running in a largish competitive race you can time each lap, mile or kilometre individually and thus be aware of how much slower you ran it than the previous one.

Running in the city

Those of us who live in built-up areas have to be content with the odd small bits of greenery that rampant urban expansion missed; in my case Highgate Woods. Where the experience of running outside differs from the gym is that you will be surrounded by people who have no interest in exercise and are inherently mistrustful of those who do. Men will clutch protectively at their wives as you approach, red-faced and blowing; babies will stare at you from their buggies with a look of horror that says, well, if that's what walking does to you I don't think I'm going to bother to learn; dogs will snap at your heels with the tacit condonation of their owners. You are a misfit because the solitary pleasure of running is not something that most Brits understand.

As a nation we are not very good at enjoying ourselves and will only go for a walk in the woods if we can convince ourselves that it is for an altruistic purpose. I am not being selfish, says the man walking his dog.

See? I am taking this exercise solely for the benefit of my pet. Then there will be the middle-aged group of people with binoculars on a bat watch, performing a valuable environmental duty in monitoring potentially endangered species, dads kicking footballs with kids, mums pushing prams. Apart from us runners, the only adults who seem to go to the woods for the purposes of unabashed self-indulgence are romantic couples and the weather-beaten middle-aged men who doze on benches with a can of Skol Super in their hands. As a runner you find yourself on a par with the drunks and will attract faintly disparaging looks from these superior dog-walking, baby-dandling men, may of whom will in the summer months have the temerity to wear shorts. Well, at least we runners have functional reasons for wearing shorts. These others seem to think they have some sort of aesthetic right to reveal their pasty, hairy English legs.

The only people from whom one can expect any respect are the other runners. But this raises another issue. Should you acknowledge them? Frequently you will find yourself running round the woods clockwise while another runner is doing the circuit anti-clockwise and thus your paths will cross three or four times. I used to drive a Volkswagen Beetle and there was an unspoken convention that you would always wave at other Beetle drivers you passed. There was a solidarity in it, a tacit acknowledgement that we are the only people eccentric enough to use this archaic and impractical form of transportation. Surely there should be a similar convention among runners? I must report that those round about where I live seem to ignore each other. Maybe that's just out of British diffidence. Americans probably exchange high fives and details of one another's salaries with every fellow jogger they pass. Or possibly it's just me who gets ignored by others. Perhaps they are fearful of being sued by my next of kin if any unnecessary words they cause me to utter bring on the heart attack I look in permanent danger of succumbing to.

Of course, one can always avoid meetings by running laps in the same direction as the other runners (like fish in a shoal, runners always seem to have an instinctive preferred direction). But then you will find that this engenders a totally needless spirit of competition. You are constantly trying to overtake people or getting annoyed when they overtake you. But running against the flow just instils a sense of futility. He's killing himself to run clockwise, I'm killing myself to run anti-clockwise and we'll both end up where we started. Why don't we just pair off like opposition MPs who fancy a day on the golf course and both just stay at home?

All in all, it's probably best to ignore all the live humans you come across. Think instead of the important social duty that you are performing. We runners may be social outcasts, but we are inevitably the first people to find murdered bodies in the woods. It will probably never happen to you, but it is your chance for glory in the local press so keep your eyes open.

I concentrate on immersing my senses in the sights, sounds and smells of nature that surround me – a portly crow waddling through dappled shadows of sun on a crisp bag; a squirrel burying a stolen sandwich; a tiny corgi perching on its back legs to sniff an alsatian's bottom; the air suffused with the scent of pine as if some nervous party host had overdone it on the air freshener. Sometimes on a Sunday afternoon there will be a cricket match in progress on the pitch at the centre of the wood. There is some great analogy of life here, I'm sure. I never know who's winning, or indeed who's playing, and catch only random unintelligible bits of the game as I flit past. Typically as I come into view nothing will be happening. A new batsman, usually a lower order one judging by his age and girth, will be shuffling to the crease. I dawdle a while as the bowler painstakingly resets the field, so that I can see what will happen to his first ball. The batsman plays a forward defensive. I run on and as soon as I am out of sight a huge cry of "howzat" goes up.

After a few weeks the flaw in my policy of running laps of my local woods becomes apparent. Even if my schedule demands that I should run four laps, that means that I have to run temptingly past the exit three times. My brain has the whole lap to think of some valid reason why I should hanger off next time I pass it. Pretty soon the novelty of the outside world has started to pall and the glories of nature that surround me become as monotonous as the decor in the gym. I know every nook and knoll of Highgate Woods by heart and am on first-name terms with several of the squirrels.

Running in the country

You may want to do your training in the countryside proper. Indeed you may already live there. Running in the countryside brings many extra hazards which compensate for the fresh air, exotic vistas and pleasant underfoot terrain. There are gates to be closed behind you, stiles to be vaulted, animals to be avoided and rights of way to be ascertained. In the town you can run pretty much anywhere you like, but rural dwellers are much more territorial. We complain about the absence of street signs in London, but the country is an organisational shambles. If roads are signposted at all it is usually just to inform potential trespassers that they are private roads leading to private property where farmers lurk with shotguns at the ready. I think it is all part of a deliberate ploy to confuse and deter the ramblers that country folk so detest. Despite being a blatant urbanite myself, I find myself sharing the landowner's contempt for these people. It's partly because they ramble, which is an annoyingly lackadaisical pace when you are running, but mainly because they do it in large groups which makes it impossible to overtake them without detours into mud.

The country has the additional danger of animals: cows, horses and sheep wandering all over the shop which provide three extra types of poo for you to step in (in addition to dogs' which we have in abundance in London). On a smaller scale, the unpolluted air encourages the breeding of trillions of insects which perform regular kamikaze plunges into your lungs as you slog along the towpaths and bridleways.

Sadly, running in the country does not garner for you the instinctive respect that it does in the metropolis. For a start you are immediately identified as a townie. Rural folk do not run, liking to imply that their healthy outdoor working lives negate any need to take additional exercise. Of course, we know that these days they all work in call centres or business parks, but there is something justifiable in their scorn. In nature there is no activity without purpose. As you sweat along country lanes and across fields you feel out of kilter with your environment. Cows and sheep laze and graze in the pasture. Ducks bob sleepily on the surface of the water. Gnats hover in fuzzy, motionless clouds. They all look at you and think: mug. I tried country runs a few times, but in the end I feel that road-pounding is an activity best suited to frazzled, time-poor, deadline-ridden, high-blood-pressure urban existence.

CHAPTER 10

Hammersmith Riverside Handicap

Hammersmith, London
27 July
Distance: 3 and a bit miles
Time: 23 mins 47 secs

After the annoyingly lackadaisical Tower Jog and the seven-minute head start I gave to the rest of the field in the Chase Corporate Challenge, I feel I need to cut my teeth in a proper competitive race. Browsing through the runners' magazines to which I have become worryingly addicted, I come across the Hammersmith Riverside Handicap. Rivers are not stupid, I reason, they follow the lowest lie of the land, so this should be a fairly flat course. With some pretty views of the Thames thrown in, it will be the perfect event on which to win my running spurs.

I arrive on time at the designated meeting place in Furnival Gardens next to Hammersmith Bridge to find no sign of any runners. Surely they can't have set off already? A bunch of old men in their underwear are loitering around nearby. I assume they are the escaped inmates of some local Sunset Home and wonder if I should alert the authorities. Then I notice a slightly younger man with a clipboard in their midst and realise to my dismay that these are my fellow competitors. I go over and give the organiser my name. He asks for my date of birth. "1960," I reply. "Ah, a youngster!" he exclaims. I feel a mixture of gratification and worry. This will be a very humiliating field to finish at the back of. The organiser explains to me that, as this race takes place on a Tuesday afternoon, only retired people can usually make it. "SOBs," a grey-bearded runner says, pointing at his chest, "Slow Old Buggers."

The organiser asks me for my five-kilometre time. I'm embarrassed to admit I don't have one. All the literature about racing I am currently immersing myself in assumes you are instantly familiar with your running times over various distances in the same way that young children know their age to the nearest quarter of a year. "You might want to run the first 2K at your half-marathon pace," a magazine article on cross-country running will advise, "step up to a 10K pace for 3K and then drop back to a 10M pace for the remainder, holding back a little for your big sprint finish." I haven't done a proper competitive race before, I explain to the organiser, and hazard that I will take about half an hour to complete the distance. *About* half an hour? The old-timers roll their eyes at each other and tut-tut at the woolliness of my answer (I'll be thinking Winston Churchill's still Prime Minister next). The organiser puts me with the slowest runners. There are three of us in my group and I estimate our combined age to be approximately 160. The total field can be no more than 12 (combined age off the scale).

We slowcoaches are to start first, with the leaner, fitter (and frankly older) runners setting off at staggered intervals behind us. There is no marked-off race track. A greybeard who is presumably too decrepit to run informs us that the course is three and a bit miles (or five and a-different-bit kilometres) and gives us general directions: "Turn right, over the bridge, right on to the towpath, continue for about a mile and a quarter…" I don't listen. I am incapable of listening when someone gives me directions. It's like trying to understand particle physics. My brain just won't do it. I'll just follow the others, I decide.

The three of us set off to a good old-fashioned "ready...steady... GO!" By the time we have crossed Hammersmith Bridge a natural order has developed. A grizzled man in red shorts leads the way, followed by me, followed by the other senior citizen who sits deferentially back in third place. Despite the shame of being outrun by someone old enough to be my dad, I argue to myself that there is no point in overtaking Red Shorts, as then not only would I have to set my own pace (which I've heard can lead to burn-out) but I would also be electing myself pathfinder-in-chief for the entire company and would probably get everyone lost.

Despite the summer sunshine the course seems designed to pass as many places where crops are being burned or roads are being resurfaced as possible and the air is noxious with fumes which catch in the back of my throat and further dehydrate me. I didn't bring my water bottle with me as no one else did and I didn't want to look like a wimp in front of the OAPs. In any case, gulping back water might seem a little insensitive to the elderly prostates all around me. It suddenly occurs to me that this whole race with its dubious distances, non-existent markings and elderly participants could be some huge scam by an organised gang of criminals. I have, I realise, just left my backpack with the race organiser, blithely entrusting all my valuables to a stranger with a clipboard. Well, he can help himself to my wallet, I think grimly, just so long as he doesn't drink the water in my pack.

We are still running Indian-brave-style with Red Shorts 10 metres ahead of me, and the unseen grampa maintaining a similar distance behind. I start to worry about using Red Shorts as my pacer. After all his very presence in this starter group is an admission that he is crap. But does he know exactly how crap he is? Can he guarantee to maintain a consistently crap pace? Also, the label on his running vest is not tucked in and sticks up annoyingly. As the track doubles back on itself for the homeward leg and there is still no sign of the chasing pack I decide that I should take over the lead as I am now confident of being able to navigate us safely home. Strangely, I now find that sheer etiquette prevents me from overtaking. Powering past this old gentleman would be a bit like knocking his hat off and running away. Surely one should show a little more respect for one's elders. Get real, I tell myself, it's only a matter of time before one of the other runners overtakes us both anyway. So I ease by Red Shorts gently, almost holding my breath so as not to draw attention to myself. "Well done," he beams as I pass. I hope he realises that my flushed countenance is due to embarrassment at being so patronised by someone two decades my senior and not the effort of putting on the extra pace. I resist the temptation to pop his label back in as I pass.

As predicted, within a few hundred metres I hear footfalls behind and breathing in my ear and another runner surges past. Not Red Shorts, thankfully, but the only other competitor in the field who seems younger than me. "Why haven't you got a job?" I telepath uncharitably in his direction as he vanishes into the distance ahead. Within a minute I am passed by a man of similar age to me. At least *I* don't have my shorts on inside out is the only thought I can find to console myself with as he, too, leaves me for dead. In the 100 metres up to the line I am overtaken twice more, on the second occasion by the race organiser himself. "I thought you were about to put on a big sprint finish so I had to give it some myself," he explains at the finishing line, managing to be both apologetic and patronising in the same breath.

Back in the park we all do a few token standing stretches, apart from the youngest man, and presumed winner, who rolls around on his back like a stuntman on fire. At least I didn't come last, I console myself as I try to balance on one leg to do a thigh stretch without falling over. Besides 23 minutes 47 seconds is a personal best (well, it had to be, this being my first proper race when I actually started on time and remembered to look at my watch at the end). A quick mental calculation tells me that this is a respectable just-over seven-minute-mile speed. Now at least I'll know which group to start in next time. My peace of mind is, however, about as short-lived as that of Dickie Attenborough in *The Great Escape* when he confides to Gordon Jackson that he's never been happier and then looks up to see the Nazis about to machinegun them both.

As the greybeards gather round the man with the clipboard to get their race times, the hideous truth dawns on me. The reason for the popularity of this race among the elderly is that all results are age-adjusted. I should have twigged from the race's name – the Hammersmith Riverside *Handicap*. That's why the organiser asked me for my date of birth. In view of their superior years the dotards pootling along five minutes behind me will actually finish ahead of me in the official results table. I did come last. Shit.

CHAPTER 11

Training Schedule

Running a marathon is like writing a novel. Many people like to think they've got one in them somewhere, but very few will ever get round to doing anything about it. They will, however, not stint on decrying failure in others. Thus any plan to run a marathon by a person with no record of athletic accomplishment in the last 20 years should be treated like a military operation, cloaked by secrecy. Only once you have proved to yourself that you can clock up half an hour or so on a running machine or a lap or two of the park three times a week can you casually let slip into the conversation that you are thinking of trying the Big One.

Once you have told all your friends and thus will be a laughing stock if you bottle out, you will need to rationalise your training programme. If you just continue running on your own when you feel like it, you will fail to complete the marathon for one of the following reasons:

a) *you will not do enough training and thus not be fit enough;*
b) *you will do too much training and injure yourself.*

Additionally you may be, like me, a lazy person who can only get down to doing anything when you have a deadline. There is no particular shame in this sort of mindset in my opinion. I am a journalist and know of almost no other journalists who would be capable of producing any copy if they weren't presented with a daily or weekly press deadline. Most of the population probably only do any work because they find themselves in an office five times a week where there is no option to do much else apart from drink coffee and complain about their lot to other people in the same situation. This is just human nature. A handful of people in life are driven to succeed, like Richard Branson or Bill Gates, and the rest of us end up as their employees.

Now putting your name down to run a marathon is a deadline in itself but a reassuringly distant one. Don't be fooled, though. You may have been able to get away with doing your homework on the back of the school bus in the morning, but you can't put off your marathon training to the day before. This is why you will need a schedule which will give you daily mileage targets to be met.

There are lots of training schedules to choose from. You find them in running mags, training books and on the Internet. Some are endorsed by famous marathoners, others are written by sports scientists, many are just anonymous. They are all essentially the same, so it doesn't really matter which one you opt for. Remember, if you get through the marathon successfully it will be thanks to your own dedication, self-discipline and punishing hard work. If you fail or get injured, it will be because you chose the wrong schedule and you can heap all the blame on Liz McColgan.

A typical schedule will specify a 15 to 18-week preparatory period of training to run a marathon for an individual who already has a reasonable level of fitness. This schedule will consist of a grid with lots of little numbers on it. It doesn't look very daunting until you realise that the numbers are miles you are expected to run over the course of the coming months. The good thing about having a schedule is that it liberates the important guilt motivator. Every mile on that plan is directly convertible into shame and self-disgust in your brain if you don't run it.

Personally I chose a schedule I downloaded off the website of American running guru Hal Higdon. Most non-stingy training schedules will allow you a rest day or possibly two a week. What I liked about this particular programme was that not only did it allow two rest days a week but Day *One* of the schedule is designated a rest day. What a positive move by Mr Higdon. Normally you might make excuses for putting off embarking on your programme, but with this one there is no need. And instead of waking up on the second morning feeling stiff and sore, you feel great. You have all that noble sense of achievement without any of the physical distress caused by having done any actual exercise. And, of course, if you don't get round to doing any training on the second day, you can just claim to yourself that you actually started *today* and thus avoid any guilt feelings about having missed a day's training. Obviously there is a danger that this might fall into infinite regress.

A training programme will specify a total weekly mileage but will allow you to switch days around within it to fit in with your other commitments. People in regular jobs may prefer to take their rest days during the week and put in the longer training runs at the weekend. As a self-employed writer, I can be more flexible and tend to schedule my rest days around my anticipated alcohol intake. For example, if I am going out drinking on a Wednesday night I will make sure that the Thursday is a rest day. There is no point on planning to run on a day when I confidently expect to wake up with a hangover. Alka-Seltzer can't alleviate the conscience. There is one downside to this arrangement. The couple of evenings when you are allowed to drink will, by definition, be on days on which you have had to train. On such days be sure to do your run in the morning and don't squeeze it in at the end of the day just before you go out. If you do this you will find that, when you take your first drink, your aching muscles gratefully soak up all the water content of the wine or beer and divert all the alcohol straight to your brain. Going out one evening after a 10-mile run I got immediately and horribly drunk, told some strange woman that I loved her and ended up phoning my flatmate Angela at 3.00 a.m. blubbing that I had lost my keys. A quick check the next morning revealed that they were in my trouser pocket the whole time. This brings me on to:

Boring things about training (1)

Essential incompatibility with alcohol. Abstinence is not a prerequisite for training to run a marathon but it is quite a practical solution. No matter how hard I try to organise my schedule around my social life there are frequent lapses. The danger of alcohol is that it is one of those rare instances of a poison that induces a positive feedback reaction, i.e. the more of it you drink, the more you want. A harmless single quick drink after work can quickly become a skinful. If you have a 12-mile run to do the next day, either you or your schedule is going to suffer. Giving up, at least for the three months of intensive training before the marathon, seems sensible. But by running 30 to 50 miles a week you already feel that you have become a social leper. Going teetotal just exacerbates this feeling. The other problem with abstinence is the fact that all nonalcoholic drinks are foul. Plus you drink much more of them, waiting for the hit that never arrives. So you either end up on alcohol-free lager, which recreates all the unpleasant effects of a hangover without any of the pleasurable effects of the preceding drunkenness or you down Coca-Cola or fruit juice all night and o/d on glucose.

Boring things about training (2)

Stretches. As if getting out of your warm bed and running round the park four times before breakfast wasn't bad enough, all your training runs should be preceded and followed by several minutes of stretching (or retching if you've followed No. 1 above). Stretches are like paying your gas bill or doing your income tax return. You know it is necessary and you'll be in trouble if you don't do it, but it is so dull. Sadly, unlike tax returns, you can't employ someone else to do them for you. If you're the sort of person who can put together flat-pack furniture by following the international diagrams in the instruction leaflet then you can learn your stretches from a training book. If like me you still have to get your dad to assemble your IKEA purchases for you, you should book yourself a session with a trainer at your local gym and have the stretches demonstrated by a human being. Bear in mind that not only do stretches prevent you from getting injured and lengthen your muscles, but scientific studies have shown that moderate aerobic exercise in recovery (i.e. stretching) facilitates lactate removal in comparison to passive recovery (i.e. lying crashed out on your bed).

CHAPTER 12

Liverpool Half Marathon

Liverpool
8 August
Distance: 13.1 miles
Time: 1 hr 44 mins 33 secs

My first impression on stepping off the 14.50 from Euston at Lime Street Station on Saturday afternoon is that the entire population of Liverpool is competing in tomorrow's half marathon. Just about everyone under the age of 50 is already changed into their tracksuit – a full 18 hours before the event – and warming up with a light stroll along the George Street shopping precinct. It takes a little while for me to realise that branded sportswear is merely the regional dress of Merseyside. Little surprise then that Liverpool was in a recent survey voted the Least Stylish City in the European Union.

My immediate task is to find accommodation for the night. I go to the tourist information office where a woman tells me that most of the hotels are full but I should try the hall of residence at John Moores University. I am not sure whether to be flattered or insulted that one year off my 40th birthday I still look like a student. But, as it turns out, undergraduate digs prove to be a convenient and cheap option. I dump my bag in my tiny room and wonder how to spend the rest of my afternoon. Just about all of my friends who through necessity or affectation live in Liverpool are out of town for the weekend. I'm not sure if they're avoiding the city or the prospect of having to watch me run round it.

I have read in one of my marathon training books that one should walk the course of a race the day before to accustom oneself to the route. Walking 13 miles 24 hours before I will have to run the same distance seems overly masochistic. I consider checking out the course from the back of a taxi or the top deck of a bus, but frankly it seems a bit swotty. In the end I decide to do some shopping and then stroll up to Sefton Park just to establish that I know where the starting point is. Liverpool's high street retail facilities seem to consist entirely of sportswear retailers and thrift shops. Fortunately this is the ideal combination for this aspirant marathon runner and born-again student. I pick up a few things I need (sports drink, water, energy bars) from Boots and a load of things I don't (shampoo, candles, nail clippers) from a shop where everything costs a pound.

Back at the hall of residence I check my map and estimate that Sefton Park is about a 40-minute walk. My route takes me past the red-brick Anglican Cathedral which beams down gloom from the top of a hill like Mother Bates's house in *Psycho*. I pass through Princes Park and am puzzled to find the place deserted at seven o'clock on a pleasant summer's evening. Literally there is not a soul in sight. The equivalent park in London – Primrose Hill say – at this hour would be crowded with tourists, couples, picnicking families, girls reading novels, dogs chasing frisbees, groups of kids and wistful adults kicking footballs around. Five minutes later I arrive at the much larger Sefton Park. I gaze across empty verdure stretching as far as the eye can see and not a sign that primates ever descended from the trees. What has happened? Where is everyone? Don't people up here own dogs that need walking? Or has rabies swept unannounced across the north of England? And where are all the kids? Today is the first day of the football season and Liverpool won away to Sheffield Wednesday. Shouldn't hordes of youngsters be out recreating that Robbie Fowler goal? Or are they too ashamed to show their faces because they are still wearing last season's replica kits? The deserted park, though far more beautiful than if it were sullied with human beings, really is quite inexplicable. Surely everyone can't be watching *Blind Date*? Finally a single dog appears with owner in tow and runs around in forlorn circles in the absence of any canine bottoms to sniff. Maybe I was right in my initial supposition that the entire city is running in tomorrow's race and everyone is having a quiet night in.

Confident that I have found the starting point, I hail a cab for the short hop back into the city centre. It is important for visitors to remember that, although Merseyside has the same black cabs as in London, taxi etiquette is reversed up here. Down south, having stopped a taxi, you then stand on the street and respectfully enquire of the driver if it wouldn't put him out too much to take you to your destination. In Liverpool you just hop straight in. If you hang around on the pavement waiting for his blessing to embark he will think you are mad. By contrast, in London when you reach your destination you descend from the taxi and pay through the side window. Up here any attempt to leave the vehicle before handing over the cash is interpreted by the cabby as you doing a runner and he will smartly activate the vehicle's central locking. The driver of my cab explains that his meter is broken and quotes me a £3.50 fare to Concert Square to which I happily agree. He gives the supposedly defective machine a few thumps during the journey to emphasise his dubious claim. I am not bothered. I feel we have struck a symbiotic deal – he has presumably charged me well over the going rate for the distance, yet I am still paying less than I would for the equivalent journey in London. Honour is satisfied.

I arrive at Concert Square in the city centre at about eight o'clock and find myself faced with the same puzzling spectacle as in the parks. There is an appealing terrace set out with tables and chairs which in any other city in the world – apart maybe from Omsk – would be crowded with customers enjoying the summer air and sky. But, no, it is deserted while the interiors of the surrounding bars are crammed with early evening drinkers. Liverpudlians – I conclude – just seem to have an aversion to being outside. Maybe they just don't want to be reminded of the decay and disrepair their once fine city has fallen into.

Having had a pint (rich in all-important glycogen-building carbo-hydrates), I set off to locate the Italian quarter for more of the same in the form of some pasta. Failing to find it, I end up in a vegetarian curry house and decide to take the risk to my pre-race bowels with a chick pea dhansak. I arrive back at my student digs and feel a nostalgic tug of adolescent self-pity. It is 9.30 p.m. I have no friends, no TV and nothing better to do than go to bed. My room is a whitewashed 10-foot square containing a single bed, a table, a washstand and a built-in wardrobe. I can't remember the last time I slept in a single bed. No adult has such a thing; you're either in a relationship or hoping to get lucky. Lit by a single stark overhead lamp, the place has the maddening claustrophobic ethos of the hero's room in *Eraserhead*. I can imagine sitting here alone for months entertaining grandiose dreams of how I will make my mark on an unappreciative world by writing a great novel or committing suicide.

So I decide to make an early night of it. My window overlooks Lime Street station and the tannoyed announcements lull me to sleep. That is until the train from Sheffield arrives and the night air is rent with the singing of several hundred triumphant soccer fans. I relapse back into sleep, only to be woken again an hour later as the next cross-Pennine express brings in a load of considerably drunker and consequently more vociferous supporters who fulfil a modern-day town crier's role of informing the city of the score (2-1), though perhaps needlessly repetitively, especially considering most people saw it on teletext earlier. The final wave comes in at about midnight. I fall asleep to the mingled sounds of seagulls and sirens.

The next morning I breakfast at the table in my room on pure carbo-hydrate: energy bars, bananas and sports drink. I think dismissively of the *Chariots of Fire* gentlemen athletes who would rise to a breakfast of devilled kidneys and pork chops and go on to win all the races anyway just because none of the workers had been allowed the day off from the factory to compete. I check over my kit and set off to walk the two miles or so to Sefton Park. On the way I plan my race strategy. It is important, I have been told by people who know about such things, to have a target time. Just running and hoping for the best, which was my preferred strategy, is out. From my past form I calculate I should be able to aim for seven-to-eight minute miles. But there is also the psychological element of which position I should take on the starting line-up. Should I be ambitious, start with the seven-minute milers and find myself being overtaken by everybody? Or conservative, go with the eight-minuters and get boxed in by dawdling idiots?

Liverpool's streets are strangely deserted, even for a Sunday. Of the few people I pass all are wearing sports casuals except for an old lady going to church, though it can't be long before they worship in Nike here. Just as I am wondering if I have got the wrong day, the wrong city, the wrong planet, a Mazda van pulls up and a London voice asks me for directions to Sefton Park. Mentally congratulating myself for having done the recce the evening before, I point the driver in the correct direction and wish I could do a Scouse accent for added authenticity. Incidentally, one of my plans for how I will reorganise society when the responsibility for running the country is finally handed over to me is as follows: I will pay unemployed people to dress up as foreign tourists and wander round the streets asking locals for directions at random. There is nothing more guaranteed to put a smile on the face and a tune on the lips of a person than to have just pointed a lost stranger in the right direction. You feel valued, bonded and ever so slightly superior.

I walk on happily practising my upper body stretches, which causes a hopeful taxi to pull over. Princes Park is, just as it was yesterday evening, devoid of humanity. So no tradition of the Sunday morning constitutional either up here. A maverick woman walking a dog comes into sight. "Looks like it's going to hose down," she greets me dispiritingly. At least that's what I think she says. My ears are still not yet attuned to the Scouse accent. Maybe she said: "Are you going to the Hoe Down?" In any event I just nod. Whether it's a race or a barn dance that's where I'm going, and a splutter of feedback from a distant PA system warming up at least confirms I'm headed in the right direction.

I arrive at Sefton Park at exactly the same time as the man in the Mazda, some 20 minutes after I directed him. He obviously didn't listen properly or asked for a second opinion and got lost. Our eyes meet. Although we are complete strangers I am irritated by his lack of trust in me. It soon turns out that my researches of yesterday were not thorough enough and the start area is actually right across the other side of the park. By the time I have got there, changed, queued to leave my belongings and queued again for the loo the race is about to start. I duck under the cordon and find myself crammed in with the eight-minute milers. There is no time to worry about my positioning or do any stretches. Almost immediately the starting hooter sounds and we are off.

The first couple of minutes of a large road race like this are by far the most dangerous part. You have 1600 competitors, in cramped conditions under which it would be illegal to transport cattle, all suddenly attempting to run with different degrees of physical co-ordination while simultaneously waving to watching friends. If you can avoid being tripped up, body-checked or smacked in the side of the head at this stage, the remaining umpteen miles seem a doddle. We are cheered round a half-lap of the park by a decent crowd of onlookers before we veer off and head south on to Aigburth Road. Here spectators are very much thinner on the ground. A couple of surly shopkeepers stare at us as they pull up graffitied metal shutters. But in general the Merseysiders' distaste for the outside world prevails and the first few miles of our run are accompanied at best by that hollow sound familiar to actors in Edinburgh Fringe productions – that of two people clapping.

Only one lane of Aigburth Road has been coned off for our use and cars glide right alongside us on our right. Not one driver thinks to give us a morale-boosting toot on the horn. The narrowness of the course causes some problems at this early stage of the race when there is a lot of jockeying for position. "All right lads, it's a *road* race here," a bumptious Scouser calls out, objecting to the fact that some runners have side-stepped onto the pavement in order to overtake. Frankly it's a better shot than remaining trapped behind grumpy gits like him or taking your chances among oncoming traffic. My watch tells me we have been running for 10 minutes now, but I have yet to see the first reassuring mile marker. Surely we must have gone a mile by now? Did I take my place at the start with a load of hopelessly deluded eight-minuters? Or maybe local drug addicts have stolen the mile markers in their desperation for something to sell to fuel their crack cocaine habit? Finally a sign comes into view and to my relief it reads "2 miles". I look at my watch: 15 minutes. Somehow this band of irregulars is keeping up their target.

At three miles we come to the first water point. Trestle tables have been set out by the roadside and teams of frantic volunteers are doling out drinks in plastic cups. It resembles a game from *It's a Knockout* with water being slopped all over the tables and road in the panic to shove it out quickly enough. Most of the cups are only about a third full as we grab them off the table. The scene lacks only Stuart Hall's maniacal giggle. I am badly overheating so I help myself to two cups which I drain as best as possible on the move and end up spilling most of the few feeble fluid ounces down my T-shirt. Almost immediately, external refreshment arrives in the form of rain. The last person who was as grateful for a sudden downpour was probably Noah who stood to look pretty foolish otherwise.

By now a little group of runners has coalesced around me. Apart from the Grumpy Scouser, there is Puff Daddy, a middle-aged man who gasps loudly and piteously every alternate stride, and a stocky thug wearing an incongruous woolly hat pulled down almost over his eyes who I nickname Bully Beef from his resemblance to the character from the *Dandy* comic. Bully Beef has an individualistic running style. He is built like a juggernaut, but seemingly one with no steering wheel. If he finds himself running slightly faster than the person immediately in front of him, he will just bear remorselessly down on them, leaving them the option of being crushed underfoot or hopping aside and risking the wrath of the Grumpy Scouser. This I would define as The Plate Tectonics School of Roadrunning. A woman standing by the roadside shouts out the names of those runners who are displaying them on the front of their shirts. "Cathy…Tony….Phil", she intones. Not "Come on, Cathy…you can do it" or "Go for it, Phil….only nine miles to go". Maybe she's just teaching her bored daughter to read. Four miles now and I am getting serious pain from my right knee. Typical. It is my left knee that has been giving me problems and now the one which has behaved impeccably throughout my training buckles at the first hurdle (well, not literally obviously. No sadist has yet been fiendish enough to invent the 13-mile hurdles event.) My body is like the England cricket team – there is no single individual part of it that can be relied upon.

We bear left for a while and then turn north on to Menlove Avenue. Those runners who read the *Liverpool Echo* pull-out race supplement – or who are Beatles Buffs like me – will know that this is the road where John Lennon grew up (I could score saddo points by adding that he lived at number 251). In my present wearied state, I wouldn't pay much attention if John was there himself taking tea in his back garden with his Aunt Mimi and Elvis Presley. It is now five and a half miles and my left knee has started to throb, too. Ironically, this helps alleviate my problem in the same way that carrying *two* heavy shopping baskets, one on each side, is easier than lurching along lopsidedly with one.

By Mile Six I'm feeling seriously dehydrated. Then suddenly a sign blissfully informs us that a drink station is 100 metres away. The next sign says it is 200 metres. What's going on? Are we all running in the wrong direction? Then another sign: Drinks 100m – clearly, we are now going round in circles. I continue in confusion. Several hundred metres later there are still no drinks. Are these signs mirages conjured up by my oxygen-starved brain or has someone borrowed my pedometer to measure the distances? Finally the welcome roadside tables appear in the distance up ahead. A drinks station, apart from the finishing line, is the finest sight in a race. It is also highly dangerous as for the next 200 metres the road is covered in discarded plastic cups and sponges. To compound the hazard a well-meaning woman is handing out bananas. Okay, I know Linford Christie swears by them as a quick energy boost, but the prospect of having runners in front tossing banana skins under my feet on an already rain-slippery surface does not appeal.

The glycogen hit kicks in and I take more interest in my surroundings. We are still running along Menlove Avenue which actually seems rather bourgeois, with tennis courts and Audis parked in drives. "A *Middle* Class Hero is Something to Be...?" – somehow it doesn't have quite the same ring about it. We turn left and pass Quarry Bank Grammar. This I recognise as John's old school (which also inspired the name of the Beatles' first incarnation as the Quarrymen – I warn you, don't get me started on this). It's probably a Montessori school these days. I concentrate on trying to lose Bully Beef. In events like this you inevitably find you get locked into a sort of psychological three-legged race with some other runner whom you can't seem to shake off no matter how fast or slow you run. You just seem to fall into an unbreakable stride with them – a bit like women working in the same office whose periods synchronise. After half an hour you know every nuance of your fellow runner's body language and, if you are me, thoroughly hate everything about him. You know that if you bumped into this nameless stranger on a railway platform or in a lift in 20 years' time you would immediately recognise him and probably punch him on the nose.

Somehow by the time we come back into Sefton Park at 11 miles Bully Beef has vanished, although in my confused state I can't remember whether I've left him behind or vice versa. The rain has now stopped and the trees round the park drip heavenly moisture on us as we pass under. With two miles to go I have now reached my decision point. So far I have been averaging eight-minute miles. Do I up my pace and put on a bit of a finish? As this is by far the longest distance I have ever run I am not sure of available energy reserves. I have a feeling that if I were my CD Discman, the little battery symbol on my display would be flashing urgently by now. I also have memories, from watching athletics championships on TV in the past, of seeing a runner break away from the pack and strike out for the line and hearing David Coleman's cautioning cry: "He's gone too soon..." I decide on a compromise plan. I will not actually try to overtake other runners, but I will not let anyone overtake me. After all, if any potential overtaker were any good they would be in the showers by now. We turn into the home straight and there are many more spectators now, applauding enthusiastically. A Scouse wit on the pavement makes eye contact with me and deadpans: "I'd like you to go a bit faster because you've let me down badly." He can obviously see I don't have the available energy to headbutt him. "You're nearly there," other spectators shout, hardly more helpfully. Nearly there, thank God. I'm nearly dead.

Many of my co-runners, sensibly mindful that this is the one time in the race when it's worth trying to put on a bit of a show, with camcorders and loved-ones packed by the roadside, start to sprint past me. I discreetly enquire of my body whether there is any possibility of a little more productivity, only to be turned down flatly by its intransigent shop steward. "His tank's empty. There's nothing there." Coleman shrieks in my head. I cross the line at 1:44:33, putting me just under an eight-minute-mile pace. A teenage girl hands me my medal. I do a few stretches, change and walk back across the park towards the city centre. I call my mother from my mobile phone. I am conscious of having always been totally crap at school sports days in my childhood, coming consistently last in the 100-yard race and embarrassing her. It's probably too late, 30 years on, to redeem the trauma of that experience for her, but she listens politely to my race report and seems impressed that I finished.

I walk to the pub where I have arranged to meet my Scouser friend Chris and sit down. This is one of the most blissful experiences of my life. You may think you know all about sitting down – in fact you've probably sat down several dozen times today – but, let me tell you, you haven't sat down until you've run 13 miles and *then* sat down. I've never taken heroin, but it cannot be much better than this. Chris soon arrives with his daughter, Raya. He drives me down to the Albert Dock for lunch as my knees have locked and I refuse to go anywhere where there are stairs. We park opposite the Beatles Experience museum, which is blasting out the dreadful Ringo-sung "Act Naturally". I ask Chris if he has ever visited the place. He shakes his head derisively. "Yes, you have. You took me," pipes up 11-year-old Raya. "I've been there millions of times," she tells me proudly. Chris looks awkward and silences her with a frown. She is too young to have been inculcated into the Scouser ethos. If I may explain.

The relationship with the city's most famous sons sums up Liverpool. On a previous trip I visited the Beatles Experience. When the next day I confessed this to a Liverpudlian friend he couldn't have been more uncomprehending if I'd announced that I'd gone out the previous evening and strangled a prostitute. It's not just because the place is naff and touristy like Madame Tussauds. It goes deeper than that. The Beatles Experience has dozens of rooms dedicated to the Fab Four's childhoods and early years in the city: birth certificates; school reports; proud mock-ups of the front rooms of the council houses they grew up in; John's first guitar. Subsequent rooms feature the lovingly recreated offices of *Merseybeat* newspaper, Brian Epstein's record shop and, of course, the Cavern Club. Suddenly you get to 1963 and it's as if the museum loses interest in its subjects. Displays become functional and half-hearted, as if to say: well, after that they made a few more records, took some drugs, went to India and split up. What was the loveable Moptops' unpardonable 1963 crime? One to match that same year's infamous Great Train Robbery? They moved to London.

Inspirational Viewing No 2

Logan's Run (1976)

The film is set in a post-apocalyptic twenty-third century world where what is left of humanity is forced to live in a giant shopping mall dressed in panto costumes. The catastrophe that befell the Earth is never explained, but is presumably due to ozone depletion from the huge volume of hair spray necessary to maintain the mid-seventies hairstyles that have now been in fashion for over 200 years. Farrah Fawcett-Majors, in a totally extraneous cameo role as a doctor's receptionist, is single-handedly responsible probably for a hole in the ozone layer the size of Romania.

In this machine-ruled society, human beings live solely for pleasure and are put to death on their 30th birthdays in a grandiose ceremony known as the Carousel. In this, victims assemble in a stadium wearing ice hockey masks and Freddie Mercury stage outfits. Those who do not die of embarrassment are spun round, float up to the ceiling and explode. This scene is one of several that makes this, like *2001: a Space Odyssey*, a film that is best viewed under the influence of mind-altering, class A drugs. Those 29-year-olds in the Mall who sensibly wish to avoid birthday execution are known as runners, hence the title. Logan is a Sandman, that is a sort of policeman whose job is to track down runners and shoot them with a crap gun that mainly just sets rocks on fire. For reasons too dull to go into, Logan himself becomes a runner and this is where the action should start to become of interest to us.

Sadly it must be avowed that Michael York, as Logan, is no Tupper of the Track. During his long and frankly tedious escape from the Mall, passing through various sewage works and hydroelectric power stations masquerading unconvincingly as the Mall's futuristic controlling machinery, he hardly breaks into a trot. In fact, he spends more time swimming than he does running, but this is mainly to provide an excuse for co-star Jenny Agutter to take her clothes off.

Little here to interest the marathoner then. Where the film rings true is in its accurate observation that people only take up running when they reach the age of 30. Its portrait of a society where such individuals are considered dangerous misfits and are killed on sight will probably not bring comfort to today's midlife-crisis marathoner.

Summary

Artistic merit **

Marathoning relevance *

Kitsch factor *****

CHAPTER 13

Race the Train

Tywyn, Wales
21 August
Distance: 14.2 miles
Time: 2 hours 12 mins

On my very first trawl through the schedules of running events around the country my curiosity was piqued by this dauntingly named race which takes place annually in North West Wales. Race the Train? Why on earth would any human being want to race against a train? Unless it's a mule train or something equivalently slow. Researching the event, I find it has been established for some 16 years and is based around the Talyllyn narrow gauge steam railway which once ferried slate from the Bryn Englwys quarry to the coast and is now maintained by charitable volunteers. Amazingly, it seems about a hundred male and a handful of female runners succeed in beating the train each year. I decide that this is one race I cannot miss, despite the six- to seven-hour drive from south-east England and the high possibility of total humiliation.

On the Friday, I'm doing my occasional evening job, playing piano as part of singer Frances Ruffelle's backing band at the Komedia Theatre in Brighton. In the days before a major race you find yourself being very fastidious about any activity that involves the slightest physical exertion. Any small injury or strain could put you out of the race. I think about ways I could damage any vital running muscles through playing the piano. Must make sure I don't snap a cruciate ligament by pushing down the sustain pedal too forcibly. Mustn't jump up too quickly to bow at the end of the concert. Mustn't overdo it at the post-gig celebrations and fall over. Must be careful of that ankle-twisting shingle on Brighton's famous beach.

After we've done a quick sound check in the theatre at four o'clock I announce that I am going to go for a run along the sea front. This is greeted by the other musicians as if I had informed them that I was just popping off to heal some lepers or broker a peace deal in the Middle East. I don't know why taking basic exercise so smacks of self-righteousness in this country. Maybe it's the look of suffering on the faces of all runners that suggests they must be involved in some higher altruistic pursuit. Certainly none of the joggers I pass as I run along the promenade look as if they're having any fun, in contrast to the footballers and beach volleyball players. We all have that head-bowed, slump-shouldered, teeth-gritted look like some punch-drunk boxer trying to go one last desperate round with Mike Tyson to qualify for his share of the purse. I try to get myself over the inevitable first-twenty-minutes-of-the-run blues with a mouthful of my new energy gel. Why does everything have to be gel these days? Hair gel, shaving gel, tooth gel, shower gel, even toilet gel. I squeeze a slew of it into my mouth. It has the taste and consistency of the raw cake mixture I would steal out of my mother's mixing bowl as a kid. Disgusting – to anyone aged over about 10. I drop the rest in a bin.

Brighton promenade is ideal for a training run because it has lamp-posts spaced at 50-metre intervals which is very convenient for *fartleks*. This is important to improve performance so I sprint from one lamp-post to the next, then jog to the one after, then sprint again and so on. Unfortunately this behaviour merely inspires macho competitiveness in another male runner who has pulled in behind me. Being unaware of my lamp-post *fartleks*, it seems to him that I am trying to outrun him, but after each burst I fade away. Then, just as he catches up, I try again in desperation, only once more to fail. Even though he is behind me, I can sense his racing hackles rise and a feeling of triumph suffuse his body at each perceived failure by me. I am able to assert this because I have experienced similar pathetic emotions myself. Emboldened by my evident lack of stamina, he puts on a spurt and overtakes. Now with him ahead of me the situation is even worse. He thinks I am making regular desperate efforts to overtake him and then falling back exhausted at the last moment – to his ineffable smugness. Eventually I have to take the staircase back up to the pavement level and leave him cockily alone on the beachside track.

I shower and change in our charmingly seedy sea-view hotel. I have recently bought a pair of cargo pants which I am assured are very trendy at the moment (they won't be by the time you are reading this, reader). As a boy I like the practicality of them – one can keep one's mobile phone in the thigh pocket, thus preventing it from irradiating one's testicles. However, as I get ready to walk down to the theatre, I realise that in its present position it is instead going to irradiate my already damaged knees. I can't decide which of these bodily parts is more expendable so I decide to take no chances and leave the phone in my hotel room. In the event the concert passes off without debilitating injury. On the way back to the hotel I offer to give Kate the cellist a hand with her instrument. As I sling it over my shoulder I feel a sharp twinge from my lower back and realise, as my grandmother would have put it, I have done myself a "mischief".

The next morning I take the train down to my parents' house near Oxford just long enough to do my filial duty and then borrow my dad's car for the drive down to Wales. For those of you wondering why a 39-year-old male doesn't own a car I should point out that I used to have one. I sold it five years ago and never got around to buying another. You don't really need one living in London. A car is more convenient than public transportation, but once you've factored into the equation all the time and petrol you spend driving around looking for somewhere to park it I reckon the advantage is negated. The only major downside is to your liver because you never have an excuse to refrain from having a social drink or six.

My dad roughs out five or six alternative routes to North West Wales, which he tells me I should switch between according to prevailing traffic and weather conditions. He points out exactly how many sets of traffic lights I will be able to avoid if I follow his recommended itinerary, a complex cross-country route involving a lot of B-roads and hamlets with double-barrelled names. I thank him and secretly decide to stick to the motorway.

The original plan had been for my friend Mary to accompany me, but she has cried off a couple of days previously. Presumably she thinks that the long trek down to the Welsh coast is not worth it to witness a result which is a foregone conclusion. Okay – true, the chances of my beating the train are zero, but I'm sure Roman amphitheatres were always packed out for Lions versus Christians bouts, despite the bookies' odds on the human participants being extremely long. Besides, it's the taking part that's important, as the Christians no doubt consoled themselves as they were torn apart and devoured. Another unusual feature of Race the Train is that the spectators are afforded a prime view of the event as they get to ride on the train, the better to rain down their scorn on the runners who fall behind – or possibly under – the locomotive. No doubt Mary thinks she is doing me a favour in allowing me to run this race unobserved at close quarters by anyone who knows me. Actually, quite the contrary is the case. Not only would I have welcomed her company over the weekend, but her presence was actually essential to my race strategy. I had been relying on her to pull the communication cord just as the train was about to overtake me, and then faint to cause further delay. Without an on-board accomplice my chances of not being handed a sound thrashing by my coal-fired opponent are looking slim.

So I undertake the long drive down to Wales on my own, a little sad that there is no one to appreciate the scenery with me. Coming upon Cader Idris with the moon setting over it reflected in a motionless lake below is all very well, but unshared and unvouchsafed its aesthetic value seems to be diminished. A little companionship on the journey would also have been nice because the mountains serve a sinister propaganda purpose. These natural fortifications that have over the ages kept out the Anglo Saxon invaders, are also effective at repelling all radio signals in the English tongue and the car radio will only pick up Welsh language stations.

I arrive at the Dolgach Falls hotel at around 9.00 p.m. and am greeted by Steve, the occasional barman. He looks like a policeman, which is lucky because he is one during the daytime. "I'm sorry I'm late," I say, "but I got lost and couldn't phone for directions because there was no signal on my mobile." Steve nods understandingly. "Mobile phones don't work around here because of the mountains," he explains with a touch of Luddite pride. "Though," he goes on, frowning just a little, "I did see someone using one in Abergynolwyn once." "Probably one of those fake phones," I say, "the ones that don't have any working parts that people use ostentatiously just for effect." Steve seems considerably cheered up by this thought and offers to go and see whether the kitchen could still rustle me up some supper. I dump my stuff in my room and repair to the bar for a drink.

The bar is really just a living room with a counter at one end and a quaint foot-pumped organ in the corner. The other guests are a Quiet Couple, who appear to have taken a vow of silence along with their marital ones, and a jovial bunch of middle-aged Northern folk, who do enough talking to compensate. I sit in the corner with my beer and listen in on their conversation for a while. They are discussing horse – rather than human – racing. They have clearly been busy at the betting shop earlier in the day and are trying to persuade one of their number, Terry, to look at the results on Teletext rather than wait for the morning papers. Terry, however, shakes his head and stubbornly refuses the proffered TV remote. "Me horse never wins when I check results on Teletext," he insists.

I try to place their accent. Somewhere in Yorkshire or Tyneside I hazard. It sounds as if they are playing a variant on that word game where you are penalised for saying the word "yes" or "no". In their case, the forbidden word is "the". The definite article just gets swallowed up into nothing in their heavy dialect. ("You know chip shop that were under car park.") The only time the sound is pronounced is in the second person singular, "thee". Naïve as I am, I had no idea anyone still used this archaic form. I later find out they come from Rotherham. Still, they manage to communicate pretty successfully without the use of the word "the" and soon I am wondering why we in the south waste our breath bothering with it.

Before long I have been drawn into their conversation and it turns out that three of the male Rotherhams – Terry, Allen and Eddie – all in their 50s, are runners who have come down to race the train for a second year (one of them apparently even beat it last time). The affable landlord, Keith, a Welshman whose accent has lost all its credibility from too much time working in the West Midlands, admits that he used to be a three-run-a-day, 100-mile-a-week man and has the permanent damage to his lower lumbar vertebrae to prove it. Even the Quiet Man, it transpires when the general jocularity finally coaxes a sentence out of him, is a regular runner, kept out of this year's competition by injury, but who has come down to spectate nevertheless.

I would be foolish to pass up on this assembled wealth of train-racing expertise, so I pick their brains for tips for tomorrow's run. I learn that the course runs from the coastal town of Tywyn inland to Nant Gwernol, passing our hotel about two-thirds of the way along, and then back again, about seven miles each way. It follows a roughly parallel course to the steam railway, so we don't actually have to slog across sleepers as I had feared. The overall consensus is that the race is pretty much a doddle. It is just over a half marathon in distance, although a half marathon time (which since Liverpool I now proudly have) offers little guidance due to the varying terrain. The only slight problem, I am warned, is that it is quite difficult to overtake on the first couple of miles of the return leg as the path is quite narrow there. "Oh, and you'll need your fell running shoes," Eddie adds as an afterthought. Great – I don't have any. Still at least most of the course is on grass so I am unlikely to aggravate my back problem. Thankfully, it seems the odds are not as stacked in favour of the train as I had initially supposed. It does not hurtle headlong to its destination with a full head of steam, passing and mowing down all runners in its path. Not only is it obliged to stop at five stations along the way, but the locomotive has to be turned round at the far end of the line, a process which apparently adds about 15 minutes to its journey time.

Clearly tomorrow's event is not worthy of serious apprehension, so the conversation turns to wider athletic issues. Like all runners, the Rotherhams are full of heroic tales of derring-do bedevilled by hideous injury. They tell me of a fellow townsman who ran the 90-kilometre Comrades' Marathon in South Africa, pulled a hamstring halfway through, and still managed to finish 18th. I enquire about their own backgrounds. All three of them started running in their late 30s, like me. Unlike me, they were all footballers before (Allen even played professionally for Blackpool). Only now does the sad truth dawn on me: running is what you end up doing when no one wants you on their team anymore.

As the consumed pints take over, the assembled drinkers come out with more and more fanciful stipulations about the minimum weekly mileage required to run a marathon. By the time last orders are called (with a fairly liberal interpretation of licensing laws) they are pooh-poohing any training schedule involving running less than 80 miles a week. Only later do I find out what a hard man's sport running is in Yorkshire. Annual races include the Burley Bridge Hyke (a "hike" of a mere 21 miles), the Doncaster Doddle (a deceptively named 40-miler) and the Round Rotherham (50 miles – round most of the rest of the county as well by the sounds of it). All this over moors and mountains, through streams and bogs and preferably accompanied by rain or freezing fog. For the moment, though, I retire to bed, feeling quite confident, even formulating a secret plan to beat the train. If I can do the outward leg in seven-minute miles and don't feel too tired on the homebound trek I could shower myself with glory yet. I think I probably drift off to sleep at some point during these highly fanciful reflections.

I go down to the dining room the next morning to find the Rotherhams all tucking into Full English Breakfasts. They are rasher men than me – five-rasher men judging by the mounds of pig flesh on their plates. I of course have read all the (frequently contradictory) articles on racing diet with which running mags are padded out. I opt instead for a carbohydrate-rich eggs on toast and steal all the bananas off the fruit bowl for a pre-race energy boost. The race doesn't start until 2.00 p.m. so I drive the four miles into Tywyn for a recce. Wales should be the perfect seaside holiday destination because it has signs written in a foreign language, thus giving one the exotic sensation of being properly abroad, but all the locals speak English. This resort, though, has a strange end-of-season feel about it, despite being mid August. Maybe all the traditional holiday-makers have taken easyJet to Marbella, where, come to think of it, everyone speaks English, too.

I sit on a bench on the deserted seafront for a while, wondering why seaside towns always have pay telescopes for tourists pointing out to sea, when there is nothing to look at out there apart from water and the horizon doesn't get any nearer no matter how much you magnify it. I take advantage of favourable local geographic conditions to make a couple of calls on my mobile phone. By 10 o'clock it is shaping up to be a seriously hot day which bodes badly for the race. I decide to stroll along to the race start area to register. A helpful sign indicates "Talyllyn Railway" pointing directly along the seafront. I walk along the rather derelict prom, past hotels called Arthur and Gwendolyn and a Christian hostel which tolerantly (and pragmatically in these secular days) announces that it is non-denominational. "Come And Drive This Train!" a stern automated voice shouts at me. I look round. A yellow locomotive for kids to ride on sits challengingly outside an amusement arcade. I ignore it and walk on. As I get out of earshot the train barks out another pre-programmed comment, probably questioning my sexuality. I continue along the seafront. After about half a mile I find a second sign to the Talyllyn Railway which points back in the direction from which I have just come. I retrace my steps looking for the sign I missed. But I just arrive back at the first one, pointing me defiantly back where I know no Talyllyn Railway to be. Obviously this is some deliberate ploy devised by the Welsh Tourist Board to get holidaymakers to walk endlessly up and down the seafront and buy some Portmeirion china or ride on the aggressive yellow train.

I walk back into the town. On the way I pass a road called "Talyllyn Drive". This road is helpfully marked with a sign reading "cul-de-sac", so by the *Alice Through the Looking Glass* logic of this place it will no doubt lead me straight to my destination. I head down it but it seems to be a nondescript residential street. Just as I am about to forfeit my male dignity by asking for directions I hear a toot on a whistle and see a little puff of steam rising from behind the houses ahead. I round a corner, climb up a grass bank and find myself in front of a *Railway Children*-style Olde Worlde station complete with little wiggly eaves and a stationmaster with a waistcoat. Inside I find the train limbering up. Frankly, it doesn't look much more threatening than the one outside the amusement arcade. It is green and resembles an overgrown Triang-Hornby model with a comically tall smoke stack and two men hanging outsizedly off either side of it. It is nothing like the huge belching behemoths my grandfather used to drive. Still, it's probably pretty nifty. I wish now I'd paid more attention back in my childhood when granddad used to take me to the Railway Museum at York and tell me stories of his days on the LNER. Maybe I'd be able to figure out a way to sabotage Puffing Billy here. In the event I'll just have to hope that the blazing hot weather will cause it to overheat and burst its boiler. Outside the station I bump into Steve the Barman in his daytime guise of Steve the Traffic Policeman. Sadly his authority does not extend beyond the public highway and he has no power to stop trains and is thus useless as a potential collaborator. He wishes me luck and I head off to register at the marquee.

Having picked up my race number, I drive back to my hotel. This is really rather foolhardy as I have now driven the route twice (and will have to do so a third time before the race). I am aware that this 15-minute drive amounts to something like a third of the distance I'm going to have to *run* in just a couple of hours' time. I am already feeling dispirited and realise that, contrary to racing wisdom, it is physiologically fatal to give the race course the upper hand by familiarising yourself with exactly how long and daunting it is in advance. Back in my room I lay my running vest out on the bed and begin the tricky task of safety-pinning my race number to it without simultaneously pinning the vest to the bedspread. I hear the whistle of the train in the valley outside, like a dragon challenging me to come out and do battle. I pick up my vest and it comes free, unattached to bedspread – a good omen surely. I pull it on, load up the pockets of my running shorts with glucose tablets and energy gel and stride out to meet my nemesis.

As I drive back into Tywyn I see runners with numbered bibs strung out along the road heading into the town. For a panicked second I think I have missed the race. But then I remember that there is a 10-kilometre run in the morning and these must be the participants, those by definition too wimpy to take on the train. I estimate that there must be well over an hour on the clock by now so only the fat, the old and the lost would still be out in the field. A stewardess in an orange jacket holds up a sign reading SLOW RUNNERS. Too right they are, I think to myself patronisingly. I suspect that there won't be an official race car park, so I park in the first available space in town, outside the cinema. Walking towards the starting point in my full running kit and race number I realise there is a danger I could be mistaken for one of the stragglers in the 10K race, who totter along the high street at two-minute intervals to a smattering of applause from the Saturday lunchtime shoppers. So I deliberately walk on the opposite side of the road from the runners, adopting a languid pace and pausing to look in shop windows. I even stop off to buy a pair of sports socks. No one could possibly mistake me for a competitor in the 10K race.

"Well done, mate," a Liverpudlian voice says as I pass.

"I haven't started yet," I reply coldly.

"Oh, I thought you were in the 10K race."

If looks could kill there'd be one less Scouser on this earth.

To avoid similar confusion I deliberately take a long way round to the start line, taking pains to avoid the 10K course. On the way I come across the official race car park. Here at least are the serious runners getting out of their cars. I fall into step with them and we walk towards the station like *Reservoir Dogs*. The long wooden tables inside the marquee at the race starting area are crammed with runners, many of them tucking into sandwiches and pints of lager. All too macho for me. I sit and munch an energy bar. The Rotherhams come over and invite me to join them for a pre-race photo opportunity. We wish each other good luck and say self-effacing things about how badly we expect to do. I go outside to queue for the loos and do a few stretches. Gradually people are starting to drift off down the road and I follow them to the start line on a bridge just outside the station.

Unlike most races, runners are not grouped according to predicted finishing times. Everyone is just gathered in a large unruly mob, which under different circumstances might have headed off to burn down a few English people's holiday cottages. We all mill around for a while not really sure what happens next. The Rotherhams had told me that the train will blow its whistle to start the race. What actually happens is that there is a sudden huge BANG! Everyone is temporarily startled. Briefly I wonder if the train's boiler has exploded in timely fashion and we can all go home. But the spectators start yelling and the runners lurch into a trot so I imagine this is the signal that the race has started.

Our route takes us out of Tywyn on the main road but quickly turns off into the fields. In no time at all it seems we hit the first mile marker. A runner just behind me with a sports watch reads off a time of 7:11 to his companion. We are on a dirt track now and this doesn't feel so bad. The second mile comes up 13 minutes into the race and I'm feeling quite confident. I reckon I should be able to give the train a good run for its money. Except of course the train hasn't paid any money. The train is not that stupid. The train is actually making money, having been paid by our sadistic friends and relatives so that they can ride on it and jeer at us. From this point on despondency quickly begins to set in. The sun blazes down and within another half mile I have decided that it is madness to try and beat the train. The train is driven on level rails of iron to a merciless timetable. We human competitors, by contrast, are running across an uneven surface made up of grass, stones, ruts and cowpats at a pace that I cannot possibly keep up. The train is fuelled by what's left of the Welsh mining industry, whereas I am suffering from a stitch and indigestion caused by that sports bar I ill-advisedly consumed an hour before the start.

To take my mind off my physical discomfort I start to compile a mental list of people I hate. It reads as follows:

a) *Pheidippides, for re-establishing running as a valid activity after its single function (i.e. chasing edible animals) was made obsolete by the invention of the bow and arrow.*

b) *Kate the cellist, for not having taken up a sensible instrument like the violin or piccolo. Okay, my back hasn't actually started hurting yet but it can only be a matter of time before this is added to my catalogue of miseries.*

c) *Mary, for not being on board that train at least to sabotage its irritating whistle whose triumphant blasts sing out from somewhere behind us in the valley.*

At three miles we come to the first major hill. This is the worst place that the Cambrian Age could possibly have decided to throw one up. Somehow I stumble up it on dead legs. At the top I pass the first walker. It is one of the Rotherhams (Allen, I think). I resist the urge to shout words of encouragement or disparagement as I have very little confidence in my own ability to make it much further.

By three and a half miles I want to give up the whole endeavour totally. Not just this race, but the entire project. I don't care about all the work I've already done on this book. Let it remain unfinished, like Schubert's symphony or Coleridge's "Kubla Khan". All I want to do is stop. So I stop. But quickly I realise that stopping is not enough. Nothing short of stopping, having a good sit down, a meal, a bottle of wine and a weekend in a health spa is going to make me feel much better now. So I start running again. Almost immediately I get my second wind. We are running across lush grass and there's a bit of a breeze on our faces. A couple of backpackers and some farm workers with sandwiches shout encouragement. We tumble down a near vertical drop and I try not to think how hellish it's going to be trying to climb back up it in an hour's time. A man in front of me breaks wind loudly as he negotiates a bump. He apologises profusely to all within hearing range. Considering runners regularly pee down their legs and a recent London Marathon winner projectile-vomited his way along the Mall, Wind Breaker's offence seems relatively mild.

I hit the fourth mile at a more modest 32 minutes and decide I'll just have to accept that eight-minute miles are my natural pace and there's nothing I can do about it. Let the train go as fast as it likes. Its funding will probably get withdrawn soon anyway. Running races, I ponder as I plod on, wouldn't be so bad if minutes five to 25 could be eliminated from the process; a bit like life, which would actually be quite a bearable experience if you didn't have to go through adolescence. In the midst of these reflections the track lurches suddenly and violently downhill. There is thick undergrowth on one side and a steep drop on the other with no more than 18 inches of twisting path between and even this is infested with straggling, snaggling tree roots. "Oh, Jesus Christ!" exclaims the runner behind me, obviously also a novice to this race. Despite 15 years as a professional writer, I am unable to think of a better way of putting it. Gravity and momentum carry me through and somehow I manage not to tumble head over heels before we hit level terrain again and head into a valley so verdant you'd turn down the colour control if you saw it on your TV. There is a Sponge Station at the entrance and the discarded white sponges fan out on the luxuriant grass ahead like war graves marking the passing of each brave departed runner. I hear the train's whistle again but it seems to echo round the valley – lingering and mournful – I can't tell if it is behind or in front of me.

I find I have become lost in my thoughts. Why do I only like girls who aren't interested in me, I muse as we clatter over a cattle grid? Or is it that girls who aren't interested in me have a misleading way of appearing very interested in me? Will I ever fall in love or will I end up some sad loner doing runs like this for pleasure? Despite the morbid overtones, this sort of maudlin brooding is actually quite positive. At least I'm not thinking about dying any more. I pass the five-mile marker. "Only nine miles to go," I find myself thinking. This wrenches me out of my reverie. Since when has the prefix "only" ever been applied to the predicate "nine miles" unless one is travelling in a jet aircraft?

Back in the real world I notice that we are passing close to my hotel and I keep an eye out for Keith the manager among the spectators, just in case there's a chance of a bit of al fresco room service. It's seriously hot and there's been only one drinks station so far. Then I hear the train again, closer and definitely behind me this time, its whistle almost drowned out by the banshee shrieks and laughter of its passengers. Somehow these sounds of merriment are transmuted in my befuddled brain into the death cries of terrified victims. It seems to me that a Tyrannosaurus Rex is bounding after me devouring all those who have fallen behind. A frisson of panic passes through me. I must keep running, I mustn't look round, is all I can think. I am still trapped behind Wind Breaker who lets rip another one downwind. I put on a spurt and slip past him hoping his pungent detonations might deter the T Rex a little.

We come into yet another meadow flanked by imposing hills. It's probably beautiful but, sadly, aesthetic appreciation is one of the first casualties of exhaustion. All it means to me is another valley to run through. We're past six miles and surely must nearly be at the turnaround point. Looking up I am faced with confirmation of this fact which comes in the form of good news and bad news. Firstly, the good news: to my right I can see a long ribbon of runners on the return leg. The bad news: they are some two or three hundred feet up the ridge. I blink away the sweat to check I am seeing right. How did they get up there? Somehow I doubt there is a funicular railway or convenient escalator round the other side of the hill. I can now see the turnaround point just a couple of hundred metres ahead of me at the end of the meadow. I know I can make it to this symbolic goal. Just as I feel triumph swelling up inside me, the train darts suddenly out of a cutting on my right, like a snake out of its hole, and shoots past me, its passengers hanging and hollering from every available window.

Disappointing as it is to be pipped at the post, I take hope. I *almost* beat the train on the outward leg and the engine still has to be shunted round before it can set off on the homebound run. This should give me an ample head start. The race is as good as won. I can't see what all the fuss is about really. With hindsight I realise that the scene at the Nant Gwernol terminus must have gone something like this: even after the engine has been turned round the driver treats himself to a second cigarette; the fireman pokes around in the gift shop, perhaps buys some souvenir fudge for his niece; the guard finishes the *Daily Mail* crossword and allows an indulgent extra few minutes waiting for any last-minute passengers before blowing his whistle. They are in no hurry to set off because they know something that I am just about to find out.

How can I put it? The return leg of the run is murder. First of all we have to scale the north face of a sheer towering hill without equipment or oxygen. Literally we are scrambling up a 45° incline following a path that is no more than 25 centimetres wide, forcing us to place one foot directly in front of the other like a tightrope walker or risk toppling backwards down the hill. "Fuck" is my less-than-eloquent response to this death-dealing new terrain. The twisting path then alternates between the following options:

a) *it goes uphill (exhausting);*
b) *it goes downhill (if anything, worse);*
c) *it goes horizontally along the ridge (worst of all as you need one leg a foot shorter than the other to make any progress).*

Overtaking is impossible, so if the person in front slows to a walking pace in exhaustion or despair, everyone behind has to do the same. Soon we are strung out in a convoy like cars on a narrow country road behind a smug farmer creaking along on his tractor.

This is not a road race, this is a fell run. And that's "fell" in the *Lord of the Rings* sense of "foul, sinister and serving some evil purpose". Quickly my death list is resurrected and a new name is added to it: the Rotherhams. They've done this race before. They could have warned me about this. And then straightaway, what do you know, speak of the devil, Eddie Rotherham pops up behind me. I know it is Eddie because he is wearing a baseball cap marked "Eddie". He greets me cheerfully and I ask him, between pants, how much more of this hellish ascent we have to endure. "What goes up must come down," he tells me with irrefutable but unsatisfying logic. He seems unperturbed by the ankle-twisting terrain, which even a mountain goat would think long and hard about before tackling, and somehow has breath left for a cheery "all right?" or "all right, luv?" for every race steward or stewardess we pass.

A blonde Germanic-looking woman up in front suddenly stops and sits down in the middle of the track. She doesn't seem injured – she looks more like someone who is opposing the building of a new by-pass, as if her action is intended to protest against the inhuman evil of this entire enterprise. We clamber over or around her with the relentlessness of soldier ants. I'm amazed that more provisions have not been made for casualties. Anyone who lost their footing on this Wall of Death would roll all the way down to the bottom of the hill. Maybe the St John Ambulance people are waiting with nets and stretchers down there in the valley below. The only comfort I can extract from the current situation is that Eddie is *behind* me. Largely this is because of the impracticality of overtaking, but at least for the moment I am beating him. I know that one of the Rotherhams is quite a useful runner, but is it Eddie or Terry? "Fast Eddie" seems to trip off the tongue, but isn't that the character played by Paul Newman in *The Hustler*? My oxygen-starved brain can't access my memory banks. Are these the early indications of altitude sickness (and we are many hundred feet up now) or the fact that all available blood has been diverted to my legs? Maybe it's Fast Terry and Steady Eddie?

After an eternity that would have fazed Sisyphus we finally reach the top of the hill, where a steward in a day-glo yellow jacket is stationed. But there is no respite. The track plunges straight back down into the valley below, like a big dipper. "No one ever stops to look at the view,", the steward observes ruefully. I pause for a nanosecond or two to take in the vista – truly magnificent, the contours of the surrounding hills shaded with incongruous purple patches of heather like a Van Gogh. But pressure from less aesthetically appreciative runners behind has already shunted me into the rocky descent, which involves stamping through a couple of shallow streams, stumbling over shale and a lot of swearing. We hit a third stream which has not yet decided whether it is a stream or a dried-up stream bed and has settled for the compromise option of being a boggy quagmire.

Mile Eight and I have reached a new stage of being, a sort of quasi-Buddhist state of fatalistic detachment. I no longer want to stop, but I don't really want to go on either. Death no longer seems such an attractive option, but there again neither does living. I don't think. I exist to run. I run therefore I am. Running is Beauty, Beauty Running. This is all I know on earth and all I need to know. We have now entered a rocky chasm. A torrent froths alongside us. A viaduct passes overhead. I'm sure this would all be very scenic if I was able to look at anything other than my feet. I concentrate on steering them across the precarious downhill slope strewn with discarded sponges and loose slate that we are running on. There is a strange detachment about this process. It's as if the feet don't belong to me but to some robot lander on Mars that I am guiding remotely from Mission Control many millions of miles away. "See you at finish," a voice murmurs in my ear and Eddie slips politely past me.

By Mile Nine I am desperate for anything horizontal to run on, be it tarmac, grass, rubble, quicksand. I must have trodden on a shamrock for my wishes are granted and we are back in the fields again. We reach the steep hill that we freewheeled down so casually nine miles ago. Hardly anyone has the energy to take it at a run – instead we all trudge up it heads bowed, like prisoners on a chain gang. To make things worse just as we reach this symbolic nadir the train, with its braying circus mob of passengers, nips past us with a cheeky toot on its whistle.

I'm trying to think of something positive. I'm trying to think at all. The only comforting thought I can seize upon is that no individual part of my body has let me down on this occasion. Knees, ankles, even my supposedly dodgy back are all performing well. If my body was an England cricket team it would build up quite a commendable total and give everyone false hope for the future.

Miles 12 and 13 are probably the worst. By this stage my whole existence has been reduced to three simple principles:

a) *put one foot in front of the other*
b) *follow the ankles of the person in front*
c) *don't fall over.*

I think I must have drifted off into this brain-dead solipsistic universe for about 15 minutes. It is the spectators, thicker on the ground as we near the town, who bring me back to reality, their intrusive presence reviving me like smelling salts. Let me say a word or two here about spectators. Now, no one would attempt to run a 14-mile race without doing some serious preparation: reading books on running, taking some advice from a veteran, going to the gym, jogging in the park. Yet people seem to be allowed to spectate at a race like this with no training whatsoever. What is the result? They all shout "Keep going!" If they had studied – or just thought about – it at all they would know that the most useless and annoying thing you can shout at a runner is "Keep going", especially in the closing miles of a race. After having already run over 90 per cent of the prescribed distance, "Keep going" is definitely a thought that had occurred to me. "Stop right now" had also featured on that *Terminator*-like menu of options that scrolled up on my mental VDU, but had been rejected in favour of "Keep going". I've been keeping going for a dozen miles now and it's a policy that has seen me almost to the end of this hideous experience and is unlikely to be abandoned at this stage. There are useful things that spectators might shout, "Only two miles to go" or "Train delayed by passenger on the track at Rhydyronen", but no one needs to remind me to keep going.

"Keep going!" a spectator shouts.

As I keep going I am at an increasing loss to understand the mentality of people like the Rotherhams who pay good money to do this year after year. At least I am subjecting myself to this ordeal for charity and it feels like I'm suffering far more than any of the people I'm collecting for (okay – I'm not , but I've just run 13 miles and I'm indulging myself in some self-pity here). What are charity runs all about? Do they just serve to assuage middle-class guilt? Look at me, I'm suffering too. And all my friends have sponsored me to do it, so they're suffering financially. See? The bourgeoisie can have a rough time, too. Is this all just some form of inverted snobbery like dressing in grunge fashion was a few years ago?

We're back on the road now with the town in sight. I am at the exact spot where just three and a half complacent hours ago, from the comfort of my car seat, I felt smug about the struggling 10Kers. I know I should get down on my knees and beg their forgiveness but, in my present state, I doubt I would ever be able to get up again if I did. A little girl shouts something in Welsh from the roadside, probably "Keep going." We enter Tywyn and I know the finish line is less than a mile away – which is a good thought – but I also know that I've still got to run that mile – which is an almost unbearable one. I fantasise that I might fall through some wormhole in hyperspace which will dump me at the finishing line without having to run it. But in the end I know I will, and somehow I do. At the last junction before the station I see Steve on points duty. He seems to be contemplating taking advantage of a gap in the stream of runners to allow a couple of patient motorists to pass. "Let me through, Steve," I shout piteously, knowing that if I stop now, 200 metres from the line, I will crumple, collapse and never start again. He relents, waves me through and I fall, despairing and dead, over the finishing line in 2:12:46.

Just two minutes, a couple of stretches and a cup of water later I am strolling round the finishing enclosure thinking, "That was all rather fun." What is wrong with the human brain? Why is it seemingly incapable of retaining the experience of excruciating pain? I know that just five minutes previously I wanted to die and now I could cheerfully sign up to do the whole thing over again.

I drive back to my hotel and soak for a long time in the bath. The train whistles wildly somewhere off in the valley, no doubt on its lap of honour. All right, I know you won. Just have the good grace to shut up about it. I lie on my bed and could easily become as attached to it as my running vests have in the past. But I force myself to get up before fatigue overwhelms me. The race organisers are hosting an evening barbecue for all participants. It is a disquieting prospect, being in a marquee with a thousand runners, but at least everyone will have the perfect ice-breaking line: "What time did you do?"

I drive back into town and take the now familiar walk to the starting area. Tywyn High Street on a Saturday evening makes Liverpool look positively vibrant. In the total silence I swear I can distinctly hear the lap of the waves on the shore half a mile away. Maybe we runners are like outlaws in the Wild West. Rumour has gone around that we are hitting town and all the honest townsfolk have locked themselves behind their shutters. Back at the marquee I find there is a long queue for food. Hungry as I am, I have definitely had my fill of standing in queues with runners (normally for smelly, overflowing loos). So I go to get myself a beer instead and bump into the Rotherhams at the bar. We compare finishing times. It turns out that Terry (the modest, quiet one) beat the train by a couple of minutes; Allen, despite his early mishap, somehow slipped past me and came in in under two hours; and Eddie, my running partner for about a mile on the ridge, simply because he was too polite to barge past me, finished in 2:10. In short, they all beat me despite surrendering somewhere between 15 and 20 years in age to me. I go over to the results board in search of comfort. It turns out that I came 511th out of 764 finishers (764 doesn't sound a lot of competitors, but I presume if they trawled the hospitals and ditches they'd find a lot more). The wooden spoon goes to someone called Natasha Lee. "What if I come last?" she had said to all her friends beforehand, and she did. My heart goes out to her. Men's and women's results are also listed separately. I finished 454th out of 616 in the men's event. A quick calculation tells me therefore that 57 women beat me. Clearly no point in attempting to chat up any of them – I'd be blown out of the water after my opening line. This leaves 91 women who might theoretically be impressed by my finishing time, though sadly there are 453 men in the marquee who are better qualified to muscle in on them. My odds don't look good. I wonder where that Natasha Lee is?

The awards ceremony starts. The Victor Ludorum goes up to accept his prize for his winning time of 1:20. He looks like Damon out of Blur. He also looks like he could still have beaten me even if he had been forced to lug his prize – a 24-inch television set – on his back round the course with him. With his pop star looks and proven ability to run faster than anyone else in the marquee, he is more competition than I can take. So I abandon the thought of talking to any girls and go off to sit on my own. This is not as loserish as it would be at most parties, as the very state of sitting is so blissful that I don't care that no one is talking to me. Once all the various age bands and categories of winner have been announced and rewarded, a rhinestone band takes to the stage and starts playing old Kris Kristofferson numbers. People get up and dance. To be fair on them, most have run 14 miles that afternoon but I suspect that their stiff-legged unco-ordination is due to more than just muscle fatigue. It's always alarming when the best dancer on a dance floor has ribbons in her pigtails and a dummy in her mouth. Some of the other runners are holding informal competitions to see who can build the largest castles out of empty lager cans on their tables. A couple of food fights have broken out. All in all, it is too grim and I slip away.

The next morning I take my leave of the Rotherhams. "See you here next year," Allen predicts confidently.

CHAPTER 14

Personal Trainer

Once you have a marathon training schedule you will find yourself obliged to run something upwards of 450 miles over the four months leading up to the marathon. If – unlike me – you have a nine-to-five job and/or a relationship to support, you will probably be obliged to rise an hour or so earlier in the morning than usual to fit in your daily run. So where on earth do you find the motivation to put yourself through such torment? Engaging the services of a personal trainer is a convenient, but not cheap, way to overcome the sloth that is the natural impediment to this challenging routine.

Unfortunately it rankles with most normal people to pay someone £30 to ring your doorbell at 5.30 a.m. and then force you to run round the park three times. That's not to say it wouldn't be quite an amusing gag to play on someone else – a sort of Personal-trainer-o-gram. Imagine some hapless friend being woken up unexpectedly at the crack of dawn by a huge muscleman and being told that they are going for a run. The friend would probably do it out of sheer terror and early morning disorientation, and pay the trainer at the end, too. But actually volunteering to have your sleep patterns disrupted is a harder concept to embrace. My subconscious is very ingenious at coming up with excuses to stay in bed at that hour of the morning. I'd probably just offer the trainer double his fee to go away and leave me to sleep.

It is no surprise then that I put off finding a personal trainer for about six months. In fact, my first session came about as a result of a charity polo match I found myself attending. Now if the couple of dozen or so people who play or watch polo on a regular basis will bear with me for a minute I will explain to the uninitiated what a very silly and largely incomprehensible game it is. It is played in one of two or three locations in the Home Counties on a huge field stretching away seemingly to infinity. For 90 per cent of the match you, the spectator, sit bored, unable to make out what all the horses clustered off on the distant horizon are actually doing. For the other 10 per cent of the time you are gripped with utter terror as the whole herd gallops straight towards you, the riders' mallets whirling in huge arcs as they attempt to transfer all the momentum of half a ton of horseflesh travelling at 30mph into a solid wooden ball propelled in your general direction. As only very rich people can afford to play polo and their equally affluent friends and relatives are the only people who would be bothered to sit through the spectacle, it is an obvious occasion where money may be raised for charity.

I am invited to a polo match one Sunday afternoon in June by the National Missing Persons Helpline. To do my bit to help those less fortunate than myself and give thanks for having survived spectating the match, I decide to bid for something in the auction afterwards. Lot 10 turns out to be a session with a personal trainer. This would be the perfect way to get my body and conscience into shape simultaneously. The lot comes up and I raise my hand confidently but still half hoping that some Argentine millionaire will push the price up beyond my means. The said playboy plutocrat fails to bid and a couple of moments later I find myself being frog-marched off by a charity volunteer to write out a cheque for £120. In exchange I am handed a voucher for an hour-long session with Tony in Wandsworth. I must confess that this item was to languish on my mantelpiece for a number of weeks before I found the opportunity to redeem it.

In the meantime an actress friend mentions that her "resting" colleague Claire is a personal trainer and I should give her a try. So suddenly from a position of having no personal trainer I find myself with two of them. I wonder if I should put them to the test and make them battle it out like gladiators for the right to train me: doing pushups in front of me until one of them keels over. More practically, I suppose I could just do a session with each of them to see who I preferred. As one is a man and the other a woman it would give me an opportunity to get each sex's perspective on fitness training.

One Saturday afternoon I am invited to watch some friends play in a cricket match on Wandsworth Common. Now cricket is only marginally less dull (though slightly safer) than polo so I take the opportunity to phone Tony and see if he can fit me in. The address he gives me turns out to be a portakabin pitched in a scrubby yard round the back of a shop on Wandsworth High Street. There is no one about and I sit on the step wondering if I am in the right place. After 15 minutes Tony arrives with his daughter. He is not tall but his muscles are. He unlocks his studio and shows me in. The sparse interior is equipped with a ghettoblaster and a punch bag. Its pine-panelled walls are decorated with an acupuncture chart of the human body, oddly devoid of sexual characteristics, and several topless photos of Cindy Crawford, rather over-amply endowed with them.

I tell Tony about my marathon quest and he listens without particular enthusiasm. Then abruptly he asks me if I have insurance. All at once I feel trapped. Clearly this is all some hard-sell scam and Tony will now get me in an armlock and not let me go until I buy an endowment policy off him. But, no, he is using an analogy. "Self-defence is like car insurance," he informs me gravely. "You hope you'll never have to use it, but one day you might be glad you've got it." He goes on to tell me how he was beaten up at the age of nine. He swore to learn to defend himself and subsequently earned black belts in kung-fu, aikido, and karate. Certainly these days no group of fewer than 10 heavily armed individuals would risk provoking an argument with him.

The strange drift the conversation has taken becomes clear when Tony tells me that he is primarily a kick-boxing tutor. Despite the fact that I am here to learn to run he tries to convince me of the importance of learning self-defence anyway. "Have you ever been beaten up?" he asks me. "Yes. Once. I ended up in hospital," I reply. Tony nods significantly. I don't mention that I was drunk on the occasion and would not have had the bodily co-ordination to use self-defence skills even if I had possessed them. Besides, as a born coward, I believe I am better off learning to run away from trouble than to fight back. After all, only a desperate – or very fit – mugger would chase me for 26.2 miles in order to get hold of my wallet. Tony and I are at loggerheads on this issue, but, unsurprisingly, it is the will of the man who has a 6th degree black belt that prevails and so we do an hour of kick-boxing. Actually it is quite therapeutic. Once I have overcome my natural pacifism I kick and thump Tony's punchbag with zeal, imagining that it is Queen Alexandra or the toadying Olympic official who added those one-and-a-bit extra miles to the marathon.

The week after my session in Wandsworth I give Claire a call. She comes round to my house one Tuesday afternoon. She is a much more reassuring physical presence: in her 30s, a little on the plump side; where Tony had pecs she has specs and of the two she looks the more likely to turn out to be an undercover insurance salesperson. I tell her about my session with Tony and she is dismissive. "Male trainers are no good on stretching," she tells me. "Men are too impatient. Stretching is the key to everything." She's right of course. I hate stretching. It's like doing the washing-up after a meal – quite a sensible long-term investment, but leaving it till tomorrow is so much more attractive. Claire puts me through a series of exercises, scoring my performance on a clipboard. First she makes me step up and down the step to my garden 30 times, which is much harder than it sounds. She then does a flexibility test. I have to put my head between my legs as if I have a nose-bleed and inch my fingers along my calves. "Average", she comments as I finish, before adding, "Actually most men are *below* average." I can't work out whether to feel complimented or belittled.

She asks me what exercise I have taken recently. I tell her that I ran the Liverpool Half Marathon a couple of weeks ago. "I could never run that far," she tells me, but manages to include a slightly scathing tone in her voice, implying that males are somehow pathetic for wanting to do so in the first place. "Men use sport to compete against other men rather than to better themselves and obtain fulfilment through improved health," she opines. I'm sure she's right but I must say I don't think this impending marathon would be quite so attractive if I had to run it all on my own and didn't get to trounce some elderly, unfit fun runners along the way. "Anyway," Claire goes on, "you can't run with breasts." She indicates her bosom as if it was somehow my fault. Well, maybe all male competitors in races should be forced to wear a pair of comedy breasts to redress the biological injustice, a bit like those "empathy pouches" that Californian new men strap to their stomachs to simulate the discomfort of pregnancy.

To be fair on Claire, her disdain is not reserved wholly for the male sex. Most of her clients are female, she tells me, and many seem to regard their personal trainer as merely a style accessory. Apparently they will often make calls on their mobile phones while doing those vital stretches.

This seems quite a sensible way of multitasking to me, but as Claire is a bit of a stretching fascist I keep my opinion to myself. Once we get off sexual ideology, the session goes smoothly. Claire at least knows something about the discipline I am interested in and she demonstrates correct running posture and technique to me. "To get maximum power you have to use your arms as well as your legs," she tells me. "Yes, I know about that," I reply. "It's called crawling. I'm thinking of using it towards the end of the race." I don't think Claire is a big fan of my flippancy. But instinctively she knows how to respond. She starts to tell me about "blood pooling". Apparently if you stop moving suddenly all your blood pools in your brain and you die. This of course is exactly the right tactic to adopt with a hypochondriac like me. Is she joking? I worry, suddenly serious. Would she dare joke about my life?

To be honest I never got round to booking another session with either Claire or Tony. Not because I had anything personally against them (though I must admit I was a bit scared of Tony). It's just that running seems to me to be a solitary activity. If I want to take exercise in the company of another person I'll play tennis or volleyball or something else that engages my competitive urges. Running for me is about freedom – from other people and from rules – so I don't feel I need someone tagging along telling me how I'm doing it wrong. I know this is not a very orthodox outlook. The runners I pass in the park on my long Sunday runs usually seem to have opted for some form of companionship, running in groups, in couples or with a Walkman clapped to their ears. Personally I find that opportunities for introspection are rare in this age of the Internet and 24-hour digital satellite interactive TV and for me running is a chance to spend a bit of quality time with myself. To others this prospect is perhaps as alarming as that of being stuck for two hours in a lift with a stranger.

CHAPTER 15

The Beast

Corfe Castle, Dorset
5 September
Distance: 13 miles
Time: 1 hour 57 mins

Having Raced the Train and lived, I must now obviously seek out greater challenges. Thus it is that, just a fortnight later, I find myself down in Dorset to compete in a 13-mile cross-country race ominously named the Beast.

Once again I had selected this event as part of my pre-Marathon training on the unscientific basis that I rather liked the name. My mother, who has kindly driven me down to the south coast, enquires of a race official why the event is called the Beast. "What else could we call it?" he replies, matter-of-factly, as if the Trade Descriptions people would be down on them like a ton of bricks if they tried to get away with calling it The Not Particularly Pleasant. She passes on this veiled warning to me and goes off to visit the nearby ruins of Corfe Castle abandoning her firstborn to his grisly fate. I'm not too worried. I'm feeling much more confident about my running these days. A friend whom I haven't seen for six months told me last week how much I had changed. Is it my new runner's haircut? I enquired. My sleek form and glowing skin? No, it's just that you're not cynical any more, she explained. Running as a cure for cynicism? Cellulite maybe, but cynicism?

Perhaps it is because running has put me in touch with my feminine side. After all, it allows us men to gain a female perspective on the world because it is the only public event I know of where *we* have to stand in colossal queues for the loos. The queues for the women's loos before a race are pretty horrendous as well, but the men's are considerably longer.

The biology that gave us the anatomical convenience of being able to pee standing up also endowed us with the constant need to compete against each other and, as ever, there are at least three times the number of male entrants in today's race as female.

I register and pick up my pin-on running bib emblazoned with the Beast logo. As I head for the starting line I find myself walking next to a man wearing number 665. "The Neighbour of the Beast," I say to him and he smiles thinly like a man who has heard the joke before. I wonder if there is a premium entry fee to obtain the number 666. Is it an honour that the macho competitors fight over, like all the hoods in *Reservoir Dogs* wanting to be Mr Black? Or is this number left unused out of superstition, like office buildings that have no 13th floor? I follow the herd down country lanes to the official start line – well, to be honest it's just a scrubby bit of farmland. Once again there are no special starting places for competitors anticipating running particular times. In fact, a race steward warns us, there will be no mile markers along the route, which will be particularly galling for those runners in possession of expensive sports watches who will have nothing to record their split times against. Someone tells me that this is not a race where anyone will be recording a PB (personal best). That's what they said about Race the Train and I almost died *en route*. I begin to feel vaguely apprehensive.

The starter raises his pistol and it clicks feebly. The front runners set off anyway and the rest of us follow. I am near the back of the pack and as we pass the starter his pistol finally fires on the third attempt. I file away this observation for possible later use. Officially, I presume, this means that the 250 or so runners who have already passed him could be disqualified for a false start. I may need to take advantage of this technicality in 13 miles' time. We start off on a dirt track which heads immediately uphill. This is the ideal starting gradient in a race as it stops you making the mistake of going too fast in the initial euphoria, as I did in Tywyn. An unforecast sea mist further blesses the opening few miles by shielding us from the sun. I find myself behind a fun runner who is wearing huge splayed clown's shoes. Only when I pass him do I realise that they're his actual feet. A trail of ribbons delineates the moorland path that we must follow, which has been further marked out by a thoughtful incontinent bovine.

I experience the now familiar sequence of feelings. By one mile I am burning up inside and want to rip off my shirt. Within another half mile even this would not be enough and I feel the urge to slit my skin to release the heat welling up under. I know this phase will pass. At a mile and a half there is a little knot of spectators gathered at the top of a rise, my mother among them. She cheers me on and I feel a vague sense of guilt at my retardedness. At my age I should be making her feel proud with grandchildren and a second home in the south of France, not by taking part in some glorified school cross-country run. A montage of embarrassing childhood performances, which my mother has been forced to witness, flashes through my head: various sports days and not forgetting the school carol service at the age of nine when I was asked by the singing teacher not to sing but just to open and close my mouth in time to the music. Lots of the big stars mime at gigs these days, but back then it was shaming.

We file through a gate where a sign instructs us to Please Shut the Gate. This freezes some of us townies in momentary indecision. After all we want to be seen to be obeying the Country Code at all times, but shutting a gate when you know that you are being closely followed by several hundred other people who will just have to open it again seems unergonomic and slightly vindictive. This will be a particularly humiliating situation for the last person in the race who will have his or her despondency compounded by being the only person who actually has to shut the gate.

After a couple of miles we come across the first serious impediment in the form of a stile, for which there is a 30-person queue. Having queued for the lavatories 20 minutes earlier, it is most vexing to find oneself standing in line again with exactly the same bunch of people. A few of the men take advantage of the wait to have a discreet leak in the bushes. I'm disappointed at the lack of initiative among the local yeomanry. An enterprising farmer with a chainsaw could hack a path through the hedgerow and charge everyone 50p to get through. I'm sure most of us would pay the money just to get moving again instead of hanging around here hopping from one foot to another to stop our muscles seizing up.

The next section of the race takes us through a wood following the dried-up bed of a stream. The stream, with the wisdom of gravity, went downhill, but we are bounding upwards along its stony furrow. Prematurely exhausted, I reach the top of the hill where we come to flatter land, but the path is overgrown with stinging nettles which the local farmers are presumably receiving some huge EU subsidy for allowing to grow unchecked. In a race situation it is impossible to pick one's way through, avoiding each nettle in a nancy sort of way, so I formulate a theory that if you run fast enough the nettles don't have time to sting you. Ten seconds later I am able to report that there is no botanical justification for this theory. Added to the stings with which my calves are now fizzing, I have a nagging stitch in my right side. Maybe it's peritonitis, my subconscious prompts worryingly. Stitches tend to occur in the right side, don't they? But which side is the appendix on? Left or right? I try to recall. It would make sense for nature to distinguish the two conditions – one an inconvenience, the other potentially fatal.

By about 35 minutes in we are on fairly firm farmland, running through a disused quarry. My second wind kicks in and I start to feel good for the first time. But nature quickly responds with its own wind and blows away the mid-morning sea mist, exposing us suddenly to the sadistic sun. "Ah, Mr Taylor, I've been expecting you," it says, stroking a Persian cat. We reach another stile and, infuriatingly, all the runners I have just overtaken are able to catch up with me again as I kick my heels in the queue. I'm beginning to suspect that this race is organised by New Age hippies or maybe the Revolutionary Socialist party in the way it is undermining the very spirit of basic human competition, taking away our incentive to run faster than anyone else.

Unusually I have so far failed to identify a Personal Nemesis. Normally there is someone who will overtake me or annoy me in some insignificant way so that I will swear undying revenge on him (or preferably her) until the end of the race. Maybe I should just target runner 666, the Number of the Beast, if ever I can spot the person wearing this shirt. The Beast is not so physical a presence in its eponymous race as the train was last month, but it seems to exert a sinister unseen menace. I brood on the nature of the Beast. Could it be a puma whose ancestors escaped from a travelling circus and who has been living wild ever since, preying on sheep and perhaps the odd runner who gets detached from the pack? Even if its breath was on my back, I doubt I could run any faster at the moment. Indeed what I am doing scarcely qualifies as a stagger. To call it a stagger would be to do a gross injustice to stags and drunks the world over. Under the blaze of the sun I am progressing at no more than a totter. I welcome the next stile and the rest break the queue affords. I scramble over it when my turn comes and hit some more flat ground.

We come out on to a main road and I am pleasantly surprised to hear from a steward that we have completed six miles already. But we have now left the cover of the woods and the sun has us all to itself. It is on our backs and seriously on our case. We pass a farm where cows are backed up against the fence presenting their udders in the mistaken belief that we are a very large team of milkers. To paraphrase an old joke: the only tits that are being felt around here are us, Ermintrude. We cross over the main road and head out on the long naked farm track towards the cliffs. The flies are hovering over us, but thankfully the vultures have not yet arrived. "Not so bad so far," I say to another runner with a bravado belied by my shagged-out exterior. "There's a nasty surprise coming," he replies, nodding ahead towards the sea. Nasty surprise? Is the Beast some sort of kraken waiting to devour any runner who topples off the cliff? "What is it?" I ask, trying to sound blasé. "Steps," he says. "Surely not the teen-pop band?" I think, but my informant has pressed on ahead.

We reach the coast, swing right and run along the grassy clifftop. The sea looks blue and inviting below. The attractions of a dip are just outweighed by the 300-foot drop on to rocks that would precede it. Suddenly we come to the Nasty Surprise. These proud tall cliffs which have defied generations of invaders suddenly dip down into a natural harbour and we are obliged to follow. Steps have been provided, sheer, shallow and made out of the slipperiest stone local masons could lay their hands on (I am no geologist, but if this isn't soapstone what on earth could be?). The cove we descend into may have been handy for ambushing gullible Normans a thousand years ago, but it is not a welcome detour to those who have already run eight miles. We reach the bottom. By this stage of what is becoming a hot early September day, even horizontal movement has become pretty hellish. After a couple of scant minutes at sea-level, we are faced with a near vertical climb up 200 steps back up to the clifftops. Sadly there is nothing for it. The steps are wide enough to travel in single file only. Any dilatoriness from me at this stage would just create another bottleneck. So up I have to go.

So dead am I by the time I get to the top that I have little munificence to appreciate the views over the sea that the clifftop offers. Green-edged water fades into the brown ocean shelf and little white yuppie yachts bob on it. A ploughed field way down below with fresh furrows looks as if God has scraped His fingernails across it to bug the angels. We soon come to another cove and – thank goodness – we don't have to descend into this one, but are instead obliged to make a large detour inland. All this so a few management consultants can sit on their weekend yachts reading the Sunday papers.

"Four miles to go," a helper tells us – well, helpfully – as he sloshes out water at a drinks point. "One bad bit, then it's all fine." Bad bit? What's he talking about? Didn't we just do the bad bit? To take my mind off the prospect of another Bad Bit, I get chatting to Caroline from the New Forest Runners. She tells me she is in training to do a triathlon. "Why?" I ask with a simplicity that fails to disarm her. "What better way is there to spend a Sunday morning?" she replies. Several hundred things occur immediately but I opt for the one closest to hand. "Sitting on your yacht, eating croissants and reading the *Sunday Times* like those people", I tell her, waving back at the last cove. But she knows I don't mean it. Have I not, after all, elected to spend my Day of Rest wearing running shorts and slogging up cliffs? She smiles and tells me apologetically that she has to hurry ahead to rejoin her team-mates. She pulls quickly and easily away from me. Oh God, I was clearly being a bore. Maybe I should hire my services out. Many professional marathoners use "rabbits", or pacers, in races to push them to a better performance. If I could just improve my running a little and make sure my conversation was just as dreary, people would be scurrying ahead to Personal Bests just to avoid being stuck with me.

As Caroline drifts off into the distance ahead I realise one of the bad things about cross-country runs. You have an uninterrupted view all around you, which means that you can see exactly how far in front of you the better runners are. There is no comforting illusion you can entertain that they are all bunched just round the next street corner and you're really not that far adrift. In this case they are dots on the distant horizon. And – oh horror! – they are going up another near vertical staircase. This is the Bad Bit, the second of the Nasty Surprises. Exactly the same as the first Nasty Surprise, surprisingly. This sheer ascent has 166 steps (I count them to keep hold of my sanity) and this time I really think I will not make it to the top. I just have to imagine that I am a machine, like those ones that they have on display in IKEA that test the durability of the furniture by opening and closing a drawer 10,000 times a day. Right foot up, left foot up. Right foot up, left foot up. Don't look up. I reach the summit – somehow – and there, just to make things a tiny bit worse, a steward with a clipboard informs me that I am in 168th position. As a person with no Big Finish this is not what I want to hear with just a couple of miles to go. It will be very depressing to have dropped a further 50 places down by the end.

As promised, the terrain is pretty flat from now on – mainly grazing land. Dorset must have the most laxative grass in the world judging by the huge quantities of animal droppings bestrewing our path. I have now entered what I recognise as the transcendental phase of the run. This seems to occur after about an hour and a half, probably as a side effect of glycogen depletion. My thoughts wander far beyond the mundane reality of tramping across fields. I meditate on sheep. What is the point of being a sheep? They shit all over the grass. The shit makes the grass grow. The sheep then eat the grass and produce more shit. The Shit and Sheep cycle. What is the point? "What's the point in being a person?" an astute sheep looking me in the eye from a safe distance seems to reply. "You run thirteen miles to end up where you started, and you don't even stop to sample any of the grass."

The fields are more cultivated now, decked out with roly poly hay bales, surely a sign that we are nearing civilisation. A runner behind me shrieks and I hear him crash to the ground. Here's a new point of race etiquette. Do I stop to help him or let the people behind do it? Luckily, in the time it takes my weary brain to process these thoughts, I have left him far behind. Besides, it seems to make more sense to let the people who are in more danger of tripping over him deal with the problem. At least there's one person who's not going to overtake me with his big sprint finish.

One last hill. Often it is faster, and more restful, to *walk* up hills. I stride up this one and find myself overtaking a runner who is going through the physical motions of running but doesn't seem to be advancing. It's as if gravity was acting horizontally on him. We're not far from home now and the ruined splendour of Corfe Castle rises slowly above the moorland ahead of me, looking slightly better than I feel. Down one more dip and there ahead of me I see the best word in the world suspended on a banner between two poles: "Finish". If I were dyslexic, I'd go and live in Helsinki.

My finishing time is 1:57 and, thanks to Horizontal Gravity Man, I have actually advanced one place to 167th position. There are no medals, but we all get a souvenir T-shirt. It is symbolically yellow like the Maillot Jaune in the Tour de France. Everyone has won. Maybe the race was organised by those Marxists after all.

CHAPTER 16
Running Club

You may wish out of a desire for sociability or added motivation to join a local running club. You may even harbour the hope that fraternising with like-minded individuals could lead to romance. A word of warning on this score: men should be advised that you will not meet many women, mainly a lot of other men who want to talk about their PBs over various distances. And women should bear in mind that most of the men you will meet are likely to be skinny-legged specimens with prominent Adam's apples who witter on about split times. You should also be aware that the divorce rate among marathoners is three times the average in society, and even higher where both partners are runners. This statistic may seem off-putting, but it should be pointed out that it assumes that relationship break-ups occur *after* one or other partner starts running. It seems to me just as logical (and more likely) that people take up running after their relationships have already gone wrong, as a way of getting away from their partners. And if both of you start to do it simultaneously, then your marriage is already ancient history.

You can get in touch with your nearest running club through your local library or, if that's been closed down, then via a running site on the Internet. The name of your club will normally be that of your town or area, combined with a noun that will give you an idea of how seriously the members take their sport: Runners or Harriers (a dedicated organisation whose members participate in and frequently win local athletics events); Chasers or Striders (a group which emphasises fitness rather than competitive aspirations); Staggerers or Totterers (a glorified drinking club). My local bunch sound pretty keen, branding themselves the Muswell Hill Runners. Their Internet home page informs me that they hold training sessions on Tuesday and Thursday evenings and a long run around Hampstead Heath on a Sunday morning.

I join them for an initial evening session, but don't really take to it. Running around residential streets partially clothed under street lights makes you feel sordid. People assume you're up to no good. In fact, you yourself feel you are up to no good. I decide it seems much more sensible to take the opportunity to get up early on a Sunday and put in eight miles before brunch.

I arrive at the rendezvous point at Highgate tube station just before 11 o'clock and am pleasantly surprised to find about 20 fairly athletic-looking individuals, of whom eight are women, already gathered there. I seem to be the only person who has brought a bottle of water. There doesn't appear to be any formal system of introductions so I just sort of blend in. Most of the other runners seem to know each other and chat as they do their stretches. At 11 o'clock a man called Steve, who appears to be the leader, gives a signal and we set off to face our first obstacle: the pedestrian crossing over the Archway Road. Once on the move, the group comes to resemble a sort of peripatetic cocktail party with men running alongside girls they fancy and giving it some of the old chat. Two men behind me are having one of those blokes-who-don't-know-each-other-very-well conversations about the state of the economy. As a gatecrasher, I content myself with eavesdropping on the arcane discussions going on around me. One man is telling his neighbour how he did 5K last night and that he's going over to Amsterdam in a couple of weeks and hoping to do 10K. A bystander would think they were druggies. "Very energetic for a Sunday morning," a woman selling flowers on Highgate High Street comments as our little crocodile passes.

After five minutes I find that I have drifted to the back of the pack. Is this because I am the crappest runner? Or because I don't know anyone and bringing up the rear of these groups is the equivalent of loitering in the kitchen at parties? Well, I might as well be doing this run on my own if I'm not going to interact with the others, I think to myself. I step up my pace and force my way back into the pack, to rejoin the party so to speak. But by now everyone is embroiled in their own conversations in their own little cliques. I now resemble the party guest who ends up sitting in the middle of the living room flicking through the host's CD collection trying to pretend he's just looking for some music to put on rather than admit he's a friendless bore.

About 10 minutes into the run the two Blokes run out of things to say to each other at about the same time that they run out of breath to say it with. We're on Hampstead Heath which is full of families, footballers, dogs and, confusingly, other running clubs out on their own Sunday morning runs. At one point my concentration wavers and I almost find myself press-ganged into the Highgate Harriers.

There is a whole etiquette that governs this form of Social Mobility. For example, you must learn how to spit over your shoulder without breaking the flow of the conversation as it almost certainly would if you did it in someone's living room. Then there is the dilemma of talking to someone who is running at a different speed from yourself. Two men chatting just ahead of me become more and more separated until their conversation is forced to an end by the laws of acoustics with one participant shouting his concluding remarks over his shoulder at a distance of about 20 metres from his colleague. Clearly one must be aware of the relative ability of other runners before engaging them in conversation. I make the mistake of buttonholing Steve with questions concerning the club's history. I just naturally assume that, as the leader, he will be much fitter than me. "I'll talk to you at the top," he grates out from gasping lungs halfway up a long gruelling incline.

Luckily at the top of this hill is the first of our three stopping points. This gives a chance for the slower runners to catch up and for the faster ones to get a breather while pretending to be just waiting for the others. By this stage the cocktail party has reverted to something much more primitive. We now resemble a nomadic Neanderthal tribe. It is a blistering hot day and, as the possessor of a bottle of water, I suddenly find myself, along with another man who has a bottle of sports drink clipped to his belt, elevated to Alpha-male status in the group. A woman asks me for a sip of my water. "No, it's mine, mine. Keep your dirty thieving hands off," I rant with thirst-deranged eyes in imitation of some actor in a desert in some film, but then relent and let her have some.

A propos of the ascent we have just climbed, the conversation revolves around the uphill topography of different roads in the locality. Hazelwood Road is particularly bad I learn from the gathered elders, and Shepherds Hill can be a bugger. These running veterans can estimate distances like aboriginals can tell the time from looking at the sun. "How far have we run so far?" I ask. "Oh, just over three miles," the sage says with an obligatory but inexplicable squint at the sky. Their familiarity with local terrain can be quite disheartening. Steve informs me that a lap of Highgate Woods is two kilometres. My own calculations had guessed it as half as much again and I will now have to downscale my recent mileage retrospectively.

After a five-minute rest we run another couple of miles and I am forced to grapple with some further points of etiquette. For example, should one strike up a conversation with someone one happens to be running next to? I assume it would be rude to ignore the person so I tend to chat. After a few minutes of small talk one man suddenly interrupts me. "Sorry, I've got to speed up here." Obviously he is familiar with the course, so is this a strategic racing decision or is it the running equivalent of saying at a party, "Excuse me, I've just seen someone I really must talk to"? A few minutes later a woman I am chatting to says to me, "Please run on if you want to". I don't know whether to take up her invitation. Is she genuinely embarrassed about the slowness of her pace or is she, too, telling me that I'm a bore? By the end of the run I'm becoming quite paranoid. Eventually I find myself running in silence alongside the other friendless beginner in the group.

We reach the second rest point. It is hot and people seek out shady patches and defend their territory like animals in the wild. Looking round I notice that quite a few runners have dropped out and there are now only nine of us left. It is like some Japanese game show. I mention to a woman that my knees are a bit sore after running the Beast last week. "A bit sore?" her incredulous glance seems to say. She goes on to tell me in great detail how she is running without her anterior cruciate ligament which she tore last year. According to her doctor she shouldn't be running at all. Not to be outdone, several of the other runners inform me how they, too, are here today in spite of fearful injuries which should by all rights have them confined to wheelchairs. There are people around me with no kneecaps, with snapped, torn or wasted away cartilages and bones. I soon begin to feel that I am somehow cheating by running with a full complement of bodily parts. To have fallen over on the current run is also important, I discover. One man shows everyone his bloodied knees with all the pride of a seven-year-old. The others immediately begin to compare scabs and scars from falls incurred on previous weeks' runs. I resolve to put a sachet of tomato ketchup into my pocket for next time. Runners, I am beginning to realise, make undertakers or medical students look positively joyous. Most of their conversations seem to revolve around two topics: (a) injuries they have sustained, and (b) races they are planning to enter (with the hope presumably of acquiring a few more).

For the home leg I go with the advance group of faster runners. I have an incentive to keep up with them as, not being familiar with the route, I will otherwise end up abandoned and alone on the Heath like a kid who has lost his mummy. Luckily there is not much conversation among this élite group until one of them informs me that there is only about half a mile to go. Still feeling quite fresh, I speed up. Here I encounter my final poser of running-club etiquette. I am starting to catch up with the front runners. But how competitive is this run? Does one treat it as a race and try to win or should we all be more concerned about the taking part in a British sort of way? I might be committing a terrible *faux pas* by powering past people higher than me in the club pecking order. I chicken out and come home a safe fifth.

I jog home through Highgate Woods and ponder on the morbidity of the runner. How do they end up like that? Actually the answer is pretty obvious. From my experience you spend the first 20 minutes of any run wanting to die. Assuming that you do five runs a week, that makes 100 minutes a week you spend wanting to die. That's over three and a half days a year of solid death wish. This qualifies you to be a manic-depressive at the least; or, looking at it differently, one could argue that this makes you a very balanced person, like the Renaissance scholar who would keep a human skull on his desk, a *memento mori*, so that he would never forget his own mortality.

On getting home I find that for the first time I have developed jogger's nipple. This is surprisingly painful, like a wasp sting. It is also irritating. Knees can get sore after a run, but at least they perform a useful function during the experience. Nipples on the other hand are a totally redundant bodily part, on a man at any rate. I have never had the remotest use for them and now they are giving me gyp. Can one have them surgically removed, I wonder? Would the Muswell Hill Runners be impressed if I told them I was running without any nipples?

CHAPTER 17

New Forest Half Marathon

New Milton, Hampshire
12 September
Distance: 13.1 miles
Time: 1 hour 38 mins 3 secs

My alarm summons me from sleep at 6.30 a.m. on Sunday. For a self-employed childless person like me this is an unknown hour. The only time I ever get up this early is when I'm going on holiday. My body is not fooled on this occasion, though, and I drowse for a while, dimly conscious that there is a little devil and a little angel likeness of me perched on the headboard of my bed. The angel is exhorting me to get out of bed at this ungodly hour, catch a train down to the south coast and run around a forest for an hour and a half before returning home. Meanwhile the little devil is blowing chloroform into my lungs. The truth is that I have never in my life regretted having gone for a run. I cannot recall a single instance when, on coming back from a race or just a jog around the woods, I have sincerely wished I'd stayed in bed and had some bizarre dream about sitting my O-levels with no trousers on instead. But unfortunately I rarely remember this fact when I am lying in horizontal comfort. Finally, I force myself out of bed, put on my running kit and jog round the garden to check the fitness of my gammy left knee. I have only had three hours' sleep after Tara's 30th birthday party the night before and would quite like a sick note for the day but for once my knee refuses to play ball.

With nothing else for it I take the tube down to Waterloo. The 7.50 to Southampton is waiting conveniently at the platform when I arrive and I take a seat in a carriage with six or seven other early morning passengers. As I unfold my newspaper I become aware that a repetitive taped announcement has been booming round the concourse for several minutes. I attune my ears to the station's muffled acoustics and make out the words: "Would all passengers please leave the station immediately due to a reported emergency...would all passengers please leave the station immediately due to a reported emergency..." Naturally everyone ignores this warning. A minute passes. The message continues to reverberate around the station. A couple of passengers peer nervously around to see if anyone else is going to crack. One man gets up and leaves the train, no doubt a foreigner. We stiff-upper-lip Brits are terrified of appearing foolish and would be much happier to die in a terrorist bomb blast than lose our dignity by fleeing in panic from what will almost certainly prove to be a false alarm. There is a sudden jolt and to our relief it is not a detonation but the train lurching into motion. It pulls slowly out of the station and we slump back gratefully behind our Sunday supplements, leaving tricky death/embarrassment decisions to be faced by the passengers on the stationary trains we leave behind.

By the time the train has rolled through half a dozen suburban stations it begins to take on the familiar reek of bananas. I sense that I may not be alone in heading for today's half marathon. A man getting on at Winchester greets a female acquaintance whom he has obviously not seen since the same event last year. "How have you been?" "Fine," she replies, "apart from breaking my ankle." Aha. That tell-tale morbidity signals my first positive sighting of runners. Soon there is a constant flow of passengers going to the loo due to early-morning over-intake of water. Any neutral observer would probably think we were on our way to a cystitis-sufferers' convention. When I finally manage to get in for a pee myself, I find the waste bin is overflowing with energy bar wrappers, banana skins and empty Evian bottles.

The train pulls into New Milton just after 10 o'clock and unsur-prisingly half the passengers disembark. We move into the town in a long and largely silent drove. All around us windows are shuttered up. Locals cower in their cottages. The runners have hit town. We locate the starting area without problem. New Milton is a small town and many of my companions have obviously done this race before. We pass the

Conservative Club whose window boxes have clearly been laid out by a colour blind person on an Equal Opportunities scheme. All the shops are closed. What do the people here do on all the other Sundays in the year when there's no marathon to watch? We arrive at the green to find a village fête atmosphere with a couple of marquees, families, dogs, a few stalls. There is the usual long queue for the woefully inadequate lavatory facilities. The marathon and half marathon taking place today have attracted 1,300 runners of whom, from my experience, at least half will go to the loo at least twice in the hour before the race. The public conveniences are already reeling under the unaccustomed pressure of the systematic evacuation of several hundred nervous bowels. I sensibly walk down the road to the local café, pay 60p for a cup of diuretic tea and use their facilities instead.

I change into my running kit in one of the tents provided and at a quarter to eleven we gather on the road next to the village green. Race stewards hoist aloft a series of signs, like Roman legions' standards, which are inscribed with predicted finishing times. We jostle and join up with our relevant legions. I toy with the macho idea of going on a suicide mission with the crack infantry on "65–75 mins" but settle more realistically for casting in my lot with the cannon fodder on "90–105 mins". The standard-bearers march forwards towards the starting line on the High Street and we follow in dutiful cohorts.

Sadly there is nothing very athletic or aesthetic about a bunch of distance runners gathered together. Skinny limbs, greying hair, beaky noses, male pattern baldness, mismatched manmade fabrics. Frankly we look more like the Home Guard than any credible army. A short speech from some local dignitary and we are off, shuffling, side-stepping and stop-starting along the high street as each one of us tries to find our natural position in the pack. Then, as soon as I have found an area where I can run comfortably at my preferred speed, the usual sensation of wanting to give up kicks in. That feeling of desiring, needing, to quit has a sort of eidetic realness even though I am aware that it is false. I know from experience that I won't stop, that I will see this race through. It is a bit like when at the beginning of the World Cup or European Championship you have the idea that the England football team could play well and win the tournament. It seems so real to all your senses, yet you know rationally that it is an illusion. The advantage of running in competitive races as part of training is that you don't succumb to this feeling of despair because you are aware that you are surrounded by hundreds or even thousands of people who are not going to give up (although probably they, too, secretly want to). If we human beings ever perfect telepathy, I am afraid it will be the death of events like this. Competitors would tune in to each other's thoughts and all just form a pact after half a mile and agree to quit right now. It would cause puzzlement and possibly one or two boos from the spectators when a thousand runners suddenly stopped, turned round and walked back to the changing tents. Of course, none of this is very likely to happen. It is just one of those oxygen-starved fantasies my brain conjures up as my body makes the tough transition from anaerobic to aerobic breathing.

We're leaving the town now and a two-year-old kid swings on a gate and waves at us. "Bye-bye," she says, "bye-bye." Now I am not a great believer in the out-of-the-mouths-of-babes theory of innate wisdom, but this seems a logical, pleasant and non-patronising thing to say to a bunch of runners. The other spectators, of course, are getting my goat by encouraging me to "keep going". An unseen dog barks insanely from behind a hedge as we pass. His owner's voice yells at him to shut up. "But surely, Master," the animal replies, "you've trained me to watch out for dangerous and potentially psychopathic individuals and here are several hundred running past our gate. They're in their underwear for Christ's sake." We reach a road junction where we are observed by a smattering of unappreciative spectators. There is one couple who clearly haven't had sex for about five years. They are leaning on the bonnet of their Range Rover, not speaking, both looking in opposite directions, neither of them at the race.

We fork off right towards the forest and a runner passes me pushing a baby carriage in front of him containing a not-at-all-puzzled-looking baby. This sight is on the increase in races and parks these days – parents taking their offspring for a run in aerodynamic, three-wheeled baby buggies. But what's the point? In addition to the fact that they are wilfully encouraging the joyriders of the next generation, I don't see the necessity for parents to keep fit. It's childless adults on the threshold of middle age like myself who have to obsess with losing their youthful looks and figure. Once you have done your reproductive duty it is your biological right, and possibly even duty, to let yourself fall apart. Genetically you are now redundant and, besides, your children are going to despise and be embarrassed by you anyway once they reach adolescence, still more so if you are trying to look trendy and young.

Despite the bucolic suggestiveness of its name, the New Forest Half Marathon is actually run on road. In fact, it is only after three miles that we finally enter a bit of token woodland. This, for most of the runners, signals a chance to relieve the bladder. Half-dressed men burst out of the heather at regular intervals, pulling up their shorts, like apprentice flashers who have got it the wrong way round. We reach the first drinks point and I opt for water as I recently read in a running magazine that glucose drinks taken in conjunction with strenuous exercise traumatise your teeth. This is one part of the body that I hadn't previously thought I had to worry about. Frankly there's not a lot the teeth have to do in a race apart from get gritted during the uphill sections and smile when we pass the race photographer.

Racing in the countryside where there are no cheering spectators or urban ambient noise is an eerily silent experience. Apart from the odd pleasantry exchanged by club runners who find themselves next to each other and the slap of running sole on tarmac, the only sound is that of massed gasping and groaning. Close your eyes and you could imagine you were an extra in a porn movie. Running next to me is a man who takes a noisy slurp of air every other step like a contestant in the World Milk Shake Drinking Competition. His breathing combines with that of the other runners who surround me to set up a complex 7/8 time signature. A woman grunts, a man gasps, the Milk Shake man slurps, another man hisses and so on. You can hum Pink Floyd's "Money" in perfect time to it. Dum DEE da DA dum dee da is now threatening to lodge itself in my brain. This is very dangerous for my stride. It is impossible to run in 7/8 time unless you are an amputee spider. I try to put the tune out of my head and take an interest in my surroundings.

A New Forest pony stands by the roadside swishing its tail at this stream of futility passing it. I am struck by the placidity of nature in the face of all this human indignity. A stocky sweating man in a singlet with a tapestry of tattoos on his scarlet shoulders and upper arms slogs past me. His machismo is impressive. That ink alone must weigh pounds. We're back on country roads now which we will follow for the rest of the race. The brief detour into the forest was presumably just to prevent disgruntled participants asking for their money back. Sensing our sudden shadeless vulnerability, the sun comes out and does its bit to spoil my day. I grab a sponge from a water station and dab off the sweat. I realise now why the humble sponge has earned its epithet of "magic". Even when its water content is pretty much exhausted there is still something refreshing about a sponge crushed in your hand. Maybe it's just some childhood throwback to one's favourite teddy bear.

We have reached Mile Five now and pass a sign saying "Photographer Ahead". Suddenly runners' shoulders go back, looks of relaxed contentment are forced on to faces that had previously been etched with despair, comfort sponges that have been clutched in hands since the last water station are ditched and joshing conversations are struck up between previously silent neighbours. I do my best but the photographer ignores me as I pass, correctly realising that there is no way I will ever be persuaded to part with money to be reminded that I once looked like *this*.

The middle miles of a race are taken up with clock-watching. The novelty of your surroundings has worn off, but you are not yet near enough to the finish to entertain any fantasies about an early end to this torment. You live for the sight of the next day-glo yellow mile marker up ahead by the side of the road. With the aid of my brand new digital sports watch with individual lap timer I am able to provide an accurate dissection of the agony of each mile. Assuming that you are aiming, like me, to run approximately eight-minute miles, it goes as follows:

Minute 1   *Bask in glory of having passed another milestone (literally). Subtract miles run from total distance and tell yourself that you can do it.*

Minute 2   *Head down, teeth gritted. Don't dare look at watch.*

Minute 3   *Head down, teeth gritted. Resist very strong desire to look at watch.*

Minute 4   *Sneak look at watch, hoping it'll be showing five minutes. Feel aggrieved.*

Minute 5   *Can't believe watch has only crawled along another minute. It feels like three or four. Mentally draft angry complaint to sports shop manager about selling defective merchandise.*

Minute 6   *Entertain hope that some imperceptible downhill gradient has speeded you up and the next mile marker will shortly be visible up ahead.*

Minute 7   *Scan road ahead anxiously for mile marker. Should definitely be in sight by now.*

Minute 8   *Entertain conviction that some imperceptible uphill gradient has slowed you down, hence non-visibility of mile marker.*

Minute 9   *Mentally draft angry complaint to race organisers about inaccurate placement of mile markers.*

Minute 10 Give up and walk.

Hopefully at some point before minute 10 you will pass the mile marker and start the whole sequence again.

Running on country roads is a whole different discipline to navigating the straighter planned urban streets. As the lanes twist and wind with the contours of the landscape, the stream of runners constantly crosses and recrosses the road. This is not necessarily to "run the tangents", that is to secure the advantage of taking bends on the inside. As far as I can work out our motion seems largely random, following some abstruse principle of chaos theory. This just serves to annoy passing cars who frequently have to slow to a halt to let us cross. The drivers vent their subsequent road rage by revving up their idling engines and pumping carbon monoxide directly into our gasping lungs.

In the last couple of miles I experience the now familiar demoralising feeling of being passed by loads of people, who, unlike me, have been doing some speed training and thus have a Big Sprint Finish. I overtake four and am overtaken in turn by maybe 40 – among them some of the thinnest legs I've even seen that are not attached to insects. I cross the line in a gap between finishers and the race announcer has time to check my number and look up my name: "…and Russell Taylor crosses the line," he announces over the PA to the indifference of everyone except me and my ankles. My finishing time is 1:38:30. Three minutes off my Liverpool time and for the first time in an hour and a half I'm pleased I didn't stay in bed this morning.

CHAPTER 18
The Runner's Diet

Scientists disagree on the perfect diet for the runner. Nothing surprising in that. Scientists disagree on most things. There are two good reasons for this:

Firstly, scientists are really no better at their jobs than the rest of us. Unfortunately in this secular age where most of us have dispensed with the idea of an omnipotent Supreme Being, scientists are expected to step into the breach and take over the role of infallible explainers of the reality that we have been so unwittingly born into. Unsurprisingly they frequently don't live up to our high demands.

Secondly, it is a common misconception that the purpose of science is to create certainty. Possibly this is the idealistic big-picture aim, but in the short term science is around to create doubt. It is actually vital for scientists not to agree with one another. Say, for example, all scientists were to announce jointly that global warming is caused by man-made pollutants or that eating red meat is bad for you. We'd all adjust our diets and/or our CO_2 emissions accordingly (or, more likely, we wouldn't bother) but there'd be no more need for any scientific reports on these subjects. Governments would be jolly pleased because they could gradually withdraw university funding and cut research grants. Scientists would thus be making themselves dispensable. This is why there will always be some boffin in the wilderness (a professor at the University of Alma-Ata perhaps) who will tell us that global warming is caused by meteorites or that red meat stops you getting rabies or something equally absurd. No matter how far-fetched the claim, it has created doubt, which means there will have to be a whole new lot of research commissioned to sort it all out. And, of course, it won't sort it all out, not if scientists have got any brains (and they've got lots – look at all those letters after their names). Remember, scientists have to eat too.

Eating, ah yes, that's where we were. Just remember that some of this dietary advice is disputed by scientists, but that's not science, that's economics.

Carbohydrate and fat

The two substances stored in the body which provide the bulk of the energy for running are carbohydrate and fat. Carbohydrate is things like pasta, rice and potatoes and fat is, well, fat. Of the two, fat has twice the energy content of carbohydrate, gram for gram, and the average young male will store 100,000 calories of this. However, the amount of carbohydrate stored by the body is much lower, about 1,500–2,000 calories. This means that you can run for 119 hours on fats but only 1.6 hours on carbs. So, by burning pure fat, theoretically you could run about 30 marathons in a row and get rid of all that unsightly flab at the same time. But for some annoying reason, which no doubt scientists disagree on, human biology doesn't work in this convenient way. In fact, the body oxidises only about 150–200g of its fat supplies during the course of a marathon. The rest of the energy comes from carbohydrate burning and we only store enough of that to run about 20 miles. The maths is fairly simple. Running a marathon is impossible. Take it up with the scientists or God. We're stuck with it.

Of course, flying was once considered impossible and we got round that. The best way to cheat nature is for the runner to load up the muscles with as much carbohydrate as possible. Experiments have shown that long-distance runners perform three times better on a high-carb diet than on a high-fat diet. Fat we have aplenty – even skinny people like runners – so the runner's food intake should consist of 60–70 per cent carbohydrates. This basic prejudice has been inculcated into most of us over the last few decades. Carbohydrate is Good (vegetables, pasta, rice) and fat is Bad (butter, oil, dead animal blubber). This is not a licence to go mad at the Eat All You Can for £6.95 at your local Indian vegetarian restaurant. Excess glucose is converted by the body and stored, annoyingly, as fat. There is evidence that glucose is more readily absorbed if five or so small meals are taken throughout the day. Runners are highly anti-social creatures who tend to go running at most times when normal people sit down to meals (breakfast, lunch, dinner) so this grazing habit isn't particularly difficult for us to adopt.

The basic form of carbohydrate as used by the human body is glucose. Glucose is transported in the blood and stored in muscles and in the liver as a substance called glycogen. Now another annoying thing about human physiology is that, although glucose can quickly be mobilised via the bloodstream from the liver to the working muscles, the stored glycogen cannot be transferred *between* muscles. Thus on a long run your thighs may be crying out for the stuff, while your biceps will be sitting up there Scrooge-like on several grams of it and refusing to share it round. Ah well, at least you can always rely on there being plenty of muscle power left up there for that big victory wave to the crowd.

Glycogen is also important for the functioning of the central nervous system. When the body's reserves start to get low, runners may suffer from a condition called hypoglycemia. This causes dizziness, weakness and hunger and is better known to marathoners as "the Wall". It normally occurs after about 18 to 20 miles of a race when glycogen stores reach a critical minimum You become listless, depressed, overwhelmed by a sense of spiritual exhaustion and despair. You lose the will to go on. You want to die. It's not unlike the effect created by listening to the Pink Floyd album of the same name.

Proteins, vitamins and minerals

The other components of our diet are proteins, vitamins and minerals. Although protein is sometimes used by the body as an energy source, most scientists agree that an exercising athlete eating a balanced diet does not have any additional requirement for proteins or vitamins – apart, that is, from the scientists who have sold out and are working for the drug companies which produce the elaborate and expensive dietary supplement pills that line the shelves of all health food shops. Many athletes take these supplements anyway, out of paranoia, just in case their competitors are gaining some minuscule physiological or psychological advantage by popping them. It is probable that these pills are simply a rip-off and most of the contents just end up being excreted by our bodies. Most likely, all we are doing is nurturing a super race of vitamin-boosted flies feeding on the sewage around sports training grounds and parks.

One day they may rise up and take over the earth.

As for minerals, a post-race glass of tomato or orange juice will replenish all the potassium and sodium lost in 3 litres of sweat. Right after a run is an excellent time to force yourself to drink something worthy and nutritious, like a can of that vile V8 combined vegetable juice that you optimistically buy from the supermarket when you first start your health kick. Under normal circumstances you'd spurn the stuff even as a mixer for vodka, but when you are craving *any* liquid after a 10-mile run it slips down a treat. If like me you are a hypochondriac who enjoys buying pills even if they are of dubious value, invest in an iron supplement, as there is some argument that vigorous exercise destroys red blood cells. If you are a woman, a bit of extra calcium is always useful to offset the risk of osteoporosis.

Water

Runners can lose 1–6 per cent of their body weight during a marathon through water loss. This comes through a combination of sweating, moisture expelled in exhaled air and urination (if you can be bothered queuing for the portaloos). Dehydration is the number one health risk in running a marathon and all training guides stress this danger. You must drink *before* you are thirsty we are warned, as if this was something very unusual. Well, actually we do it all the time, don't we? Otherwise our social lives would be very dull. (Can I get you a beer? No thanks, I don't feel thirsty yet.) So the rule of thumb is apply the same mentality when on the run as you do when sitting in a pub: have a drink every 20 minutes (though obviously not an alcoholic one). An easy way to ascertain whether you are dehydrated (well, easier for boys than girls) is to monitor the colour of your urine. It should be pale or straw-coloured. If it is amber, then it is overconcentrated with waste products and you are dehydrated. Don't be an amber gambler, as the road safety adverts used to say. In practice, there is clearly not a lot of communication between the various bodily organs. It is quite common to find yourself coming back from a training run simultaneously dying for a drink and a pee.

Runners are advised to drink more than the two litres of water a day recommended for adults and so one of the first things you should do is get your daily fluid intake up. But do not make the mistake that I did and have your bathroom floor retiled (and thus your loo out of service for a couple of days) in the week you decide to get serious about your training. Many runners use isotonic drinks (Lucozade, Gatorade etc.). These contain glucose at the same concentration as your body's fluids and replenish your carbs at the same time as rehydrating you. They are especially useful to take on the move after 90 minutes or so of a marathon when glycogen supplies are getting low. Runners, however, drink them on all occasions. Gin and isotonic is rather nice. Some of these sports drinks claim to enhance your performance by 33 per cent, but sadly that doesn't mean that if you drink three of them at once you will do the race in no time.

There are two other bodily chemical substances that you need to know about:

The runner's enemy: lactic acid

Glucose is broken down in the body by a substance called ATP. This is not another name for a cashpoint machine, but it is our body's hole in the wall as far as providing us with energy is concerned. ATP stands for adenosine triphosphate and is able to hold 38 per cent of the energy it liberates for use by the muscles. The rest is dissipated as heat. So the next time you are burning up on a long training run, don't blame yourself for being out of condition. Blame the ATP for letting go of that other 62 per cent. Really! It's had millions of years of evolution to get its act together. Anyway, the whole physiological process of liberating energy is vastly complicated, involving both aerobic and anaerobic components and something called a Krebs Cycle which would make your eyes glaze over. Importantly for us, though, hydrogen is released as a by-product of glucose breakdown and it combines with oxygen to form water (or sweat to you and me). If, however, your little lungs are not pumping hard enough, and there is not enough free oxygen, then the hydrogen combines instead with pyruvic acid to form lactic acid in the muscles. Lactic acid is Bad. It inactivates enzymes used in the energy transfer process and produces the condition that we call feeling knackered.

The runner's friend: beta-endorphins

Beta-endorphins are hormones secreted from the anterior pituitary gland of the brain. Their production is stimulated by exercise and induces euphoria and pain tolerance, the so-called Runner's High. They also reduce anxiety, tension, anger and confusion, control appetite and are about as addictive as heroin. If it weren't for beta-endorphins, I wouldn't be writing this book, and you probably wouldn't be reading it.

Before the race

There are two normally accepted legal ways of improving a marathon performance.

No. 1 Carb loading

Carbohydrate loading (or glycogen supercompensation) simply means that a week before the race you eat very little carbohydrate (less than 100g per day) for three days in order to deplete the glycogen stores in you muscles. Then, three days before the race, you switch to pigging out on 500g a day of the stuff and your gasping muscles suck it up like a sponge. This is why most marathons have a pasta party the day before the event. Carb loading might work for you, but you may never be able to look fusilli in the face again.

No. 2 Caffeine ingestion

Caffeine ingestion has an ergogenic effect, that is it gives you an energy boost. Apparently it does this by facilitating the burning of fat and thus conserving the body's glycogen reserves. To benefit from this technique, two and a half cups of coffee should be drunk 60 minutes before exercise. Be warned, though, that coffee is also a diuretic and thus you may find yourself standing in the portaloo queue for one extra pee when everyone else is on the start line.

Fat and protein should not be eaten in a pre-race meal. They are digested slowly and may hang around in your stomach and give you cramps. You will notice that there are no hamburger or hotdog stalls in marathon starting areas. In any case, unless you are super confident, your last meal should be taken at least three hours before the race as tension reduces blood flow to the digestive system.

Peas

Lastly, a word about this most indispensable of foodstuffs. Obviously the runner's larder should be well stocked with pasta, rice, fresh vegetables, sports drinks, dietary supplements (well, you don't listen to advice do you?) and most importantly a packet of frozen peas. These are not for consumption but to be used, wrapped in a tea towel, as a cold compress to ice the inevitable injuries you will pick up on your training runs.

Inspirational Viewing No 3

Marathon Man (1976)

Here at last is a serious film about running. Dustin Hoffman plays Thomas Babbington Levi (aka Babe), an aspiring marathoner. He pounds the track; he gets involved in "race rage" incidents with other runners; he is attacked by dogs; he keeps a stopwatch in his jogging pants; he fills out a training log; he has posters of Abebe Bikila on his wall; in the predominantly Hispanic and black area where he lives, even the local lowlife look down on him and call him "creepy" and "twinkletoes"; he is patronised by waiters in expensive restaurants for not wearing a tie. In short, he is the lowest of the low in society's eyes and every serious runner will identify with him.

Then suddenly the film takes a leap into the realm of pure fantasy. Dustin manages to get an attractive German woman to be his girlfriend and she is even prepared to stand with a stopwatch timing him as he slogs round the waterfront in New York. Then we see them having sex. Dustin rolls on top of Elsa and she groans "No vay. Not again. I can't." We wonder if Dustin has fallen asleep and this is a dream sequence. But gritty realism soon reasserts itself with the arrival in town of Babe's shady business-man brother, Doc.

Doc, played by the excellent Roy Scheider, has pretty soon been bumped off by some nasty Nazis. This is the point everything goes wrong for Dustin. He gets mugged in Central Park by two middle-aged heavies, one of whom has a club foot and whom he embarrassingly fails to outrun. His girlfriend turns out to be a Nazi as well, just showing that you never can trust those Germans. And, of course, famously he finds himself strapped into Laurence Olivier's dentist's chair for an involuntary check-up. In trying to extract information and teeth in equal measure, Sir Larry hasn't reckoned with the fact that Dustin is a marathon runner. "When you run 26 miles you don't give in to pain," Dustin opines earlier in the film. By his own admission he hasn't actually run a marathon at this stage and so lets out a few squawks as the drill bites.

By this stage the athletically minded viewer may be beginning to fidget. Frankly, Dustin hasn't really done much running since the opening title sequence. In fact, we have to wait until the last half hour of the film before he finally gets down to some serious road pounding. He is dressed only in his pyjama bottoms, and shoeless, so he manages to emulate the barefoot feat of his hero Abebe. Admittedly, Abebe hadn't just had all his teeth drilled out and didn't have three gun-toting gangsters in hot pursuit to spur him on.

Naturally, Dustin manages to dispose of all the Nazis and by the end of the film we find him training again, but with a new maturity and determination. We are left to ponder on the nature of greed, suffering, loss, experience and exactly how Dustin managed to explain away to the police the five corpses he left in his trail.

Summary

Artistic merit ****
Marathoning relevance ***
Kitsch factor *

CHAPTER 19

Cabbage Patch 10

Richmond-upon-Thames
26 September
Distance: 10 miles
Time: 1 hour 9 mins 27 secs

I have entered another race, partly to relieve the monotony of running round the local woods and partly because it is important for a serious runner to amass statistics, personal bests over the various set distances (including a 10M PB). This gives us hard data from which to calculate a potential marathon time and also with which to bore other runners we meet at events like this. After the rigours of the Train and the Beast I feel I need something a little more genteel and so opt for this 10-mile run along the Thames round Twickenham and Ham due to its homely name and convenient location. What on earth could the Cabbage Patch be I wonder as I take the train down to south London. Are we going to be running round someone's allotment?

The Cabbage Patch turns out to be a pub in Twickenham. I am easily able to identify it as I walk from the railway station by the inevitable clutch of skinny men in tracksuits with beaky noses, specs and prominent Adam's apples hanging around outside. I draw in a lungful of air. I love the smell of Ralgex in the morning.

The first priorities are as ever to (a) identify where the start line is and (b) go to the loo. Having ascertained the first vital piece of information, I join several dozen other runners in a queue in the deserted lounge bar upstairs. The pub toilets are a particularly unpleasant place first thing on a Sunday morning as they still bear the stains of Saturday night's revels, including a generous caking of congealed vomit. This is my most unpleasant pre-race lavatorial experience so far. I make a note to book myself a colonic irrigation before all future events.

The function room of the Cabbage Patch is doubling up as a changing room for the morning and I find myself a space in the corner. I put on my kit while the runners around me go through a pre-race ritual that resembles some ancient fertility rite, anointing their nipples and groins with exotic balms and unctions (well, Vaseline actually). Back outside in the pub car park I survey the assembled competitors and note an air of professionalism that I have not come across in previous races. There is a profusion of muscled thighs and running club colours. I note a healthy number of Muswell Hill Runners, their red and black banded vests giving them the look of anarchists. Runners strut around in their tribal groupings, discussing race strategies and necking sports drinks. This is clearly going to be a serious field.

At a quarter to 10.00 we are rounded up and herded on to King Street for the start. The Sunday morning shoppers stare at us as if we were lots in a slave market, making us feel vaguely exotic but contemptible at the same time. I squeeze myself through the crush to take up a position as near the start line as I can. I have decided that it is psychologically better to go with the front runners. Being overtaken will spur me on to better efforts. A klaxon signals the start of the race, followed immediately by the massed blipping of several hundred runners activating their sports watches, like the electronic chirping of a swarm of cyber-insects.

As I am contemplating paying my subscription and joining the Muswell Hill Runners I decide that I will adopt them all as my Personal Nemeses today, as a sort of voluntary initiation ritual. Two miles into the race I am overtaken by a pair of them: two girls, one of them with very nice legs. I give chase – not out of any form of sexism I might add. As I have mentioned before, it is pretty much impossible to get sexually aroused when running. With limbs and heart pumping frantically there just isn't enough blood to go around to the less vital parts of the body, if you get my drift. In fact, chaps, your "old man" does not look at his dapper best during or indeed after a race. Shrunken, shrivelled, wrinkled – now is when he earns this disparaging nickname. In the general competition for blood and water, only the appendix and the hair take a lower priority over him. Some trainers maintain that athletes should have sex before a race. This is nothing to do with any performance-enhancing benefits. It's just that no woman would want to have sex with you for quite a while afterwards.

Anyway, my motivation for following the Muswell Hill woman's legs is simply that they are far more attractive and more memorable than the spindly hairy male specimens I would otherwise be obliged to lock on to. We track the river along Broom Road, which some wit with a spray can has rechristened Vroom Road in our honour. On our left we pass Teddington TV studios where a row of blue plaques proudly remembers the immortal work laid down here by the likes of Harry Worth and Kenny Everett.

The Muswell Hill Runner is getting away from me with an awful inexorable inevitability. Her imperceptibly longer stride is giving her maybe a couple of metres a minute on me, but that is enough in the long run (which, of course, this is). My decision to start at the front of the pack has already backfired on me and I am feeling demoralised by the frequency with which I am being overtaken, and by people with the most bizarre running styles. I am passed by one man who runs with his arms jammed rigidly to his sides as if pushing a very heavy wheelbarrow. Then there is a woman who trots along primly upright, like a lapdog begging for a biscuit, with her hands perched daintily, high on her chest. Another woman strides as if she is leaping invisible hurdles at each step, but she progresses at exactly the same speed as a man running alongside her with a stooped slack-limbed Groucho Marx posture. A man next to me runs with one arm twitching by his side, like a landed fish, the other held with little finger extended as if he is about to stir a posh cup of tea. Then there is the strange style favoured by one middle-aged runner – his arms held close to his sides, with forearms extended at right angles like the exterminator and sink plunger of a Dalek. And there's a woman whose body twists round like a screw propeller with each stride. It's amazing she attains forward motion and doesn't bore herself into the ground. Behind her is a man who jerks his head from side to side as if being slapped repeatedly round the face by an imaginary assailant. Amazingly, all of these people are serious runners, and most will finish ahead of me today.

As I pointed out earlier, one of the reasons I chose to run the New York Marathon was for the advantage of doing the bulk of my training in the summer months. The problem with training at this time of year is that it favours the very first and most important exertion you make on Race Day (getting out of bed), but severely hampers most of the subsequent ones (like running in the actual event). Just when I would have appreciated a continuation of the recent monsoon season, an Indian summer seems to have arrived. The heat is oppressive in the open and even more unpleasant in supposed shelter. We cross to the east bank of the Thames over Kingston Bridge and find ourselves in an underpass filled with superheated car engine fumes. As we double back along the riverbank some winos taking the midmorning sun offer us encouragement from a park bench. "Go on, chaps, go on," they shout waving cider bottles, excited at having for once come across some people who *they* are able to patronise and feel vaguely sorry for.

I am amazed to find that I am doing each of these first few miles in well under seven minutes – much faster than my usual racing pace. This is mainly due to the fact that this is a proper race with serious runners. There are no fancy-dress funrunners here or fatties whose workmates put their name down for the race for a laugh without telling them. Today's competitors are people with racing pedigrees as long as your arm and expensive sports watches to go with them. As I strain to keep up with the field I can't believe this will all be over in just six weeks. I remember experiencing a similar feeling before my university final exams (I feel I'm in better shape for the marathon than I was for those). We hug the riverbank for a while and then deviate off through some residential avenues. Speed humps are an extra element you really just don't need in a road race. Although they are designed to calm traffic (and infuriate drivers), they are also effective at breaking the stride (and possibly the ankles) of runners. Some of us opt to tackle them while others veer off on to the pavement and court the risk of stumbling over loose paving stones or colliding with baby buggies.

At about seven miles, a man with a British Airways shirt and a bumbag streaks past me. He cannot seriously be keeping up that pace, I think. He'd have won the race by now if he was. Sure enough, like a discourteous motorway driver, he is content just to overtake, pull in right in front of me and drop his pace so it is fractionally less than the speed I want to cruise at. I am obliged to overtake him in return. Five minutes later he zooms past me once more and does the same thing. What's going on? I feel like I'm being man-marked here. Still, this is clearly a challenge and as my original Personal Nemesis has no doubt finished the race by now, I decide to adopt BA Bum-bag instead. We cross Richmond Bridge and with only a mile or so to go we are still keeping up a cracking pace. On the towpath I edge ahead of BA Bum-bag again and this time try to hold off his challenge. But he has calculated his spurt and slack cycle to precision and his last burst takes him past me literally on the finishing line.

I pick up my complimentary finisher's T-shirt and drift back to the Cabbage Patch with it draped over my shoulders. "Run out of steam, have you, luv?" a passing old lady enquires. I am annoyed by this apparent allusion to my vanquisher of last month, combined with her inability to recognise an athlete who is "warming down" in dignified manner after having set a PB. I glower at her and walk on.

Back in the changing room, tables have been set out against the far wall for sports massages. Chaotically overcrowded, it resembles a scene from a Crimean War field hospital. I feel a bit stiff so I approach a couple of clientless masseurs. Bob, bespectacled with a shaving-brush beard, starts the massage while his colleague Andy regales us with a story about agonising deaths occurring among orienteers after being bitten by rogue insects. That morbid mentality, it's unmistakable. "Are you a runner?" I ask Andy. He nods. They both are. Bob explains that he was a long-distance lorry driver and long-distance runner – not the most sociable combination of work and leisure activities, so he turned to sports massage to meet people.

"Is your *tibialis anterior* painful?" he enquires, rubbing the bottom of my shin. "If you mean the bit you're prodding, yes," I reply. "Shins are always a good way to tell a runner," Andy, a fount of useful facts, informs me. He asks me to feel his shin. I run my finger obligingly along it. "Like a hacksaw blade," I tell him, and he puffs up proudly. This is the runner's equivalent of a boxer getting you to feel his biceps, except obviously it's not considered quite so sexy by girls you're trying to impress in bars.

Back outside there is now a symbolic unity, like in some heavy-handed socialist realism film. Where once people were sporting their running club colours, now everyone is wearing their race souvenir T-shirts and are all dressed in uniform white. This is not to last long.

People start to jostle round the notice-board in the car park where the results have been posted in superquick time. Running is largely practised by thin men with beards who are also exactly the sort of people who spend the rest of their leisure time playing with their PCs and thus events like this boast the very latest computer technology. Additional print-outs are being pinned up by the minute as the slower runners come home. I'm not sure this is such a good innovation. In the old days, presumably, the results would have been mailed out to running clubs a few days after the race. Runners would have found out their times and positions maybe a week after the event, when tensions had cooled and memories dimmed. Like instant video replays at football grounds, technology here just seems to provoke confrontation.

There are dark mutterings about how well the Muswell Hill Runners have done. There are six of them in the top 20. If only they knew it, they'd be deeply grateful to me for not having joined yet and thus not dragging their average down with my mediocre contribution of 209th place out of a field of 668. The results sheet further informs me that I completed the course in 1:09:27 and that this equates to 6.56 minute miles. An old man complains that there is no over-70s category. Why should he hand 12 years to some of these 60-year-old whippersnappers he grumbles. I discreetly check his time and am mightily relieved to find that I beat him.

CHAPTER 20

Psychic Reading

A sign attached to a lamp-post on Muswell Hill Broadway announces that the local branch of the Royal British Legion will be hosting a Psychic Fayre on Tuesday night. My eye is caught by the yellow day-glo notice, perhaps from its resemblance to the mile markers in a race. Why do they spell Fayre like that, I wonder? Surely if they were really psychic they'd realise that it just irritates people. I walk on but the seeds of an idea have been planted.

So far my preparation for the marathon has consisted of mugging up practical dietary and training advice in countless running handbooks. But running a marathon is more than just a physical challenge. Perhaps a psychic reading might offer the possibility of a transcendental approach to the endeavour which has been hitherto lacking. I'm too embarrassed to go on my own so I phone Tara to see if she is free on Tuesday. She is currently without a job, a boyfriend or a flat and her beloved Tottenham Hotspur's form could do with improvement and she agrees that she, too, might be in need of some spiritual enlightenment.

The Royal British Legion, Muswell Hill and Highgate Branch, turns out to be a dingy ex-servicemen's club set back from the main road. Those who once fought for king and country are now rewarded with "TV, Snooker, Bar Billiards and Dancing Saturday Nights". Men who half a century ago swept across the North African deserts in Sherman tanks now get to ride the Stannah stairlift down to the bar. It is a depressing place and the New Age visitors being entertained today seem oddly out of kilter with the establishment's militaristic past. The entrance to the Psychic Fayre is barred by a huge bearded man sitting behind a table from which it looks like it would take lifting equipment to extract him. He demands an entry fee of £2.50. We pay up and go in. Tara wonders what his speciality is. "Clairvoyant," I reply, "He obviously saw *us* coming a mile off."

We find ourselves in a room decorated with drab brown seventies wallpaper. An elderly man with a heavy limp moves painfully across the floor, making his way towards the faith healer's table. He sits down. Oh, he *is* the faith healer. This is not a good start. Seven or eight different psychics, mainly women but a couple of men, are sitting behind trestle tables arranged along the walls. A dozen or so potential clients tiptoe nervously around the room, deciding which reader to choose. We feel desperately unspiritual as we crane our necks trying to read the list of charges which is always displayed on the psychic's table in a place of minimum visibility. "Do I want a woman or a man?" I wonder aloud. "Women are more spiritual," Tara advises and I tend to agree. Besides, one of the men is called Tim. Psychic Tim? No, I don't think so. I pass along the row of tables. Selena, Angeline – they all sound like lap-dancers to me.

Choosing one's psychic is only half the problem. One still has to decide which reading to have. Crystal ball? Pendulum? Crystal healing? Or maybe Palmistry? Which would be most relevant to predicting a marathon time? Tara selects her reader – a man who claims to be channelling the spirit of the Grey Wolf – and takes her seat. I cannot make up my mind and sit down for a while in the lecture area in the centre of the room. The faith healer is giving a talk to a gaggle of people while they wait for their appointments with their chosen psychics. He smiles winningly through absent front teeth and I wonder whether some conventional dentistry might not be of more use to him than his own techniques. After a couple of minutes I have to admit to myself that I have no interest in faith healing and that I am just being indecisive because I am embarrassed. I bite the bullet and select a female psychic sitting in the far corner of the room, partly because she is called Sandy and looks a bit like Sandie Shaw, but mainly because there is no waiting list as she doesn't currently have any clients. I opt for a composite package which includes palm, tarot and pendulum readings for £30.

I tell Sandy about my mission to run the marathon and ask her what spiritual guidance she can offer me. Despite her clientless state, she doesn't seem very enthusiastic about this customised reading. Nevertheless she takes my hands in hers and examines my nails. This immediately takes me back to my prep school where junior boys would line up before lunch to have their hands inspected by sadistic prefects. The tiniest trace of ink would necessitate being sent back to the washroom to excoriate the offending stain with a pumice stone. "You're the sort of person that works on nervous stress", she tells me, perhaps sensing my repressed childhood anxiety. "You will always create stress whether it is there or not. But you use it as creative energy rather than get ulcers from it." Is she calling me neurotic? Surely my nails aren't *that* bitten? Sandy goes on to check the general shape of my hands. "You're sensitive, quite creative", she opines. A safe guess – as I don't have the word H-A-T-E tattooed across my knuckles it's reasonable to suppose I won't take affront at being accused of being pleasant and interesting. "You're practical," she goes on, turning my hands over, "and open to influences," she adds as if it was written on the other side. Well, I'm listening to *you,* aren't I, I think, but just nod positively.

It quickly becomes apparent that my palms don't have a great deal to communicate about the coming marathon experience. Fair enough I suppose. Apart from getting slapped a lot in exchanging high fives with children along the way, palms are fairly extraneous to the process. Sandy tells me a bit more about my various lines. Apparently I have a long life line, but I expect everyone does. Somehow I can't imagine a palmist ever saying to a client, "Actually yours is extremely short, so do you mind giving me cash rather than a cheque?" She goes on to tell me about my heart line and all the romantic fulfilment it promises for the future. I am beginning to think that consulting a psychic is a bit like going to see a professional flatterer. Looking around me I note that all the other clients are women, presumably with unappreciative husbands and boyfriends.

Perhaps sensing my restlessness Sandy says she is going to see what she can psychically intuit about me. After playing what is basically a variant of Twenty Questions she concludes that I work in advertising. Not far off, I suppose. But maybe her credibility would be more intact if she stuck to divining things that I don't already know the answer to. She is telling me that she can feel that I have a potential for three children when I suddenly remember that I have left my mobile phone switched on. It hasn't actually rung but I fear that it may be interfering with the psychic signals. I reach discreetly into my pocket and switch it off. Sandy is still nattering away about how I will have twins, but apparently I won't ever settle down to family life. With all due respect to my unborn progeny, I remind her gently of my interest in the New York Marathon in November. She suggests we move on to the tarot reading. I take the pack and deal out the cards as directed by her.

I turn up the Traveller. Well, that's a good start. "This is the first card in the major Arcana," Sandy tells me, "and represents going blind into a new area." Can't say much fairer than that, I suppose. The next few cards are all Coins, presumably some sort of warning about the cost of living in New York. Then I get the Chariot. "You have endurance, but you will find it a struggle," is its message according to Sandy. "Your fitness will have to be built up." Well, thanks a lot, Mr Chariot, for stating the bleeding obvious. The next card is the Page of Swords which Sandy interprets as an indication that I will be spending a long time abroad. "Does that mean I'm going to run a very slow marathon?" I ask her, but she ignores me and moves on to the next card. The Wheel of Fortune tells me that success in the marathon won't be the end of it. I will do it again. Next is the Fool. Well, that's what everyone's been telling me since I announced my plan to run this race. "No," says Sandy, "it marks a new beginning." So, what's that? A false start? I think Sandy's getting a bit annoyed with my flippancy and she tries to side-track me onto non-marathoning issues by telling me that my next card, the Empress, indicates that there is a pregnancy in my family. There isn't, hasn't been and is unlikely to be. Then comes the Emperor indicating that a particular man will help me, an older well established person. I have a dreadful vision of that octogenarian that beat Angela carrying me over the finishing line. Sandy points at the next card. "The ten of Wands is about self-doubt," she tells me, but seems refreshingly free from it herself. Luckily for her, tarot cards appear to be able to yield multiple levels of interpretation, many of them self-contradictory, so at some point if she talks for long enough she will arrive at something relevant to my situation. Finally I turn up the Hierophant. Sandy tells me that this indicates that a female person connected with me has back pain. Oh God, she's back on to this bloody pregnancy again.

Astonishingly I find I have started to become embarrassed on her behalf for her getting things wrong. This is ridiculous and so British.

Would you feel bad about your dentist if he pulled the wrong tooth? No, you'd refuse to pay and sue him. Basically, Sandy has been talking a lot of rot and we both know it. At this point I would like to beat a dignified retreat and I think she wouldn't be averse to seeing the back of me either. But I notice that I haven't yet had my pendulum reading, which is included in the price of the consultation.

Sandy duly produces the pendulum. It is not some weighty bronzen bob from a grandfather clock, as I had expected, but a flimsy little girly trinket of the sort one sees advertised on the QVC channel. Sandy explains that I have to ask the pendulum a series of simple questions. If, in response, the pendulum wobbles, it means "yes". If it swings back and forth in a straight line, it means "no". I look at her just to check she's not taking the piss. Am I really supposed to ask personal questions of a bit of Woolworth's jewellery? Oh well, I've paid for it, so here goes. I fix the pendulum a steely gaze and, feeling really quite foolish, enquire of it:

"Will I do the New York Marathon?" The answer comes – "yes", but weak. The pendulum is hedging its bets here.

"Will I bottle out of doing the New York Marathon?" This is a trick question, just to see if the pendulum is on the ball. It doesn't fall for it – "no". Weak again, though.

"Will I do the marathon in under four hours?" "Yes". Strong this time. I feel a flush of pride, immediately followed by a sense of my own patheticness that a blob of metal on a chain has made me feel good about myself.

"Will I ever do another marathon?" A big "yes" from the pendulum. Hmm, worryingly that's what the Wheel of Fortune said.

Sandy looks at me expectantly. Clearly I still have another question, but I have run out of inspiration. I am tempted to ask:

"Have I just been completely ripped off?"

That would be tricky for the pendulum. As it is supposed to be totally all-seeing and all-knowing it would be obliged to give the blindingly obvious answer "yes" to such an easy question and discredit itself, or answer "no" and also discredit itself by telling a blatant fib.

I waive my right to the final question. Sandy hands me a cassette of the reading and asks me for £30. I almost expect her to produce a videotape from a hidden camera showing me asking questions of her jewellery and demand another 30 quid or she'll send copies to all my friends. I hand over the cash and debate whether to ask for a receipt – after all, this is research for my book – but I decide it would seem a deeply unspiritual act after my reading. Besides, I doubt the taxman would gamely sign off "psychic consultation" as a valid business expense. I thank Sandy and go off to look for Tara. Sandy gets up and heads off probably for a ciggy break. I watch her out of the corner of my eye. She is barefoot. *Was* it Sandie Shaw?

Tara's reading is over and she has joined a group of people listening to a middle-aged woman in a shawl give a lecture on psychic auras. I sit down as the lecturer is telling Tara that she can clearly discern her aura which is purple. Tara is visibly pleased, as if she'd just been complimented on her nail varnish, but I can't really work out why. How can one be vain about the colour of one's aura? I mean, what colour is a healthy aura supposed to be? Blue? Red? Gold? There is almost no hue which would not have sounded good (apart from brown maybe, because of course that was last season's colour). The lecturer tunes in to the negative chi being radiated from my presence at the back of the group and soon winds up her talk.

Tara and I repair to the bar for a drink. Over a pleasantly cheap beer and vodka and tonic Tara tells me about her reading. The Grey Wolf was certainly playing the percentages in his predictions. He foresaw travel for her in July/August ('summer holiday possibly?' Tara wonders) and financial problems in December ('could that be Christmas shopping, maybe?'). Still she is broadly satisfied. The Wolf said all the right things: that she would find a boyfriend in July (subsequently borne out), accommodation in April and a job in September. As for Tottenham's season, the Wolf wisely refrained from making any optimistic predictions. After all, Tara's credulousness goes only so far.

CHAPTER 21

Henley Half Marathon

Henley-on-Thames, Oxfordshire
10 October
Distance: 13.1 miles
Time: 1hour 37mins

By this stage in my training programme I am heartily sick of races. I have done eight of them in the last five months and am bored with queuing 30-deep for unflushable lavatories; bored with the mingled smell of grass and Deep Heat in changing tents; bored with the taste of sports drinks and the sodden running vest you get from trying to drink them on the run; and bored with listening to stick-legged, knock-kneed men in shorts talking about their 10K PB. In short, all the paraphernalia that comes with a race day. But there is one event in the running calendar that I would be a fool to miss. The second most prestigious road race in the country after the London Marathon itself – the Great North Run.

Sadly, entries for this heavily oversubscribed event closed back in March, so I have to settle for entering the Henley Half Marathon on the same day instead. To my annoyance almost everyone I have mentioned my marathoning aspirations to has asked me if I'll be doing the Great North Run. Brushing aside my own lack of foreplanning, I convince myself that Henley presents several obvious advantages. Firstly, all serious runners will be up on Tyneside doing the Great North Run, thus leaving me with an easy field. Secondly, I don't want a glitzy high-media-profile event. This is to be my warm-up for the New York City Marathon – in just four weeks' time – and it should be as low-key as possible.

Thirdly, and most importantly, Henley is a 20-minute drive from where I grew up, thus giving me a chance to combine the race with a visit to my aged parents who will greet my arrival with slaughtered fatted calf etc. I walk through the door and my mother's first question is to enquire why I'm not doing the Great North Run, which she has just seen an item about on the six o'clock news.

Still, for once I have the luxury of being able to get changed and perform my pre-race ablutions in the comfort of my parents' home and then being driven straight to the start line. On arrival I limber up with a quick jog round the adjacent playing fields. The PA announces that today's oldest competitor is aged 75. I could have done without this knowledge. For the whole of the race I shall now be terrorised by the thought of being overtaken by this man.

The Half Marathon course is in two loops based around the starting point at Henley Rowing Club. On the first leg we cross the Thames, pass through some outlying hamlets and then describe a long loop round the water meadows back again. There are no mile markers along this course, so we élite athletes who need to know exactly how far we have run in order to pace ourselves for the remainder of the race are reliant on the course stewards for this information. I am by now experienced enough to be able to listen to my body and estimate how far we have run – quite feel like stopping = 1 mile approx.; definitely feel like stopping = 2 miles; desperately feel like stopping = 3 miles. But of course I don't stop.

By Mile Three we are following the long sweep of the Thames back towards the town and runners are strung out along the riverbank, with little knots of individuals coming together here and there like crystals forming on a thread suspended in a supersaturated solution. People who probably don't know each other and certainly don't speak to each other instinctively coalesce in a pack. Perhaps they are "drafting"(the technique of using other runners' bodies to shield you from the wind – although, as the idea is to avoid the wind, it should really be called "draft dodging") or maybe it's just some instinctive form of tribal bonding. In any case, I never seem to end up in any of these groups and always find myself running on my own. The disadvantage of this is that when I am overtaken, it is by several runners one after the other, which is demoralising. At about five miles into the race, as ever, I begin to drift mentally: I wonder why I'm not in one of the groups. I have never been very clubbable. At school I never knew the stringent entry requirements for being in someone's gang. Which football team do you support? Which of the girls out of Abba do you fancy? (It had to be the dark-haired one; fancying the blonde was considered predictable and naff.)

A man overtakes me at about five and a half miles. He, too, seems to be a solo runner. He has a peculiar running stance with his hands on his hips, like Michael Flatley. Has he got a stitch in both sides? Despite overtaking me, he isn't gaining much ground. It looks like he's volunteered for the job of my Personal Nemesis, so I push my pace to keep up with him. We overtake a novice. How do I know he's a novice? Easy. As I draw level with him he glances over his shoulder. I recognise that paranoid reflex. Please, God, let there be *someone* still behind me, it says.

At six miles we pass back through Henley town centre to the general indifference of oarsmen and tourists alike. One of the good things about running a road race is that it ensures that you will always enjoy any return visit to the location (unless you are foolish enough to sign up for the race again). By whatever form of transport I may visit Henley in future, be it walking, riding, boating or motoring, it will by definition be more pleasurable than today, stumbling half-dead across the bridge – unless, I suppose, it's on an open wagon being taken to a place of execution, but that's rare in the Home Counties these days.

We pass the start point and head back out along the Marlow road. Michael Flatley is still just a few metres in front. I have been staring at his back for about three miles. Apart from playing the rear end of a pantomime horse, there is probably no other field of human activity where you spend so much time admiring someone else's back view. The sweat stains on Flatley's white running vest have formed themselves into a sort of Rorschach inkblot test. The perspiration has funnelled down from both shoulder blades in a blurred T-shape. What does it remind me of, I ponder as we run. A vulture, the Weimar eagle, the Angel of Death, Christ crucified... all run through my head in rapid succession. An hour into a half marathon is not a good time to seek a positive life-affirming outlook.

I force myself to keep up with Michael Flatley because it is vital to beat – or at least to do your damnedest to beat – your Personal Nemesis. You see, if you decide that it really doesn't matter about beating him –

after all he's only one guy in a race, no one else knows he's my PN, not even him, so why should I kill myself to finish this race ahead of him? – if you continue with this thinking, then it doesn't really matter if you beat anyone else at all in the race. In fact, you might as well come in last. By an extension of this logic, you might as well stop now and save yourself any further effort, or better still, not have bothered to enter the race in the first place. In fact, what's the use in doing a marathon at all? Indeed, what's the point in exercising? You're going to die anyway – at best you're just putting it off by a few years. You might as well die right here and now by the roadside. This is why it's important to beat your Personal Nemesis. I put on a spurt and edge past Mr Flatley.

We run through the grounds of what was once a stately home and then cross the Marlow road. "How far have we gone?" I shout out to a steward. "Oh, more than halfway," he replies cheerfully. This is uselessly vague to someone who is running a marathon in four weeks' time. I need precise measurements so I can work out my various split times in order to run at my optimum ergonomic pace. Oh, who am I fooling? Frankly, I'm just hoping to *survive* New York next month.

We begin to ascend a monster hill leading towards the village of Fawley. As we slog up this mile-long incline I am overtaken by a man in a Reading Road Runners shirt, with a dog on a lead running ahead of him. The dog is also wearing a Reading Road Runners coat and looks by far the freshest of the competitors, though a little miffed that his running mate will not allow him to stop to investigate the dead squirrel lying by the roadside. I can't see if the dog has a race number. I wonder if the man will allow his pet to maintain its short lead over him at the finish line or whether he will yank the poor beast back at the crucial moment so he can take the honours.

Several other people overtake me in this nightmare climb. I have now discovered the best tactic when you are passed by another runner in a race. It is one I borrowed off Red Shorts in the Hammersmith Riverside Handicap back in July. My previous options when overtaken had been to (a) scowl, (b) pretend I hadn't noticed the person, or (c) put on a spurt and try to stop them getting past, especially on a dangerous road bend with oncoming traffic. A more mature and effective ruse, I have now realised, is to say "well done" to him as he passes. If he is younger than you, he will feel embarrassed. If he is older, he will feel patronised. If he is of roughly the same age as you, then your sporting word of congratulation will make you appear gracious in defeat, while at the same time implying erroneously that you must be pretty good in the first place and that anyone able to pass you must be fairly special. If the person is a woman, then I revert to (a), (b) or (c) above.

Breathlessly we reach the summit and I ask the next steward how far we have left to go. "It's downhill all the way," is all he replies. Maybe I look like I'm on my last legs, but actually what I am seeking from them is not "You're gonna be okay, son"-style deathbed platitudes, but hard data. Besides, if there was any more uphill left I'd have asked him to call me a taxi. Still, it turns out he was not exaggerating about the downhill bit. We descend the hill it took us 15 pain-racked minutes to climb in about two. Sadly, downhill stretches in running races can never compensate for their uphill counterparts. Being equipped with legs, you cannot freewheel like a cyclist and in fact running down a slope puts extra strain on the knees and the backs of your legs. The only good thing about the absence of mile markers and the unreliable stewards is the seductive thought that I might suddenly round a corner and see that magical finish line just ahead. Unfortunately, the last two-mile stretch is along the A 4130 – a road which I have driven down many hundreds of times. So I know exactly how far it is back to Henley. And it's far enough in a car.

Not only am I suffering physically today – from having run 10 miles pretty fast on a hottish day trying to beat this stupid Irish Line Dancer with the proto-Fascist sweat stains – but I cannot rid myself of the demoralising thought that today's finishing line is only half way. My legs too have become blasé. They no longer get excited at the sight of a finishing line. "You're only going to do another race once we finish this one," they grumble as they plod along. Thankfully for once my Personal Nemesis seems to have nothing left when I overtake him for about the seventh time halfway along the final stretch of road and he fades away behind me. I finish in 1:37:38 – a new Personal Best. I am presented with my medal by Miss Henley who appears to be about 12. You know you're getting old when beauty queens start looking like children. Thank goodness I didn't bother to travel 250 miles to check out the infant Miss South Shields.

Inspirational Viewing No 4

The Running Man (1987)

This is the opposite of *Logan's Run*. Instead of the perfect future society, we are shown a dystopia where the élite sit around watching game shows while the oppressed underclasses hunch around braziers on the streets down below. Like *Logan's Run* the movie tells you far more about the decade it was made in than any likely future. It is directed by Paul Michael Glaser, who in attempting to rid himself of the naff 70s tag that *Starsky and Hutch* left him with sadly succeeds only in linking his name to a terrible naff 80s film instead.

Both the film and the eponymous game show within it are misnomers. In fact, Arnold Schwarzenegger, as wronged hero Ben Richards, does far more chainsawing and garroting than running. As with most action movies, it makes the elementary error of assuming that people run only when they are being chased by someone with a flame thrower. Admittedly, Arnie does break into a canter when escaping from a prison camp at the beginning of the film, but he is clearly carrying far too much upper body weight to do even a decent 5K.

Still, his performance, captured on security video, gets him selected to appear on the Running Man game show and some satire on the genre follows. This is at its best in the programme's female house dance troupe who wear leotards, flip back their big hair and do lots of ripply arm waving and peek-a-boo hand movements. It is a brilliant send-up of terrible Paula Abdul videos. Then, when the film's credits roll, it is revealed that Ms Abdul did the choreography and one has to contemplate the unthinkable notion that the dancing was supposed to be good or sexy. In any case the dancers are all white, so something has gone seriously wrong with the future, and dance music itself has not evolved beyond Prince in his pre-symbolist phase.

Apart from a reference to Mandelaburg airport, the only true piece of clairvoyance comes in references to Quake in 97. Ah, the modern viewer thinks, a clever prediction of the computer games phenomenon of the nineties. But, no, it's an earthquake which devastated LA in that year. The dire music that the people of the future are forced to endure now makes sense. Presumably the district where all the cool black rappers lived was at the epicentre of the quake and somehow the suburb where all members of pomp synthesizer bands resided was left unscathed.

Maria Conchita Alonso provides the love and Hispanic interest. Her English is almost as incomprehensible as Arnie's and most of their scenes together cry out for subtitles. She survives being pursued by larger-than-life villains Buzzsaw, Dynamo and Professor Subzero but sadly her movie career was not so resilient and failed to outlive this giant turkey.

The film displays the arrogance of a decade (in this case the most stylistically bankrupt decade ever, i.e. the eighties) to presume that its fashions and values will last beyond the turn of the third digit in the date. Did the designer really think that people would be wearing powder-blue suits with narrow lapels and shoulder pads over baggy white shirts and loosely knotted skinny black ties and sporting wedge haircuts in 2017? Or did the costume budget run out and the actors have to turn up in their own clothes? One can only be indulgent and presume that the art director was aware of the ironies of retro-chic and this is why, 30 years in the future, instead of having sophisticated modern computers, people all have crap old-fashioned ones with green writing on a black screen.

Just for the record, the title song was composed and performed by John Parr. Now here is one man of whom all memory was collectively erased the second the champagne corks had popped on 1 January 1990. Delivered in one of those horrible hoarse, bellowing eighties voices, his composition boasts a chorus that sounds like a Reader's Digest collection of all the terrible meaningless lyrics of that dreadful decade and must be reproduced here for posterity:

"No more lonely nights
With a restless heart
Roll the dice
Make a brand new start."

Like *Logan's Run*, this film tells you almost nothing about running and marathoners may rightly demand their video rental money back. Arnie's main contribution is to kill a lot of people and make corny sub-Roger Moore wisecracks afterwards. The film should really have been named the Punning Man.

Summary

Artistic merit *
Marathoning relevance *
Kitsch factor ****

CHAPTER 22
New York

In the fortnight leading up to my departure for New York I have two marathon dreams.

Dream No. 1: I am running the marathon and I spot my mother standing by the roadside. I stop for a chat and we go somewhere for coffee. Some hours later I realise with horror that I forgot to finish the marathon. And now it is too late. How could I have forgotten? And how could she have let me forget?

Interpretation: deep-seated resentment towards mother (after all, she threw away my priceless 1967 Dalek annual).

Dream No. 2: I am running the marathon but it is a dream marathon. Dream marathons have a tendency to go through buildings, up staircases and sometimes even through people's living rooms. I have just emerged from a warehouse when I see a sign saying 25 miles. I feel fine. Then I see Chris and Ceili from my local pub, the Prince of Wales, ahead of me. Now Chris and Ceili are very able contenders in the Tuesday night quiz but have never struck me as runners. I can't believe they can be beating me at this late stage in the race. Then I look again and see I have misread the sign and we have in fact covered only 15 miles.

Interpretation: deep-seated feeling of inferiority at my ignorance of the periodic table, English league football grounds, prime ministers of New Zealand and other vital quizzing subjects.

I wear my best suit to check in for the flight to JFK (actually it's my only suit – £125 from last year's sale at French Connection) and am rewarded for my smart presentation with an upgrade to Business Class. The suit is a fickle garment, though. Once I have boarded the plane the very item that gained me admittance to Club Class immediately betrays me. You see, any genuine business traveller on a 747 which gets into New York in the early evening wouldn't dream of wearing anything as uncomfortable as a suit for a six-hour flight. Thus all the other passengers in the cabin are in smart casual dress with their business apparel packed away in their luggage. They stare contemptuously at my formal attire, which labels me as an interloper as surely as if I was wearing a lapel badge with Upgrade written on it. I try to feel superior. After all, I am flying to New York to run 26.2 miles and not just to park my arse in a couple of meeting rooms in order to pick up some Air Miles for my winter skiing break.

After we land at JFK the co-pilot earns the only round of applause I have ever heard for the stock "arrival at airport" intercom speech. After blahing on about ground temperature and onward connections he concludes by saying, "and I'm sure you'd all like to join me in congratulating the honeymoon couple who are aboard and I hope their married life will be just as happy as I thought mine was going to be."

I join the queue for US immigration and don't anticipate any problems. There are only 20 or so people ahead of me and I am the sort of person who never gets stopped at customs. I'm not sure exactly what quality this is that I possess – a sort of instinctive anonymity, I suppose – but I know that it is not of much benefit elsewhere in life. For example, I cannot get served at bars and no taxi will ever stop for me in the street. But the upside is that I never have any problems arriving at airports. On this occasion, however, the immigration officer stares at my passport for an impossibly long time, then consults a book and makes a phone call. "Have you ever been in trouble with the police?" he asks me finally. I cast my mind back for possible offences. I have been so dully law-abiding all my life it is an embarrassment. My sister and I were once stopped by a policeman for running across a bridge when I was about 12. That's it as far as my brushes with the law go. Could this childhood misdemeanour be stored on an Interpol computer somewhere? I hope not, as running across bridges will be an important part of the marathon I have come here to take part in. As for my criminal record in New York, I've only been here once before and I've never so much as asked a policeman for the time. "No, never," I reply. Perhaps he can sense my guilt about the bridge-running incident because he takes my passport away and makes me wait in a little room with a forlorn-looking Mexican couple.

Twenty minutes later my passport is returned without explanation and I am waved through to US Customs. The customs officer, not wishing to look any less diligent than his immigration colleague on such an evident contrabandist and illegal alien as myself, immediately instructs me to open my suitcase. Again this never happens to me. He takes out each item carefully and scrutinises it with that mixture of concentration and disdain seen in old ladies rooting through merchandise at jumble sales. He sniffs (literally and metaphorically) at my embarrassingly large collection of toiletries. Then he dismantles my running shoes and finds the little orthotic inserts taped to the underside of the insoles by Brad back in Camden Town. This is just the sort of cunning place where a smuggler would stash packs of crack cocaine (although why anyone would import it from Britain to the US is a mystery). The officer gets quite excited by his find. I explain that I am a pronator and an abductor. He takes this as a voluntary confession to more un-American activities. Sadly his imagination cannot transform these lumps of plastic into anything illicit and he is forced to accept my flimsy cover story that I am running the most famous marathon in the world along with 35,000 other people in this city next week. As I repack my suitcase I ask him why I was singled out. "You've got a common name," he replies. Well, this is America, I muse as I head for the taxi rank. Maybe I can sue my parents.

I have allowed myself a generous 10 days in New York before the actual race in order to spare myself the debilitating effects of running a marathon while suffering from jet lag. What I have not allowed for is the "food lag". Now, in the week before a big race you must taper your training regime. Training at this time would be a bit like revising the day before your exam. There's no point. If you can't do it now, it's too late. With a marathon there is the added danger that you might actually impair your performance. You have already built up the necessary muscle strength and stamina. Heavy exertion now would just deplete your glycogen reserves needed for the ordeal ahead. Most training guides recommend very light exercise or even none at all in the days leading up to the race. Obviously this must be accompanied by a reduction in calorific intake, otherwise you are going to put on extra pounds that you will then have to lug 26.2 miles around the city. Unfortunately, cutting down on food is hard when one has just come to the USA, where people seem to eat at least twice as much as anywhere else and portions in restaurants are huge. Within 24 hours of arriving I am suffering from "food lag": a constant state of exhaustion and listlessness caused by gastronomic overindulgence.

Of course, to say that Americans overeat is not to imply that they are a bunch of gourmands. Quite the contrary, they are extremely fussy about what they overeat. Katina's Diner on Seventh Avenue, Brooklyn, where I go for breakfast on my first morning, has a bewildering submenu of choices. This leads to an awkward Anglo-American stand-off. The waitress has to ask me a whole raft of supplemental questions when taking my order. How do I want my eggs cooked – over easy, over medium, sunny side up? What sort of toast do I want – whole wheat, white, rye, English muffin? All these culinary minutiae are vital to an American, but as a Brit you just feel you are making a fuss (which, of course, we hate). The waitress, probably fearful that her employers will be sued by me if they do not provide waffles cooked to my precise requirements, continues to demand detailed specifications. She is embarrassed because she appears to be coercing a customer. I am embarrassed because I keep having to ask her to explain the terminology (over easy?). It is a distressing experience for both participants. Then, just as my food arrives, an advert pops up on the TV in the corner: "Remember: genital herpes does not have to ruin your life". Maybe not, but it's just ruined my breakfast.

This is a country of strange contrasts. I poke around a few shops, which is always my preferred way to get a feel for the culture of a new country. In a drugstore I am amazed to find that they sell enemas for parents to administer to their children. Then the next day I find myself roped into helping a friend of my host move houses. I haul a few boxes from the friend's car to his third-floor apartment. Strangely, he does not lend a hand but remains upstairs throughout. When I enquire about this seeming rudeness it is explained to me that he cannot leave his baby alone even for the time it would take to descend to street level and pick up a box, in case he is reported for abandoning a child by one of his neighbours. "Mao's Cultural Revolution and Political Correctness in the United States. Compare and contrast."

Being away from England in the first week in November necessitates missing Guy Fawkes night, but this is easily compensated for by the two big events in New York this week: Halloween and the upcoming

Marathon. There is a jack-o-lantern in every window and a Marathon story in every paper. The *New York Times* letters page is running an ongoing correspondence on the issue of "slowpokes". Disgruntled club athletes have written in to complain that "fun runners" should not be allowed to compete in the Marathon, as they just clog up the road, slowing down the serious competitors and spoiling their chances of attaining a PB. I am appalled by this attitude and am almost tempted to write an angry letter in response. After all, one should not forget that these middle-aged or unfit people are running the Marathon for that once-in-a-lifetime sense of personal achievement and often to raise money for charitable causes. Their presence is absolutely vital to the race: after all I need there to be a load of crap runners whom I can be sure of beating very easily. The *New Yorker* carries a feature on the dangers of over-consumption of water. All marathoners are well aware of the risk posed by dehydration in long races. Now it seems a woman died after the Chicago Marathon from hyponatremia, a condition brought on through drinking too much water. So that's one more thing for us runners to worry about. Drinking too much water will be fatal, as will drinking too little, and there is a narrow survival band between the two conditions.

I have picked up a niggling foot injury, so after a couple of cautious jogs around Prospect Park I decide to abandon even light training for fear of aggravating it. My preparation in the week leading up to the race thus involves only some seemingly eccentric and antisocial behaviour:

1) *Shunning any person who is sniffing, coughing, sneezing, purulating, sweating or showing any other indications of infectious illness. Two days before a marathon is not the time to go down with flu.*

2) *Scrutinising restaurant menus for shellfish, eggs, raw meat or other potentially toxic ingredients. Likewise, a bad time to contract food poisoning.*

3) *Belying my supposed level of super-fitness by acting like an old person and taking huge amounts of time to sit down, stand up, pick up objects etc. Slipped discs and pulled muscles are also not to be desired.*

During this time the New York climate shifts through the whole gamut of meteorological possibilities. At the weekend it is shirt-sleeves weather.

Then on Tuesday gale-force winds suddenly whip through Manhattan, accompanied by driving rain. At the end of the week there is a sudden cold snap. My own paranoia runs through a similar spectrum: I am convinced that I'm going to be ruled out of the race with, respectively, sunstroke, pneumonia and frostbite as the week progresses. These random weather patterns are good news for the sports stores who for this week every year make a killing out of marathoners' neuroses. On Monday they have a run on sunblock. By Friday they are shifting woolly hats and gloves by the truckload.

There remain two pieces of psychological preparation I have to undertake for the Marathon. Some while ago I decided that while in New York I must get a haircut from a good old-fashioned Italian-American barber. Walking down Seventh Avenue in Brooklyn I come across just the place. The window has a bleached-out look and the display has clearly not been changed for 20 years. It features a framed faded photo of the New York Yankees' droopy-moustached World Championship-winning team from 1978. The proprietor is obviously so out of touch that he did not notice last week's ticker-tape parade that marked his team's winning of this year's World Series (and a fair few in between). This is the establishment I've been looking for. I go in.

Inside there is total silence except for the hum of something – a strip light possibly or a tongs warmer. If this were a Coen brothers movie, there would be a fly buzzing in the window. But there isn't. The fly died some years ago. There is a row of big old-fashioned barber's chairs but only one is occupied, by a customer who appears to be asleep or dead. Maybe he passed away during the interminably long process of having his hair cut. The single barber, an old man dressed in white coat and check trousers, shuffles slowly across the linoleum floor. Everything he wants seems to be placed at opposite ends of the shop. There is one person ahead of me in the queue who sits reading a sports paper. I look at the doddering barber anxiously. Will he make it to me?

The room is cluttered with obsolescent furniture. There is a manual till with big keys on stalks like an old fashioned typewriter. A portable TV with Martian-like antenna that doesn't look like it's been switched on since they invented colour. A rocking chair stands in the corner and in the centre of the room there is a ride-upon model car for kids. The waiting customer who is in his 50s could well have been the last person to have a go on it. The whole room is in washed-out brown. The only thing that is not brown is the incongruous climber plant in the window. Its tendrils curl desperately towards the sun, their progress a little faster than that of the barber. There has been no sound in this room since the barber cheered the Yankees in '78.

I sit down. The single waiting customer soon abandons his paper and succumbs to the torpor, head slumped on chest. Another man comes in, wearing a baseball cap and Yankees jacket. Funny how elderly men can wear such things in this country. He hangs up his jacket and goes to the back of the shop. The trickle of urine rings out in the silence. The man returns and takes a seat. He is obviously familiar enough with the place to know where the lavatory is, yet doesn't say a word of greeting to the barber. The clippers buzz cheerfully but there is no ice-breaking "See the game last night, sir?" or "Been away this year, sir?" Finally the barber drags a huge mirror up from the far corner of the shop and hoists it behind the customer's head. This effort looks like it will finish him off. Opportunely the customer wakes up and nods silently. He pays and leaves, still with no audible word exchanged. The next customer steps up to the chair. The barber leans over and mutters to him, like a priest administering last rites. The customer immediately drops into unconsciousness as if hypnotised. The barber sets off on the slow journey to the far side of the shop for his clippers. I have a feeling that this was what the world was like in prehistoric times, when millions of days passed unrecorded before they had names like Tuesday or Saturday. Animals grazed, fought, slept, mated, grazed some more, all in their own uncommunicating worlds. Events repeated themselves and played themselves out in an eternal dumb cycle. As I wait my turn I resolve that I will fight the silence and provoke conversation and possible controversy by asking the barber for a "runner's haircut".

When my turn comes, I seat myself in the huge chromium chair, haul my feet on to the footrest and make my bold request. The barber doesn't dignify me by nodding, frowning or indeed react to my demand in any way other than to shuffle off in search of his clippers. He returns and without further ado he strikes me a glancing blow to the side of my head with them. I swear I hear a "flump" and feel a distinct breeze as a huge swathe of my beautiful hair falls to the floor. His clippers have clearly been set to "sheep shear" mode. I try to protest but it is already too late. One side of my head is ecologically devastated. He'll have to continue now to even it out. Maybe he misheard me and thought I asked for a "gunner's haircut" and presumed I'd been drafted. Or, more likely, this is just the haircut he has been giving since 1934. And if it's been good enough for four generations of Americans, it's good enough for me.

I make polite small talk. The barber responds and, like a monk released from his vow of silence, suddenly nothing now can stop him from talking. His name is Edde, he's Italian by birth and he's 78 years old. He retired once but got bored at home and came back to work. Incidentally it took Edde many long minutes to convey this basic biographical information to me. I am now beginning to realise why none of his customers talks to him. For a start, although his English is probably good, his accent is incomprehensible, to this Brit at least, and there's only so much encouraging nodding and agreeing one can do before the conversation starts to become a little one-sided. Secondly, I am reluctant to distract his shaking septuagenarian hands as they wield the cut-throat razor in close proximity to my jugular vein. The unaccustomed sound of social intercourse has roused the waiting customer from his slumber. He tells me that his son is running in the Marathon too. The son's running number is five thousand and... well, five thousand and something (dad doesn't remember exactly). But, anyway, I should say hi to him if I see him in the race. So, er, what? I buttonhole all male runners with numbers in the 5000s and ask them if their dad wears a baseball jacket and had a haircut on Wednesday?

By now Edde has transferred most of the hair from my head to the floor. He finishes off by cutting my fringe, ruler straight and Herman Munster high. I look 10 years younger, he tells me as he unties my bib. How can this be, I mentally question, when he has, with a dexterity that belies his years, cut off the brown hairs and left all the grey ones still attached to my head? He seems to notice the horror with which I gaze at my crew-cut reflection in the mirror and jokes that he has a special glue to put the hair back on if I'm not satisfied. I smile as best I can. Despite everything, this is the runner's haircut I wanted. Very low wind resistance. I give Edde a big tip. I am just relieved that the experience is over and we both lived.

My second mission is to have a pedicure in order to give my feet a treat by way of an advance apology for what I am to put them through on Sunday. A beautician's shop just along Seventh Avenue from Edde's is doing a special deal: manicure and pedicure for $15. Having never had such a thing before, I've no idea if this is a steal or a total rip-off aimed at beauty therapy virgins like me, but I can't resist the thought of a bargain. Why not go for the job lot and treat my hands, too? I don't want to go high-fiving any spectators with sharp unkempt nails and risk ending up on the wrong end of a $10m lawsuit for malicious wounding.

The hardened marathoners among you will be tut-tutting at this point. A pedicure? No proper runner has a pedicure before a marathon. Not because it is vain or wimpy but simply because no proper runner — that is one pounding out 50+ miles per week — has any toenails left before a marathon. The fact that none of mine have dropped off is withering evidence that I have been skimping on the mileage.

In the beauty salon I am assigned Conchita, a plump broad-faced Hispanic teenager who if she speaks more than three words of English does not deign to waste them on me. Her own name is not included in her vocabulary and I call her Conchita because of her resemblance to the Spanish tennis player Conchita Martinez. She refuses to smile and only speaks to issue orders to me using her full lexicon: "right"(foot or hand) "left"(ditto) and "water"(stick one or both of the previous in). Small talk with her seems even more doomed than it had been with Edde so I sit in silence and survey the room. Needless to say I am the only male customer here in this Woman's Realm and, as Conchita scrubs aggressively at my feet with a pumice stone, I try to make sense of the arcane rituals going on all around me.

After a few minutes Conchita indicates that my pedicure is complete by abruptly and wordlessly leaving the room. I move over to the manicure table pointed out to me by the manageress and sit down. A grey-haired bouffante woman in a check suit smiles at me and indicates with a circular hand movement that I am sitting at the wrong side of the table. Embarrassed at my ignorance of beauticianary procedures I quickly switch sides, fearful of earning an admonishing look from Conchita. The manageress comes over and tells me that the rest of the clientele have been trying to guess why I am having this pedicure. They have come to the conclusion that I must be getting married. "What, in open-toed sandals?" I want to protest. Oh well, this is America, after all.

Conchita returns, sits at her side of the table and abandoning her modest vocabulary grabs my right hand and starts to slap lotion on it. It is a strange experience, sitting just across the table from her, close enough to clinch, sharing my body space with a person who is ignoring me. She even manages to pick at my fingernails with a scalpel-like implement while gazing over my shoulder into the middle distance. It is as if I am some lower invertebrate life form or maybe her spouse.

In the absence of any conversation of my own I listen in on other people's. The manageress is giving a manicure to a recently arrived customer, a hard-bitten, fox-faced woman in her 40s with Patti Smith dyed black hair and a fake leopardskin coat. Patti is clearly taking advantage of the salon's special offer for some cut-price therapy ($15 for half an hour's individual attention must compare favourably with most New York shrinks). She moans unceasingly about her job and her boyfriend (she has obviously stopped off for this impromptu treatment *en route* from one to the other). "You're looking great," the manageress tells Patti to stem the flow of self-pity. She catches my eye and raises her eyebrows apologetically. A girl's gotta get a tip somehow, her look says.

Conchita finishes my manicure. I know this because while continuing to ignore me she moves over to another table and starts work on a new customer. I pay the manageress who seems grateful for this brief break from Patti's whinging. I take my change and try to think of a single thing Conchita has done to merit a tip. I can't think of any, so I give her one anyway just to see if I can get her to smile. No smile, but I discover that "thank you" is also in her vocabulary.

The next day I go down to the New York Marathon Expo by the East River to pick up my race number and other official paraphernalia. One of the traditional problems of running in a race which attracts 35,000 runners is that it can sometimes take ten or fifteen minutes to cross the starting line. This tended to render one's official finishing time highly inaccurate. Technology has now come to the rescue and this year we runners will each be equipped with an electronic chip which will give us a personalised time for crossing the start and finish lines and various other points along the route (though as far as I am able to ascertain the device is not sophisticated enough to detect and subtract time spent in the portaloos.) It is about the size of a 10p piece and attaches to the runner's shoe. I am tempted to keep it in my pocket and at some point just before the race start to attach it secretly to one of the dozens of police motorcycle outriders that precede the marathon. Possibly the race organisers might be suspicious when the official timings show that a 39-year-old runner competing in his first-ever marathon came in first having maintained a consistently blistering pace always 10 metres ahead of the front runners. Of course, the risk is that the cop might decide he'd earned his Sunday double-time rate and pop off for a bagel somewhere halfway through.

I pick up my race number, shoe tag, complimentary T-shirt and cap. I wander round the rest of the Expo and collect all the other freebies on offer at the stalls, mainly energy bars. One stall is promoting upcoming signings with various famous marathon runners, most of whom have African names and none of whom, sadly, I have heard of. What a shame that marathoners seem destined for obscurity. If Rosie Ruiz was here signing autographs, people'd be queuing round the block.

The night before the race I go out for a light pasta meal and then return home to check over all my kit for the next morning. New Yorkers have a sensible habit of leaving unwanted clothes on railings so that any needy person can help themselves. Earlier in the week I took a shabby jacket and grubby pair of pants off a neighbour's fence. I should explain that there is a lot of hanging around involved before the start of a marathon and sensible runners will bring some old clothes, or a binliner with arm holes cut in it, which they can wear to keep out the cold and then discard once the race starts. I try on the jacket and pants and decide I would probably look smarter in the binliner. I lay out my running kit and pin my race number to my old faithful shirt. Training guides advise you never to attempt a marathon wearing shoes or clothes that you are not used to. Over the huge distance we will be running, unfamiliar shoes can pinch, brand new shirts can chafe and untested shorts can induce unpleasant groin rashes. Boring, safe running kit is good for runners, but not so helpful for your loved ones who will be waiting for you along the route. It is a little-known fact that it is almost as exhausting to watch a marathon as it is to compete in one. I found this out the previous year when I was standing on the sidewalk watching for the various people I knew in the race. Your friend, whom you are trying to spot in a crowd of 35,000 moving at an average speed of 8mph (needles and haystacks come to mind), has helpfully informed you that she will be wearing a white T-shirt (along with 14,867 other people, she omits to mention). As your head sweeps back and forth scanning the runners as they speed past 10 abreast, your vision begins to blur and you get a migraine. Mentally apologising to my family I lay out exactly the same blue wicking vest and baggy black shorts that have seen me through all my training runs. Some friends have suggested that I should write my name on my shirt. This will ensure that all the spectators I pass will root for me and shout my name out. I'm not so sure I want this. From my experience of races so far, I tend to get very irritated by spectators – and that's over distances only half of what I will be running tomorrow. No, I decide. Amid all the Scotts and Carries and Sue Anns and Forrests I will be the Man with No Name. It worked for Clint Eastwood.

I have spent the previous few nights sleeping on a mattress on the living-room floor of the Brooklyn apartment where I am staying. Tonight, Tony, my host, has generously offered me the use of his bed (without him in it, I hasten to add). I retire at about 11 o'clock and set the alarm for 5.00 a.m. I feel too excited to sleep. Tony's alarm clock seems to be ticking the phrase "Krypton factor krypton factor krypton factor" in my ear. I drop off a couple of times, but keep waking in a panic that I have overslept. From four o'clock I no longer dare sleep but just lie listening to the clock which is now ticking: "First class upgrade first class upgrade first class upgrade". I have probably managed a total of about three hours' fitful dozing. I lie on my back, trying to be aware of my body and make myself appreciate that this is the fittest and healthiest I will ever feel in my life. In nine hours' time I will be half-dead. Tomorrow I will be hungover. After that it will be the long slow decline to physical decrepitude. This is as good as it gets. I must admit it doesn't feel that good at 5.00 a.m. on a dark chilly New York November's morning. I haul myself out of bed just as the alarm sounds.

CHAPTER 23
The New York Marathon

New York, NY
7 November
Distance: 26.2 miles
Time: 3 hours 48 mins 11 secs

At 5.30 a.m. I am waiting for the F train at the Seventh Avenue subway station in Brooklyn. There is only one other person on the platform – a slender pretty girl in her mid-20s. She is wearing a tracksuit and carrying a kit bag and I suspect she might be a fellow competitor. We strike up a conversation. Meghan is a masseuse (pronounced as in the phrase "the *mass use* of fluorocarbons has significantly damaged the ozone layer"). On the train into Manhattan she gives me a quick anatomical lecture on the structural flaws of the human kneecap. It would never have won God any design awards (not even if He'd had some sycophantic archangel awarding them). It has no muscles attached, just lots of flimsy tendons. Once damaged, it will never recover. This will be her first and last marathon, Meghan tells me. She's going back to swimming afterwards.

We emerge at the New York public library at 6.45 and I experience the familiar eerie feeling of being in a 1950s B-movie. At this unearthly hour of a Sunday morning the streets are crammed with thousands of people in tracksuits, moving calmly and silently in the same direction. We are ushered into the waiting fleet of coaches by enthusiastic teams of marathon volunteers. Like army dispatchers sending troops off to some distant war zone, they are thankful that we've volunteered so they don't have to do it. The New York City Marathon passes through all five boroughs of the city and its start point is located on Staten Island, to where we will now be whisked. It should be added that the only part of Staten Island we will actually set foot on during the course of the Marathon is the Verrazano Narrows suspension bridge which takes us straight out of the godforsaken place and into Brooklyn. The coaches speed us through Manhattan under a level slate of grey cloud. The buildings across the East River look like they were quarried out of the sky. At first the streets we pass along are deserted but then people start to emerge – normal people walking their dogs, or popping out for a paper and a bagel; normal people who have no intention of running 26.2 miles before lunch.

We arrive at Fort Wadsworth on the east side of Staten Island at 7.35. This huge camp is run along military lines by real US Army soldiers in fatigues. They clearly have orders to shoot deserters and eye us dismissively. "I'd like to volunteer to warm them up," I overhear a barrel-chested GI say to his sergeant as we file through the gate. The soldier's disdain is understandable. Half of us runners are wearing old jumble sale clothes which we intend to discard before the race, the rest are dressed as giant Power Bars thanks to a complimentary hand-out of yellow binliners printed with the logo of this energy-boosting snack. We do not look like anyone's army.

I do a tour of the camp, trying to be stirred by the momentous occasion. "Is this the way they say the future's meant to feel?" as Jarvis Cocker once pondered, "or just 20,000 people standing in a field?" There is very little to do except go to the loo, but this is an activity into which we throw ourselves with zeal. People are already queuing 10 deep for a single Port-a-San, but if you walk round the corner there is a bank of 20 totally unoccupied cubicles. Marathoners are not that bright really. I take the opportunity to relieve myself. Unfortunately, with the best will in the world, going to the lavatory cannot fill up all the available time till the start so I poke around the collection of marquees and stalls in search of some other distraction. An announcement on the public address system informs us that the pre-Marathon religious services are about to start. We have a choice of denomination: Christian, Jewish or Muslim. The Muslims probably find themselves better stretched for the race with all the bowing they do and the Jews get to wear little hats to keep out the cold, but sadly I am stuck with my nominal faith of C of E.

As I enter the Christian tent the faithful are droning a dreary hymn the title and only line of which appears to be "Jesus Loves Me". Only if he's tone deaf, I think, and take a place at the back. An Episcopal priest in full running kit hops up on to the podium and delivers a rousing sermon about the "inner running" he has been doing in preparation for the Marathon. This, he tells us, involves prayer, meditation and relaxation. And I'm the mug who's been slogging round Hampstead Heath in the rain, I think ruefully. The priest says a short prayer and ends it with, "Go for it! Amen." We then sing another hymn which presents a strange spectacle. I know that all men are equal in the sight of God – and in this secular age He's probably grateful for anyone He can get – but surely He draws the line at 200 worshippers singing "How Great Thou Art" dressed as Power Bars? The hymn ends and we are invited to give Jesus a round of applause. We clap dutifully. Some disrespectful souls even whistle and whoop. Now it is time for Communion featuring, no doubt, Energy Hosts supplied by Power Bars Inc, enabling worshippers to combine Absolution with Carb-Loading. I decide to pass on this and slip off to search out the so-called Longest Urinal in the World.

I wander round for a long time before I finally come across this much publicised feature at Fort Wadsworth. It turns out to be just a piece of plastic gutter pipe. But long it is. I pace it out and find it clocks up an impressive 100 metres. I take a pee and check the colour of my urine. Pale – good. I overhear a pair of peeing runners discussing how nervous they feel. One of them even claims to have thrown up. I don't really understand this. How can one be nervous about a race which only the élite few will finish in under three hours? There's so much time in this race – too much really – time enough to fall over and pick yourself up again, time to stop to tie your shoelace, to dawdle for a drink or a chat with a friend, to take souvenir photos and see the sights. It's not as if we were doing the Olympic 100 metres, where if you get a bad start you might as well just stop running straightaway with four years of gruelling preparation right down the toilet. *That's* something to be nervous about.

My bowels and bladder are now thoroughly evacuated and I don't know what to do next. It's too cold to sit down, but I don't want to tire myself by just walking round and round. The only other available distractions are to eat complimentary bagels, drink complimentary coffee or have a complimentary Breathe Right strip fitted on your nose. I find myself in front of a stage where various nondescript dignitaries (heads of participating running clubs, the Chief Warden of the park, the Mayor of New York, etc.) are making dull speeches and being greeted with good-natured indifference. The leader of the French contingent gets up and wishes good luck to his 2,500 compatriots running in the race. They are the largest foreign group. The French are natural runners – as the late General de Gaulle proved, his nation can hold their own beaky-nose-wise with any on earth. I decide to go to the loo again. Not out of any physiological need but because with a cold Atlantic wind now blowing the loos are the cosiest place to sit, especially after they have been used a few dozen times and the warmth is rising from the open cesspit beneath. As I stand in the queue, now 15 deep, one wag runs along a row of 75 cubicles banging on each door and shouting urgently: "Come on! Come on!" Terrified occupants emerge, jogging pants awry, fearing they have missed the start of the race.

Towards 10.30 this collection of hobos and Power Bars begins to assemble at the designated muster areas. From there we are shepherded by race officials towards the official starting line on the Verrazano Narrows Bridge. As we walk, people start to discard their surplus clothing and the ground we move over soon comes to resemble a bring and buy sale that has been hit by a tornado. At 10.40 I am part of a 35,000-strong crowd gathered on the bridge in a high wind, crammed too close together with many of us standing on one leg as we attempt to perform stretches. By some fluke, or unremembered lie about intended time put on my entry form, I find myself only a couple of hundred metres from the actual start line.

We are a captive audience with nowhere to go until the starting gun sounds and so various officials take advantage of the opportunity to bore us. The right-wing Mayor of New York, Rudy Giuliani, makes a speech and is enthusiastically booed by the liberal runners. Then there is the singing of the American national anthem. "O'er the ramparts we watched were so gallantly streaming; And the rocket's red glare, the bombs bursting in air", we sing lustily (or mime lustily in my case as I don't know the words). There are no rockets or bombs in the air today but instead cast-off trousers and jackets fly surreally past. An excitable man takes the microphone and informs us that, "This is the New York City Marathon." As if some of us might be in the wrong race and not yet have noticed. "I'm so sorry", we might say, picking our way apologetically through the 25,000 strong crowd behind us. "I thought this was Boston." One discipline at which the Americans are undoubtedly world-beaters is Shouting Through PA Systems. "It's a Great Day for a Marathon," the man, presumably the race organiser, is now enthusing at 250 decibels, "And This is the Greatest Marathon in the Greatest City in the World *and Everybody's Going to Win*." Cue wild applause and whoops. What rubbish, I think. If that were the case, why don't we all walk the course holding hands? I know I am not going to win this race, literally or metaphorically, but someone (and I hope lots of people) will finish behind me. Not coming last: that's the point.

A cannon goes off, there is a huge cheer and, as ever, nothing happens. A few last-minute items of clothing are hurriedly discarded and flung recklessly aside. A flight of yellow and black balloons drifts past. We start to press forward excitedly, then we are walking and finally break into a restrained trot. I'm not sure at exactly what point we cross the start line, but it seems that only about three minutes have elapsed since the gun.

We are running, tightly bunched, now and the first thing I discover is that the Longest Urinal in the World is not the 100-metre gutter in Fort Wadsworth. The Longest Urinal in the World is actually the Verrazano Narrows Bridge. To my amazement less than half a kilometre into the race, men are lined up all along the rusted iron parapet voiding nervous bladders into the bay below. "Why didn't you go before we set off?" their mothers' voices are saying in their heads. "We did, but we need to go again," they whine as the wind-chill factor cold-welds their penises to the metal girders of the bridge. Manhattan is away on the left looking like a tiny model you could reach over and pick up. It is impossible to imagine that we are going to have to run there. At least in London you can't see Big Ben from Greenwich Park. Down below a couple of boats are squirting big jets of water in the air, like whales. I don't know if this is intended to be ornamental or whether it serves some useful waterway maintenance function. I really must ask someone about this.

Everyone is very densely packed at this early stage of the race as we sort ourselves out in terms of pace. One man is running backwards. Please God, don't let him beat me. Another man in dark glasses, presumably blind, is holding hands with a hopefully sighted companion. The right side of the bridge is congested but there is plenty of overtaking room on the left. However, as I soon find out, running here leaves you exposed to the vicious whipping 30mph wind. Bizarrely, we seem to have disturbed a Japanese man who had chosen what he thought would be a quiet Sunday morning to commit suicide and is nonplussed to find himself observed by 35,000 passing runners. He climbs slowly up the parapet and vanishes over the top. Did he jump? Or was he just a photographer trying to get a better view? We are far too exuberant to allow this possible human tragedy to spoil our mood. Cars passing on the opposite carriageway honk and we dissipate energy needlessly by hollering and cheering in response. There is an *esprit de corps* that I've never felt before. If somebody led communal singing I'd probably join in right now. We are fired up with a common purpose – no matter how futile. This of course is how armies are made.

The first mile post is in the middle of the Verrazano bridge which is the highest point of the Marathon, so we have the comforting thought that it's all downhill from here on. Normally the opening 20 minutes of a race are exhausting as you fight oxygen debt. But in this case, with the freezing wind lashing us high up on an exposed bridge over an estuary, it is not possible to feel exhaustion. I simply don't have enough nerve endings in my body to register any form of unpleasantness other than sheer cold. And given the choice between standing in your underwear exposed to an arctic gale or running, one tends to prefer the second, more thermodynamically efficient, option.

As we descend from the bridge to the relative warmth of the Brooklyn–Queens Expressway, I try to force myself to be properly conscious of the moment. Here I am finally running the New York City Marathon. This should be the big occasion, the culmination of this artistic and sporting endeavour, but it feels like just another road race. It has all the usual ingredients – irritating runners who go too fast and overtake me; annoying runners who go too slow and get in my way; and infuriating runners who run at the same speed as me and bug me with their personal habits. For example, just ahead of me runs Snot Rocketer, who every two minutes evacuates the contents of each nostril in turn at a reverse angle of 45° causing me to have to sidestep smartly. He is only marginally less irritating than Happy Snapper, running alongside him, who every few hundred metres will suddenly stop dead, do an about turn, pull out his camera and line up a suicidal photo of 25,000 runners bearing down on him. "Do it once. Do it right. Never do it again." a T-shirt in front of me proclaims. I'm with you there, brother.

Interestingly, the New York Marathon has many fewer charity fancy-dress runners than London; and of the people in costume, a good number are dressed as Beefeaters or British bobbies, suggesting that the runners might not be native New Yorkers. I don't think this state of affairs necessarily implies that Americans are inherently less charitable than us Brits. It probably has more to do with their natural self-confidence versus our instinctive diffidence. We don't like to be seen to be taking things too seriously, just in case we turn out to be crap at them.

We turn on to Fourth Avenue in Brooklyn along which we will now have to run approximately 77 blocks. Here I get my first taste of the legendary vocalness of the American spectator. Luckily I don't immediately hear anyone shout my bogey phrase of "Keep going" – although Power Bars have printed up large yellow cardboard signs which read "Keep Running" with a space to put your runner's name. (If you ever take up running, reader, I urge you to buy a rival brand of energy snack.) Those encouraging us from the sidewalk tend to restrict themselves to the simple exhortation "Go!" to which they will append anything they see written on a T-shirt – names of people ("Go Terry!") or organisations ("Go NYPD!") or even countries ("Go Australia!"). I wonder if I could get a leading brand of pet food to sponsor me to have the single word "Cat" printed on my shirt.

As well as spectators we also encounter our first drinks station, supplying us with water and Gatorade (which turns out to be an isotonic drink and not, as I had previously supposed, an alligator charity). I grab two cups of water, drink one and pour the other one over my head. I'm not particularly hot or dehydrated, this is just what real marathoners do. We pass the first of the promised 15 live bands along the route. They are a leaden, leather-clad heavy rock outfit with a surly Goth female singer. Pseudo-Teutonic angst is not what you need when running a marathon and I up my pace a little to get out of earshot quicker. I overtake a luckless runner who obviously had the misfortune to contract a cold a couple of days ago. He has unwittingly compounded his discomfort by wearing a Breathe Right strip. This is essentially a piece of sticking plaster that is fitted across the bridge of the nose, its purpose being to dilate the nostrils and thus increase air supply. Sadly, if you have a head cold you just get a river of snot pouring straight into your mouth. I turn away from this unsavoury sight and watch as we pass a line of boiler-suited workers standing on the roof of their factory by the roadside. "You're nowhere near yet," a spectator reminds us gracelessly at five miles. I still have energy left to flash him a scathing smile.

Before a marathon there is always a temptation to be wildly optimistic about the pace at which you expect to run it. Sitting somewhere in comfort with a drink in your hand planning your race strategy, there seems no reason why you should not do the race in, say, seven-minute miles. However, if you allow this wishful thinking to communicate itself to your loved ones they will just be looking out for you far too early and by the time you come wheezing up they will already have gone off for coffee somewhere thinking they have missed you. My mother and my sister, Frances, have kindly flown out to support me and have arranged to be waiting for me between Miles Eight and Nine. I am running right on my predicted eight-minute-mile schedule but still I fail to see them. They had arranged to be on the left side of the road, so I hug the left lane. Running at the side of the road is always a liability. You get impeded by other runners who have stopped to talk to friends, slowed down for water, or have already given up and are walking. Plus we are now passing through Bedford-Stuyvesant – Spike Lee country – and scores of begging children's hands are held out by the roadside. It's like being in India except in this case they're actually seeking high fives and it would be churlish not to oblige them despite the retarding effect.

I am starting to crave something. It is not water or bananas or even Vaseline of which there is no shortage at the various pit stops or from obliging spectators. It is silence. It sounds deeply ungrateful on my part but I am already getting annoyed by the famed New York spectators screeching and bawling the whole time. If I were organising this race, I'd have a Peace Mile from which all spectators are banned and runners can run in silence for a few minutes and dwell on their own thoughts. Then at Mile 10 my dream suddenly comes true. We pass through Williamsburg – world centre of Hassidic Judaism. Soberly suited and hatted adults wait politely and attentively by the roadside. Not a whoop or holler passes their lips. Their children stand obediently and silently in front of them and observe the race as if on a school trip to the Metropolitan Museum of Art. This, I realise, would have been the perfect place for my loved ones to have waited for me. Not only would I have heard them shouting my name in the comparative silence, but also by wearing any colour other than black they'd have stood out a mile from every other spectator in the vicinity.

We pass another of the roadside bands (six down, nine to go), a three-piece grunge outfit who are in the process of doing a big stadium ending. The guitarist leaps in the air, hits a power chord and yells "THAN–GUEW very much." I'm sorry? Does he seriously expect people who have just run a dozen miles to applaud him, whose maximum exertion this morning so far has been to jump on to his amp during his solo? The annoying thing about the bands I have seen so far (apart from being almost universally heavy rock acts) is that Sod's Law dictates that at the exact moment I run past they will either be between songs or, worse, in the middle of the drum solo. By Bedford Avenue, the music budget is running low. A single man sits on a stoop with a beatbox and a keyboard balanced on his lap. I later find that the only bands who seem to have given any thought to what genre of music athletes in the latter stages of mental and physical exhaustion might actually want to listen to are the orchestras playing gentle ambient Eastern melodies at the two Sri Chinmoy stalls. The music may be pleasing but I'm not sure I'm going to break off from a marathon to root through the ginseng creams and essential oils they have on offer at their roadside tables.

We've run through Greenpoint, the Polish enclave, and now have to embark on our second major ascent, the Pulaski Bridge, which takes us from Brooklyn over into Queens. I pass the half marathon point, halfway up the slope to the bridge, at a respectable 1:49. I try to double this figure to work out what theoretical finishing time this will give me – an easy mental calculation for anyone not slogging up a hill after having just run 13 miles. Halfway down the slope on the other side, I work it out: 218 minutes. After several more minutes – there is just no blood available – my brain, like one of those old-fashioned hand-cranked adding machines that I dimly remember from school, finally churns out the answer: 3:38. A good time, but sadly the laws of entropy tend to determine that the second half of a marathon is run slower than the first. As we've now passed the halfway point I try to visualise the rest of the race as being all downhill. This psychological trick does not convince my feet which are now embarking against their will on their longest-ever competitive run. If I was a little fitter I'd quite enjoy this race, I think to myself, before realising that if I was a little fitter I'd try to run the race a little faster and hate it just as much. "Don't worry. Run happy" a banner on the sidewalk proclaims. I want to leap over the barrier, landing with my full weight on the person's feet, and say, "Right, now *you* try running and/or being happy." There must be something healthy about all this negativity that running releases in me.

Queens is the largest borough in New York, but frankly it passes in a bit of a blur. I recall a biggish building (later I find that this was the Citicorp tower – the tallest building in New York outside Manhattan) but that's about it. At 16 miles we cross the East River into Manhattan via the Queensboro Bridge, aka the 59th Street Bridge. "The 59th Street Bridge Song", as all pub-quizzers like me know, is the real name of the Simon and Garfunkel song that all non-pub-quizzers think is called "Feelin' Groovy". "Slow down, you move too fast. You gotta make the morning last," I sing to myself, but find these hippie sentiments rather out of kilter with the commitment required for finishing a marathon before mid-afternoon. By now all the other runners seem to have retreated into their own private hells. Jaunty banter is a thing of the past. Looking dignified is, too. I pass one woman who is crouched down in a strut of the bridge in a foetal position looking like she's bowed out of reality completely. On closer inspection I realise she's just attempting to have a discreet pee. The bridge seems to rise forever to clear Roosevelt Island. This is torture. Now, torture is bearable just so long as you know that it is finite. This is why Hell and the idea of everlasting torment is such a useful religious notion to scare the shit out of people. However agonising this current ordeal is, my brain clings to the laws of physics and the fact that this bridge will at some stage even off and then actually descend. This race itself will be over in just a couple of hours' time. My life, too, will end in its turn, but hopefully not before Mile 26. Sadly, I for one will never again be able to associate this bridge with the gentle mellow place where Paul Simon had a conversation with a lamp-post.

Finally, blissfully, the bridge levels off and then descends into Manhattan. I spot a vacant loo cubicle by the side of the road and stop for a pee, just to be on the safe side. There is no blood left in my fingers and I waste valuable seconds tugging numbly at the cord on my shorts to loosen it. I manage to pass a feeble trickle of urine, but as I tumble back out into the race I am glad I made the effort. A friend of mine had an embarrassing experience with a bursting bladder once at Mile 25 in Central Park, where crowds are densest and lavatory facilities non-existent, but sadly she made me swear not to repeat the story in this book.

The road twists round through 270° and deposits us on First Avenue where the crowds are suddenly five deep on both sides of the road. There is a charged and motivating atmosphere around us as the individual annoying shouts of "Keep going!" merge into one long encouraging roar. The advantage of First Avenue is that it is wide. This allows me to run in the middle and not get stuck at the sides with the walking wounded, the dehydrated, the high-fivers, and the banana-seekers. The disadvantage of First Avenue is that it is long and dead straight. It stretches for about three miles up ahead of me, receding to a vanishing point, an endless expanse of bobbing heads, like a coastal shelf full of seagulls in a wildlife documentary. I am reminded of that famous *New Yorker* poster that people who were pretending to be cosmopolitan used to have on their walls in the early eighties. You know, the Saul Steinberg crayon drawing with the foreshortened perspective where you can see all the way along Madison Avenue to the Statue of Liberty, the Atlantic Ocean, Europe, Asia and Australia and there, just beyond Australia, the Finishing Line. Many runners are wearing sunglasses against the glare, but perhaps we should be equipped with blinkers like racehorses.

My running number has absorbed all my sweat and hangs stiffly like a literal millstone around my neck. I'm now running in a sort of dream, or more accurately a state of reality displacement. Like an inter-planetary astronaut I am experiencing a delay of several seconds in any communication from mission control. At some point near the beginning of First Avenue I become aware that several seconds earlier I heard Angela's voice shouting my name. I turn and wave vaguely behind me in the direction I think the voice came from.

I am passing a drinks point and snatch a cup from one of the volunteers. I try to drink without taking my eyes off the road because drinks points are always the accident black spots in a marathon. The classic received wisdom from Mack Sennett films of the 1920s is that the slipperiest object in the world is a banana skin. Not so. Americans have found something even more precarious underfoot: orange peel. Orange segments are being handed out at the drinks points and the cast-off crescents of skin make the water-slopped road surface doubly treacherous. On the positive side, I think they may have discovered a cheap and effective surface for artificial ski slopes. "You can Run but you can't Haider" proclaims a witty banner on the sidewalk. This is a reference to the Austrian politician and Hitler apologist Jörg Haider who is competing in today's race. Before I left England Tara instructed me to kill him if I saw him. I'd love to oblige her but I don't feel I have the energy to kill anyone right now. It's as much as I can do to stay on my feet. Besides, I'm sure political assassination is against the New York Road Runners Club rules. No point in getting myself disqualified after I've made it this far.

I pass Mile 19, still slogging up First Avenue. There's a vague Latin feel to the surrounding music and spectators so this must be Spanish Harlem. More importantly, this is classically where runners hit the Wall. I don't feel any obvious physiological or psychological changes, but this is definitely the point by which any residual joy of the experience has evaporated. As if we weren't demoralised enough we now have to head into the Bronx for a token mile just so that the race can claim to pass through all five boroughs. "Feel the sun behind you," a woman at the Sri Chinmoy stall shouts through a megaphone as we run over the Willis Avenue Bridge. "Well, at least I'm beating the sun," I console myself. Overtaking is hard on the narrow bridge, which has been carpeted for the occasion, and I am stuck behind a stalled wheelchair athlete and a runner who has "sprfld mass" written on the back of his shirt. I ponder for a while on this and finally my brain, which has other things on its mind than doing word puzzles, works out that it stands for Springfield Massachusetts. So what happened? Couldn't he be bothered to write it all? Or wasn't there room enough on his T-shirt? Maybe he should pump some iron and get bigger deltoids; or move to a town and state with shorter names. Ames, Iowa, maybe? Lima, Ohio? One's mind meanders in a very mad way in a marathon. A conviction begins to form in me that I will finish in 3 hours 48 minutes.

Mile 20 is the halfway point of a marathon; not literally (my maths isn't that bad even with the state my brain's in) but physiologically and psychologically. This is where you run out of glycogen and hope simultaneously. Six miles more shouldn't be that bad, not after you've already run three times that distance, but it is. It's just as bad. It's a nightmare in anticipation and execution. Running the last six miles of a marathon is like running the first six miles you ever run when you are an out-of-condition slob embarking on your initial training session, only worse. It's hard to explain unless you've done it.

We hit Mile 21 and pass under a bridge on which a sign announces ambiguously "The End is Near" Having done our bit in the Bronx, we are steered back into Manhattan over the first available bridge. This engenders a positive feeling of being on the home straight. We reach the marker for Mile 22. Only four and a bit miles to go, I think. That seems close. But then I do the mental arithmetic and realise with horror that it represents 40 more minutes of running at my present rate, which has declined to nine-minute miles. Forty minutes. That's the time it takes to watch a sitcom and the news afterwards. Exhaustion is not the immediate problem. I could certainly use a sit-down, but my breathing is fine and I'm hardly sweating. The problem is that my feet and ankles are absolutely killing me from three hours of smashing into New York streets. Due to the weird sense of reality displacement, rather than my feet hitting the asphalt it actually feels as if the asphalt is hitting me, repeatedly on the soles, like some sadistic Turkish prison officer.

Just when I thought things couldn't get any worse I find I have become trapped next to a fun runner dressed as Spiderman. This immediately has the effect of banishing the pleasant tinkling pentatonic melodies from the Sri Chinmoy band which have been flowing through my head since Mile 18. Instead I find myself singing the inane theme song to my running-mate's TV series. "Spiderman Spiderman/ Does whatever a spider can/ Is he strong? Listen, bud/ He's got radioactive blood" runs round my fevered brain. I try to outpace him but I don't have the energy, and he, despite his Spidey powers, seems unable to go any faster. As we round each corner, and a fresh set of people on the sidewalk catch sight of my superhero pal, shouts go up of "Hey Spiderman!" and "Yo Spidey!" and even, inexplicably, "Hey Superman!"

Hatred is a good way of over-riding pain (I'm sure it's how soldiers get through battles) and by now you'll know who my hatred is reserved for. The New York City Marathon is proud of its 97 per cent finishing rate, which is due, according to Allan Steinfeld, the Race Director, to the vociferous personal cheering for which New York spectators are renowned. I must take issue with him on this point. It is not the fact that they shout encouragement that bothers me, it's the fact that they all shout the same things. This repetition of identical phrases from two million throats has an effect like Chinese Water Torture, especially after a dozen or so miles. I've already mentioned that a lot of Americans shout "Go!" Now this is a pretty self-evident suggestion, but is not so bad in that at least it doesn't have the negative connotations of "Keep going!" which suggests you were about to stop. More annoying are the people who slap you on the back and shout "Let's go!", the use of the first person plural imperative suggesting that they are including themselves in this proposition. Yet strangely they show no inclination to vault over the barriers and run with us. Then there is the oft-heard but mystifying exhortation "Way to go!" Whatever are they talking about? I know the way to go. I'm following the 5,000 people ahead of me. Or is it meant metaphorically? Dropping dead of exhaustion here on Madison Avenue would be a good "way to go"? Of course, the spectators at Mile 22 do not know that they are shouting exactly the same things as the spectators at Mile 21 and indeed every mile before. But by the time we get back into Manhattan I have arrived at the paranoid conviction that there is just one spectator following me along the course hollering the same inanities over and over to bug me. If I never hear anyone shout "Lookin' good, man" again for the rest of my life I will die happy.

"Spins a web any size/ Catches thieves just like flies." my brain is still singing under these ruminations. But where is Spidey? "Can he swing from a thread?/Take a look overhead," my brain prompts. But no, he's not up there, or behind me, or in front of me. He has mercifully vanished. Maybe a Doc Octopus fun runner took him out. We are at Mile 23 now. I overtake a competitor who is walking and I allow myself just for a moment to imagine how pleasant walking must be. But no, I mustn't think about it. Walking is fatal. Running may yet prove to be, too, but I know I must not walk. What about sitting down my brain suggests, and for a second it allows itself to imagine how it would feel right now to sit down. This blissful vision is so eidetic that my knees almost buckle under me. I put it out of my mind and force myself to concentrate on the route. We are now making a right turn off Madison Avenue and entering

Central Park, passing under its rich canopy of golds, yellows and greens. I know this because I later saw them in the official race video. Right now my colour vision seems to have stopped working. Still, at least I know the finishing line is close. This is a psychological boost but the road still seems to wind on forever and, worse, has the insensitivity to go uphill. At Mile 25 I spot my mother and Frances by the roadside, on the left as promised but 16 miles late. I manage to smile, wave and look vaguely dignified. By now there is no doubt in my mind that some inner destiny has intended me for a time of 3:48. Everything seems to point towards it.

This last mile should be quite enjoyable. Although my feet and ankles are in agony there is no doubt that I am going to finish and in a matter of just another few minutes. But, of course, the last mile is not enjoyable, mainly because it consists of a big loop circling tantalisingly round the finish area and then gradually curving back towards it. This seems a piece of sadism too far by the race organisers. I think of Queen Alexandra – "old bag, old bag, old bag". This last gruelling mile is enough to make a republican of anyone. Finally we round a corner and there is the finish line with its big digital clock just a couple of hundred metres ahead of us. Unexpectedly, this is not the beatific sight I had expected. I have played so many tricks on my body to induce it to keep running that it thinks this is just another one. I am in the position of the Boy Who Cried Wolf. "Oh yeah? So we just have to run to that banner that says 'Finish' and then we can stop?" my legs say cynically. "You said that about that sign with Mile 21 written on it." But despite their misgivings they plod on gamely.

They carry me over the line in 3:51:36. Once I have subtracted the 3 minutes it took me to cross the start line I am left with my predicted time of 3 hours 48 minutes. Although this is a pretty good time for a first marathon I feel slightly disappointed. I have been anticipating this exact figure since Mile 18, it is almost as if nothing I have achieved in the last hellish hour has counted for anything.

There is almost nothing good about finishing this marathon. The next hour is without exaggeration one of the worst of my life. A marathon is like a pregnancy. It is a huge endeavour that people undertake sometimes by choice, sometimes, like me, by chance. Once embarked on it you experience joy, fear and pain in various degrees. But you know you have to go through with it and that in the long term you won't regret what you've done. Now I am in the finish chute I am about to reach the marathoning equivalent of post-natal depression. For a start, it now hurts more to walk that it did to run. After running for three and three quarter hours all my muscles seem to seize up as my legs attempt to perform the unfamiliar short steps required for walking. I want either to sit down or to continue running, but with earlier finishers bottlenecked ahead of me and competitors streaming over the line at a rate of 200 per minute behind me, neither of these options is possible. We are chivvied along by armies of stewards, like worker ants, funnelling us through a sort of production line where we are unceremoniously handed our medals, have the electronic chips cut off our shoes and finally are given our aluminium blankets, which being American are of course *aluminum* blankets.

The production line spits us out metamorphosed into a flock of shimmering metallic butterflies. On the grass around me some runners are doing stretches. I have neither the energy nor the inclination to join them. The only stretch I would have any time for now would be a limo to whisk me out of this place. I pass a bench where a couple of runners are seated blank-faced and uncommunicating like old people. This is exactly what I want to do, I think, and hobble over. I sit down. Sure enough it hurts. I wonder if I will be able to get up again. I don't care. I don't want to think about this or anything else. I am reduced to a bleak minimalist state of being. I stop existing and sit there for probably quite a while.

When cerebral activity resumes I wonder what happens next. I had given no thought to this moment. Like troops returning home from World War One I hadn't cast my mind beyond enduring the nasty experience immediately at hand. Foolishly those brave men thought that they had got through the tough bit in surviving four years of dysentery, rats, mustard gas and German shells in the trenches. But then they arrived home to a bit of bunting, some pork pies and long-term unemployment. I, too, had just sort of assumed that everything would be okay at this point. Someone would have fixed things for me. But the reality is that I am alone in Central Park in my running vest and shorts on a coldish November afternoon with no public transport in the vicinity to take me back across the East River to Brooklyn. And it's a long way to Brooklyn. I know, because I ran through it about 16 miles back. I just want that limo, or maybe a helicopter. Make that one with a jacuzzi in it.

I force myself up from the bench before my leg joints stiffen in a permanent sitting position, and contemplate the problem to hand. My mother has my tracksuit and money so my first thought, sensibly, is to find her. Unfortunately my second thought is all muddled. Instead of taking the nearby exit from the park which would have led me to the exact spot where my friends and family are waiting, I follow the signs and the masses towards the Family Reunion area. Someone offers me a goodie bag but I have neither the energy nor the desire to take it. I must strike a pathetic and woeful figure as I trudge along and a concerned steward asks me if I want the medical tent. I shake my head. What I actually want is to burst into tears and shout "I want my Mummy". But I realise this would be both embarrassing and unproductive as they don't know where she is either.

I keep walking, 15 blocks in the wrong direction as it turns out. "Good job," athletes congratulate each other with handshakes, hugs and backslaps all round me. "Good job it's over", is all I can think. Behind me one runner is trying to persuade another of the benefits of a post-Thanksgiving 30-mile race. "Work off that turkey, man," he enthuses. I want to turn and shout at them that they are mad, but like in a dream I can't speak. Other runners greet me in comradely fashion as I stumble along, but I blank them. I have never been so cold, or so miserable. Any part of the race (the bitter wind on the Verrazano Bridge, the slope up on to the Queensboro Bridge, the last two miles in Central Park) was preferable to this. My feet now know that my pledge to them about how they could stop if we got as far as the finishing line was indeed just another bluff and are on a go slow.

Failing to find anyone in the Family Reunion area (largely because that was not where I had arranged to meet anyone), I turn and walk all the way back. At some point along the way I bump into my family and friends more by chance than design. My mother later tells me that I was blue in the face. Apparently I was blue when I was born and had to be put straight into an incubator. This is the closest I have got to that state since. Being put into an incubator sounds like quite a nice idea right now but sadly my mother doesn't have one. But she does have my tracksuit. I put it on and summon up the breath to make the melodramatic announcement to my assembled friends and relations that I will never ever run another marathon.

An hour, a cup of tea and a hot bath later, I am wondering whether I should put down to do London in April.

CHAPTER 24

Spitting On Callimachus's Grave

Running a marathon is a mixed experience, it involves a couple of nice bits and loads of nasty bits. Telling everyone that you ran the marathon is far more fun. It's the equivalent of my grandfather's generation being able to say that they were at Arnhem or in Burma. Like war, a marathon may ultimately be a futile undertaking, but it conveys a sense of dignity and duty to let people know that you did your bit in a stiff-upper-lip sort of way. The problem is that the average person doesn't know that much about the marathon. In fact, they often don't even know that it is run over a set distance but think the word marathon is used in its metaphorical sense of "really long and difficult".

So when back home I inform all my friends that I finished in 3 hours 48 minutes it is about as meaningful as proud new parents sending a non-parent, like me, a little embossed card with the birth weight of their baby (7 pounds 6 ounces? Is that big or small? I've really no idea). To clarify things to non-runners I could mention that 3:48 is a time that would qualify me to compete in the élite and prestigious Boston Marathon. To be strictly honest, though, I'd have to add "if I was aged over seventy". Handily, marathons are full of these statistics that may be manipulated according to the impression one wishes to create. For example, if I want people to be embarrassed on my behalf I can tell them that I came 7,659th in New York. "Oh dear..." they say, trying to think of a way to change the subject. Then, so that they realise I am actually not that bad, I merely have to add that 24,091 people finished behind me.

The week after a marathon is spent trying to draw people's attention to your achievement. This is not so hard really. The fact that your aching calves oblige you to descend staircases backwards is bound to provoke comment. Then there is your medal. Throughout December mine was displayed on the top of my Christmas tree for maximum visibility. Another visible factor is your sleek runner's physique, except that post-marathon thinness is not something you get any credit for. All that intensive training has burnt off most of your body fat and your friends look anxiously at your hatchet-like cheekbones and tell you that you are *too* thin.

The change that you yourself notice is the feeling of being fit. For those of you who, like me until now, have not really experienced it before I should explain that this is a sensation not unlike that of being drunk. You have an ineffable sense of wellbeing, a lightness and grace which seems (to you at least) to infuse your every movement and thought, an easy belief that you have a capacity to do all sorts of things that you can't. This state is something that not even the gluttonous temptations of Yuletide can quell and I decide that I am definitely going to do the London Marathon in April.

This addiction to fitness – or perhaps more accurately to the euphoric beta-endorphins produced by exercise – is the tragedy of marathon running. I can see already how easily I could get caught up in a vicious downward spiral which will lead me to enter more and more races until my knees and lumbar vertebrae crumble to powder. There is only one release and that is to get injured. Funnily enough when I first planned this whole endeavour I was quite looking forward to getting injured – provided it happened *after* the marathon. One of the advantages of training up to compete in a serious running event, I felt, was that I would then be able to get a sports injury. Now people who laze around never taking any exercise are just slobs. But total inactivity as a result of a sports injury is justifiable, even noble. Clearly one cannot validly claim to have a sports injury unless one has participated in some sport.

I have now completed a marathon and thus have the right to call myself a runner, but I trust that I still have sufficient sensitivity not to bore you with the grisly details of all the injuries I have incurred since New York. Suffice to say that I had to pull out of the London and Stockholm Marathons the next year and with my name down to run in London in 2001, I once again find myself on the physiotherapist's couch in January undergoing an exotic cocktail of treatments ancient and modern (acupuncture, laser, ultrasound) for a damaged Achilles tendon. By March I have had to withdraw from London for the second year running (or, rather, not running). I suppose I should feel proud that I am doing my bit to keep such events solvent by paying my advance entry fee and then not showing up for the race. Maybe one day somewhere in North London a plaque will be erected to me by the Association of Sports Physiotherapists and Podiatrists for services to funding their industry. In the meantime, I try to draw solace from the fact that this year's will be the perfect London Marathon to miss. The winter, even by British standards, was wretched and the foot and mouth epidemic caused all the warm-up races to be cancelled. But even so it is scant consolation for one who is seemingly doomed never to run again. I am like a broody childless woman who bursts into tears every time she passes a mother wheeling a baby carriage. Joggers glimpsed on the street become objects of intense hate to me. Even when from the comfort of the top deck of a bus I catch sight of one slogging along in the misery of the rain and the cold below I am nevertheless willing him to fall over and break bones.

April approaches and sponsors' adverts start to appear all over London depicting happy gritty marathoners slipping through Mile 19 thanks to their astute choice of mineral water. I have a sudden desire to escape all these frustrating reminders of what cannot be mine. I feel as if I am in love with someone unattainably beautiful or young. I am Dirk Bogarde in *Death in Venice*, blubbing in his deckchair. Someone is to blame for all this. Someone has placed this horrible curse on me. Some sort of melodramatic act of revenge and defiance is called for, like spitting on someone's grave. But whose? My first thought is Queen Alexandra. But then I realise that, harridan that Her Royal Highness undoubtedly was, she was only responsible for the last 1.2 miles of the marathon. In any case, spitting on a monarch's grave is probably one of those three or four treasonable offences that still carries the death penalty in this country. Another possibility might be to spit on my erstwhile flatmate Angela's grave – she being the person who induced this sad obsession in me in the first place. The major drawback of this option is that Angela is still alive. I could spit on Angela herself, but that would defeat the whole point of what is essentially a cowardly act to which the victim is unable to retaliate.

In the end I decide to restrict myself to dead people whose final resting places I can easily identify. The most obvious candidate is Callimachus, the Athenian War Ruler in 490 BC. He was after all the man who, from the selfish motivation of winning for himself immortality, took the spineless decision to attack the Persians rather than run away, and thus set in motion the chain of events that have led to my present misery. I know from my research that Callimachus was killed on the battlefield of Marathon and that the 192 Greek dead were interred in a burial mound which survives to this day on the site of the battle. As well as getting me away from London for a few days this grave-spitting option will also have the advantage of allowing me to simultaneously take in a bit of early season Mediterranean sun.

These days one cannot escape from one's country simply by going to another one. A couple of days later as I wander through the streets of Athens with its orthodox churches the size of Wendy houses, skinny stray cats and the ever-present danger of being run down by pooty scooter riders, there is the constant background *beep beep... beep beep* that indicates receipt of a text message and has passers-by of all nationalities fumbling for their mobile phones. Within a few hours of arriving, I have already received several texted enquiries from friends back home about what the weather is like – the first two of whom I was unable to enlighten as I was still inside the airport terminal at the time.

I take the opportunity to visit the Olympic stadium built for the inaugural 1896 Games. It is an impressive white edifice sparkling in the bright sunshine. So weird is it to see an amphitheatre that is not crumbling and overgrown that it seems like a film set. Apparently it is an exact replica of the stadium built by Herodes Atticus in AD 144 for the Panathenaic games – right down to the bum-aching marble seats, I note. Not a place I'd like to have sat for two and three quarter hours waiting for Spiridon Louis to come in. Sadly the stadium, like most of the rest of Athens, is closed. I belatedly discover that I have chosen to come here on the day of a national strike. Riot police and soldiers hang around in their hundreds smoking on street corners but, as it is the Thursday before the May Day bank holiday, many of the disaffected workers have presumably chosen to make a long weekend of it and register their protest somewhere agreeable on a beach. If you can't beat them, join them, I suppose. I decide to forget the Acropolis, Parthenon etc. and set off for the town of Marathon the next morning.

The injury to my Achilles (another blasted Greek) has put paid to any romantic ideas I might have entertained of running or even walking the original marathon route and I settle instead for the bus. I realise now just how lucky I was to escape injury in the months leading up to the New York Marathon. Running is something we just assume we know how to do. It doesn't occur to us that we should have any lessons or take any advice on it. We would never be so complacent if we were thinking of taking up pole-vaulting or hang-gliding. Yet most of us probably haven't refined our running technique since we scampered round the playground as infants. Imagine entering a public speaking competition if your oratory skills had not progressed since the age of three. The result would be an embarrassment.

Running the distance from Marathon to Athens in full armour must be unpleasant but it can't have been much worse than travelling the route in the overcrowded, superheated, non-air-conditioned bus in which I find myself with the driver's radio playing Greek cover versions of Spice Girls hits. Once we leave behind the suburbs of Athens the road is a long string of drive-thru towns, a bit like the Wild West – distended clusters of buildings which seem to exist just to service the highway. A modern Pheidippides would have plenty of opportunities to stop for refreshment, not to mention garden furniture, bedding plants and pet-care products. The trees that line the road are bare and blackened from last year's fires.

I am sitting next to a man whose slicked-back grey hair, reactolite sunglasses and paunch give him a scary resemblance to Joe Pesci. His English proves to be limited and as we make tentative conversation I dread that we will reach the end of his vocabulary before we reach the end of the journey. It's so ghastly when one ends up reduced to the smiling and nodding stage. Vasili manages to convey, I think, that he has been in Athens to attend a court hearing for not having a public entertainment licence in the restaurant he owns. This sounds an innocuous enough offence, until one remembers that Al Capone was only finally nailed for tax evasion.

On hearing that I am bound for Marathon Vasili advises against it. Marathon is very small, he tells me, and has no hotels. He recommends me instead to go to the beach resort of Nea Makri which is much more tourist-friendly. He himself lives there and offers to give me a lift from the bus stop in his car. What does one do when someone you suspect of being in the Cosa Nostra invites you to take a ride with him? To refuse would be an insult punishable by death, but to accept might be to end up as part of the foundations of the new Olympic stadium being built for the 2004 Games. However, the seaside sounds a tempting option in this scorched landscape, so I agree. Mercifully it transpires that there is no fate more grisly in store for me than having Vasili's brother's hardware shop and his cousin's restaurant pointed out to me as we drive past. With a promise to visit at least the second of these establishments I hop out of his car – hopefully not too eagerly – at the sea front. Various hotels are signposted but the Marathon Beach hotel sounds as if it is destined to be my home for the next few days.

My sixth-floor room has a balcony overlooking the bay where the Persians landed two and a half thousand years ago. Today the plain is dotted with high-security luxury villas. Tall hills surround the bay, their balding green tops flecked with grey outcrops of rock. Up there somewhere Callimachus stood and took the fateful decision that has today boosted the area's tourist population by one.

The next day dawns very hot and I set off to visit the museum of Marathon in search of more background detail about the battle. The bus drops me off at the side of the sort of straight bare dusty road on which one half expects to be strafed by a crop-duster. The museum is a sweaty 25-minute slog off the main road and rewards me for my efforts with a single helmet (apparently similar to ones worn at the Battle of Marathon) and statues with missing body parts that anticipate the work of the Chapman brothers by a couple of millennia. I walk back to the main road and on a further three kilometres to the town of Marathon itself, stopping off at a roadside supermarket for a few moments to bask in the air conditioning.

Just outside Marathon the word PEACE is written in giant letters in Greek and English on the road, presumably for the benefit of invading aliens. I just hope they're not members of the Alpha Centauri Striders here on a pilgrimage. They'd have wasted their time. Marathon turns out to be an anonymous town of whitewashed two-storey buildings set along a winding high street. Its population comprises about a tenth of the number of people who ran a few days ago in the London race named in its honour. Nowhere is there a single reference to its place in athletic legend. There isn't even a sports shop. Are the towns of Badminton and Rugby as modest about the sports they inspired, I wonder?

A little disappointed, I walk back to Nea Makri, taking a short cut in the hope of coming across the battle site on the way. I get lost and end up walking for what seems like hours along a straight road under the baking afternoon sun. I seriously wonder if I should walk backwards for a while to even up my tan. When I finally get back to my hotel I find that the only other guests in this slack season between Easter and summer – a German couple – have not budged since this morning but are still face down on their sun loungers as if stretched out on instruments of torture.

The hotel receptionist informs me that the Tomb of the Athenians – where the Greek dead from Marathon are interred – is a 20-minute walk from the hotel. It seems that Vasili was right about the advantage of Nea Makri over Marathon. Feeling guilty about having misjudged him, I dine in his cousin's restaurant that evening. I take a seat on the terrace just a few feet from the lapping Med and force myself to order my fifth Greek salad of the trip. Running is like smoking. Once you give up this highly addictive but damaging habit you start to get fat. While you are training four times a week you can eat as much as you like, knowing that you are going to be burning off all the calories almost immediately. When you find yourself unable to run, not only do you fail to cut down on food, but worse still you start comfort eating.

The brief twilight fades sky, mountain and sea down into almost indistinguishable shades of dark purple, like adjacent colours on a wallpaper swatch. A runner ambles past along the sea front. Bastard, I think instinctively. But why am I jealous? What's the point in me trying to run another marathon now? Even if I could get fit enough again I turned 40 last summer. This means I will be classed as a Veteran in the official race results, a person whose performance will be listed separately from the rest of the runners. My contribution will be dismissed, written off, not taken seriously. The realisation of being old strikes me with the same chilling force as it would a man who has found a bald spot or discovered that he is to become a grandfather. You cross some unmarked half marathon point in your life and suddenly you find it has begun to wind inexorably down. This is the first time I've ever been made to feel marginalised by my age. Forty's not so old these days, certainly for a man. I've never experienced the remotest urge to lie about my recent milestone. I've still got my hair and a trimmish waistline and, as a writer, I am hopefully just coming into my prime. As a runner, though, I am officially over the hill. I undertook this whole business to stave off my midlife crisis but instead I have just succeeded in reinforcing it. Perhaps sensing my depression, Vasili shuffles up to console me with a complimentary glass of house white.

The next morning I set off along the coast on the final stage of this epic undertaking: to visit the Tomb of the Athenians. The local Greeks are oddly coy about revealing the location of this shrine to what the eminent Victorian historian Sir Edward Creasy identified as one of the Fifteen Decisive Battles of the World. It is not marked on any signposts. Maybe Medes and Persians are an important source of tourist revenue these days. Following some vague directions from a waiter in one of the seafront restaurants I wander inland and, after about a kilometre, I see the green swell of the burial mound ahead of me. I am surprised to note that the car park is full of vehicles, including several coaches, and to hear the sounds of a large crowd gathered. Am I at last finding Greeks with some respect for their history?

It turns out to be some sort of an organised demo. A couple of hundred protestors are massed before a makeshift podium balefully surveyed by a dozen policemen. A man in a Lenin cap with a beard is making an impassioned speech in front of a backdrop of handmade banners which proclaim some no doubt very stirring sentiments in Greek. He finishes his oration on an upnote and I join in the applause, though to be honest the only word of the speech that I understood was the last one: *efharisto* (thank you). Despite the barrier of language it is clear to me from the profusion of beards and ponytails among the protestors and the contemptuous looks on the face of the police that this is a bunch of lefty environmentalists. A bystander tells me that the protests are over the Greek government's proposal to construct an artificial lake to stage the Olympic kayaking events here in 2004 which will devastate this pristine ecological and archaeological site. I hang around for a while in case any impromptu re-enactment of the Battle of Marathon is going to be staged but, apart from a bit of bad-tempered jostling between the police and some of the more bolshy demonstrators, there is nothing worthy of this ancient site.

I cross the road to examine the Tomb of the Athenians. It is a UFO-shaped grass-covered mound about 20 feet high, planted round with pink-blossomed trees. I circle it and am struck by the absence of any background information on this historic war grave. There is a single small plaque in Greek, but this could merely be informing us of the penalties for dog fouling; and – need I say it? – no mention for poor Callimachus.

I have reached my goal but the presence across the road of the demonstration takes away the admittedly half-hearted urge to spit on the grave. The one thing that could possibly unite the tree-huggers with the cops right now would be the sight of some foreigner desecrating a Greek national monument. They would wade in *en masse*, squabbling only over who got to hold me down and who got to deliver the kicks. Besides, I feel rather sorry for Callimachus, the man whose casting vote for battle utterly backfired on him at Marathon. He didn't even get a name check on the tomb, never mind the immortality he was promised. So let him have this tiny bit... for what it's worth.